Futurescape

Get Ready for the World of Tomorrow

By GonzyDesigns

First Edition

ISBN: 9798863443324

www.gonzydesigns.com

Disclaimer

Table of Contents

Introduction

In the vast expanse of the cosmos, there exists a small, blue marble teeming with water and land—a garden of life suspended in the void: Earth, home to a peculiar species of apes that have transcended their humble beginnings and are unlocking the secrets of the universe piece by piece.

From the moment the first sparks of consciousness flickered within our ancestors, we have sought to understand our place in the cosmos. The prehistoric hominids used stones and sticks to conquer the wilderness, drawing upon their budding intellect to fashion the first primitive tools. This early curiosity sparked the grand saga of technological advancement, turning simple apes into masters of the world.

Fast forward to the 20th century: we transformed the terrestrial world around us and set our sights on the skies. The advent of aviation, the birth of the computer, and the mapping of the human genome were but milestones in our relentless quest. Each achievement was a testament to the unstoppable force of human imagination, a leap from the realm of science fiction into reality.

Nowhere was this more evident than in our voyages into the cosmos. Inspired by visionary authors such as H.G. Wells and Arthur C. Clarke, we looked up at the Moon, that eternal beacon in the night sky, and dared to dream. The notion of setting foot on the lunar surface, once a fantastical tale penned in the pages of a science fiction novel, became a reality in the summer of 1969.

As Neil Armstrong descended the ladder of Apollo 11 and planted the first human footprints on the lunar surface, it was clear that the realm of the fantastical had become the domain of the possible. The line between imagination and reality blurred. If we could land a person on the Moon, what couldn't we do? This question propels us into the future, driving our insatiable hunger for knowledge and advancement.

In this quest for understanding, we have harnessed the power of the atom, built laboratories in space, and begun to explore the frontiers of artificial intelligence and quantum physics. These accomplishments make us wonder: If our progress continues unabated, what will the future hold?

Now, as we stand on the precipice of the future, we peer into an era where AI, neuroscience, robotics, and holographic technologies intertwine, crafting a world beyond our wildest dreams. A future where technology will redefine our existence, where energy flows as freely as the wind, and where the very fabric of space bends to our will.

The future is a tantalizing enigma, full of promise and perils, and we are its architects. Through the pages that follow, we will venture into the realm of the possible, exploring the tantalizing precipice of our understanding and technology's forefront. We will see how far our species has come and how far we might yet go. For we are dreamers, explorers, inventors—destined for the stars, with the future as our ultimate frontier.

Advanced Materials

For most of human history, society was built using wood, iron, and stone. These materials were enough to shape empires and civilizations over centuries. Yet, it was only at the dawn of the 20th century that the landscape of our material world began to evolve in earnest, giving birth to the age of plastics and sophisticated composites. Today, a new era beckons as materials with extreme characteristics come within humanity's grasp.

Picture a car that heals its own scratches, a smartphone that charges as you walk, or even a building that cleans itself. Imagine materials multiple times stronger than steel and those that remember and return to their original shapes when subjected to heat or stress. Welcome to a future where materials are not just static and passive, but dynamic, interactive, and adaptive.

Aerogels

When many picture the materials of the future, a common vision is that of shiny metals that never rust and are incredibly light. Although there are materials that humanity is developing with those characteristics, some of the most intriguing prospects are found not in the shiny and hard, but in the light and airy. Enter aerogels, a family of ultra-light materials that look like frozen smoke and are light as air, yet hold incredible strength and thermal insulating properties.

Aerogels are composed of over 90% air and appear as if they are made from smoke[1]. This is not an illusion, but a feature of their unique structure. Aerogels are made by creating a gel and then removing the liquid component, leaving behind a structure of solid material filled with air pockets[1]. This process creates materials that have low density, high porosity, and incredible insulating properties. They are up to four times more efficient than the best fiberglass insulation[2].

The extraordinary insulation abilities of aerogels can best be demonstrated through an experiment involving a flower and a blowtorch[3]. When a delicate, dry flower is coated with a thin layer of aerogel, it can survive the extreme heat of a blowtorch, remaining untouched while the world around it is reduced to ashes. If such a lightweight substance can protect a fragile flower from destruction, imagine the protection it could offer to society.

Research has already shown that this material could be revolutionary for first responders and firefighters[4,5]. Firefighters face hazardous conditions as part of their daily lives. The protective gear they wear, while currently the best available, is often heavy, limiting mobility, and can still leave them exposed to dangerous levels of heat. Clothing insulated with aerogels would revolutionize fire-safety gear. Aerogel's insulating properties and lightness would allow for much more comfortable, lightweight, and effective protective clothing. The gear would not only shield firefighters from the extreme thermal environment but also increase their maneuverability, thus enhancing their effectiveness in rescue operations.

Aerogels could play a crucial role in making everything more efficient, from engines to computers. When transferring energy, whether it's in a combustion engine or a computer, some energy efficiency is lost through heat dissipation. The use of aerogels could help everything run a lot more efficiently by minimizing heat loss during energy transfer[6]. For example, the range and performance of electric vehicles is greatly affected by temperature. With aerogels incorporated into their design, electric vehicles could potentially maintain battery performance despite temperature fluctuations[7]. The dreamed milestone of driving from New York to Los Angeles on a single charge would become more plausible not by enhancing the battery, but by harnessing the latent potential of the energy already stored within it.

Even as we grapple with the pressing issue of climate change, our power plants, from renewable-driven steam turbines to conventional combustion engines, could reach new levels of efficiency. The significant reduction in heat waste means every ounce of fuel, every gust of wind, and every ray of sunlight we harness is converted into usable power with minimal loss.

These same benefits could also be utilized for our handheld devices and computers. The bane of modern existence is watching the battery percentage plummet. With aerogels incorporated into their designs, our devices could hum along for days, perhaps weeks, on a single charge. Not because of a larger battery, but because the energy typically lost to the ambient environment is trapped, conserved, and used.

The use of aerogel for construction and building

insulation is already showing great potential[8,9]. Imagine the buildings of the future, insulated not with bulky layers of fiberglass but with thin panels of aerogel. The implications are we could maintain comfortable temperatures in our homes and workplaces with a fraction of the energy and cost currently required.

The utility of aerogels is already being felt in the fashion world, too. Companies are already making apparel insulated with aerogel[10,11]. A winter coat, instead of being a bulky monstrosity, can now be as thin and light as a windbreaker, but still keep someone warm in sub-zero temperatures. Aerogel-insulated clothing has the potential to revolutionize outdoor apparel, making it possible to stay warm and dry in extreme conditions without the heavy layers traditionally required.

But the applications of aerogel's thermal properties extend far beyond our planet. Space, with its extreme temperatures, presents unique challenges for insulation. Aerogels are already being used in Mars rovers and space suits, protecting delicate electronics and human bodies from the intense cold of space and the scorching heat of re-entry[12,13]. But we have only scratched the surface of what is possible.

Picture a future where spacecraft are insulated with ultra-light aerogel shields, significantly reducing their weight and thereby the energy required for launch. Bases on remote planets and moons could be constructed with aerogel-insulated habitats, ensuring a comfortable living environment for astronauts despite the harsh conditions outside.

Advanced Alloys

A typical idea of future materials often involves chromed spacecraft matter that is stronger than steel, lighter than plastic, and never degrades or rusts. These are the types of amazing characteristics that will be incorporated in our future advanced alloys.

Advanced alloys are made using a blend of elements to go beyond the constraints of traditional alloys. By no longer relying on the inherent strengths and weaknesses of a single element, these alloys can leverage the strengths of a multitude of elements to overcome pitfalls of traditional materials.

With their unique atomic structure, these materials can have exceptional strength, remarkable resistance to corrosion, and outstanding thermal stability. These alloys offer tantalizing combinations of mechanical, electrical, and magnetic properties.

The applications of advanced alloys span a wide spectrum of industries, captivating researchers, engineers, and visionaries alike. In aerospace, they promise lightweight materials with unparalleled strength for next-generation aircraft and spacecraft. In energy, they offer solutions for high-temperature environments and improved efficiency in power generation. From advanced manufacturing and electronics to biomedical devices and infrastructure, advanced alloys hold the key to unlocking a myriad of possibilities.

One of the newest of these alloys was developed by NASA. Known as *GRX-810*, this material was made using a 3D printing process, and offers unprecedented resilience in extreme conditions. Designed for high-temperature applications like aircraft and rocket engines, its exceptional attributes arise from nanoscale oxide particles. GRX-810 can endure temperatures exceeding 2,000°F. To put this into perspective, this is well past the temperature that would melt steel. Additionally, this material possesses superior malleability, and lasts over 1,000 times longer than other advanced alloys[14,15].

Thanks to advances in 3D printing technology that is steadily improving and continually able to work in smaller and smaller scales, soon we will be able to produce alloys with some amazing properties.

One of these will be alloys with varying compositions throughout a single component[16]. This would allow for alloys with tailored properties, such as a surface that's extremely hard and wear-resistant while maintaining a ductile and shock-absorbing core.

Similarly, localized property enhancement will also be possible with these materials[17].This is the introduction of nanoparticles at specific locations to grant localized enhancements in hardness, conductivity, or corrosion resistance.

Another amazing type of alloy that will be possible are *shape memory alloys* or *smart alloys*. In the dynamic landscape of materials science, these stand out as a fascinating breed. These remarkable metals can "remember" their original shape and return to it after deformation[18]. This phenomenon is known as the "shape memory effect" and is responsible for giving these alloys the ability to change shape in response to changes in temperature, mechanical stress, or an electrical stimuli.

Consider the limitations of current prosthetics: they may be functional, but they lack the fluidity, the nuance of organic movement. With smart alloys, we are on the brink of birthing prosthetics that don't just mimic human motion but are also able to emulate the symphony of muscles, tendons, and ligaments that create our every gesture. They have been utilized in prosthetic arm designs and soft grippers, showcasing their potential in enhancing prosthetic devices to mimic human anatomy and movement more closely[19]. Research has already gone into the development of innovative prosthetic hands and wrists using shape memory alloys to achieve a range of motion and load-bearing capacity comparable to the human anatomy[19,20]. New actuator designs using shape memory alloys are being developed for prosthetic hands, replacing conventional servo motors which are bulky and noisy, making the prosthetics more user-friendly and closer to natural human movement[19,20]. Picture a world where an amputee doesn't just get a replacement limb, but one that moves, feels, and responds with the delicate ballet of natural motion.

Yet, the potential of smart alloys doesn't stop at prosthetics. Envision exoskeletons, not the clunky mechanized suits of past predictions, but sleek and nearly invisible frameworks. These future exoskeletons, imbued with the magical properties of smart alloys, could shadow our every movement while amplifying our strength and endurance. Research has shown advancements in using shape memory alloys to make actuators for developing upper limb rehabilitation exoskeletons, which showcases a promising future for more comprehensive exoskeleton designs[21]. This research could lead to a world where the elderly, reinvigorated by these suits, could walk with the vigor of their youth. Laborers could lift and toil hour after hour without pain or strain. Athletes could leap and perform to new superhuman levels.

By incorporating shape memory alloys into the structure of vehicles and equipment, they would gain the ability to regain their original shape after enduring stress or impact. This could increase durability and reduce the need for frequent maintenance and repairs. Cars would be able to fix dents from rock strikes and hail storms, and have improved suspension systems with these alloys built directly into the frames. The automotive industry is already exploring the applications of these alloys for enhanced safety, performance, and comfort, with a significant increase in the use of sensors and actuators due to these amazing materials[22,23].

These alloys could also enhance the durability of electronics. By using them in circuitry or device casings, electronic devices could withstand more physical stress and harsh conditions, an invaluable feature in the field. This can lead to power tools and vehicle computers with unmatched durability. Moreover, the material's flexibility opens up new possibilities for wearable tech that can conform to unique shapes and bodies without breaking[24].

The adaptive nature of smart alloys can also be used to

create dynamic camouflage systems[25,26]. By changing shape in response to external conditions, these alloys could mimic the textures and contours of their surroundings, providing superior camouflage capabilities. Additionally, the shape-changing properties could be used in stealth technology, allowing drones or vehicles to alter their surface geometry to reduce radar detection.

Furthermore, smart alloys could be instrumental in creating deployable structures such as tents or bridges that can be compacted for transport and then automatically set up on site almost instantly[27,28]. This could drastically simplify logistics and save valuable time during emergency response operations or quick shelter deployments in harsh environments.

Metallic Glasses

When we think of glass, we often picture an aesthetic yet delicate and brittle material. But not all glasses shatter, and not all metals bend. Introducing metallic glass: a material that combines the strengths of metals and the unique properties of glass to create a truly remarkable substance.

Metallic glasses, also known as amorphous metals,

possess a disordered atomic structure similar to traditional glass but are made from metals or metalloids[29,30]. This unique composition yields some extraordinary properties: strength, resilience, and more resistant to wear and corrosion than their crystalline metal counterparts. This makes them more suitable for use in harsh environments, such as saltwater or desert conditions.

Being incredibly hard and resistant to penetration makes metallic glasses a fascinating candidate for the next generation of military armor. Picture a military vehicle or a soldier's body armor that can resist higher-caliber rounds without the added weight of traditional armor materials. Not only could metallic glass provide enhanced protection, but its lighter weight could also improve mobility on the battlefield[31].

Acoustic Metamaterials

The world of metamaterials is one that will be a lot more common in the future. A metamaterial is engineered with properties not found in nature, exhibiting specific characteristics and behaviors. Acoustic metamaterials are specially designed materials engineered to control and shape sound waves in unconventional ways. By carefully arranging their internal structures, scientists have unlocked the ability to manipulate sound like never before. Just as a skilled conductor guides an orchestra, these materials orchestrate the behavior of sound waves, guiding them along desired paths and creating different effects.

Crafting acoustic metamaterials requires a blend of creativity and engineering prowess. Scientists use advanced fabrication techniques to design intricate structures at the microscopic level. These structures consist of carefully arranged patterns and elements that interact with sound waves in unique ways[32,33,34]. By manipulating a metamaterial's density, stiffness, or shape, scientists can mold sound in extraordinary ways.

Acoustic metamaterials have already found their way into various real-world applications. One notable example is noise-canceling headphones[34]. By using metamaterials to control the propagation of sound waves, noise-canceling headphones can effectively neutralize unwanted ambient sounds, creating peaceful and immersive listening experiences.

These materials have the potential to revolutionize urban architecture[35]. By integrating acoustic metamaterials into buildings, engineers can manipulate the behavior of sound within spaces. This enables the design of concert halls with exceptional acoustics, reducing echoes and enhancing sound quality for both performers and audiences. It would also allow for the design of buildings that are completely soundproof while allowing air to pass through. At a larger scale, these materials could redirect seismic waves to protect buildings and even entire cities from earthquakes[36].

The military would gain a significant advantage from using these materials. They could be used to lower the sound profile of vehicles and weapon systems. However, even more impactful applications are possible. By redirecting sound waves around an object and releasing them on the other side, acoustic metamaterials can theoretically render underwater objects like submarines invisible to sonar[37,38].

Self-healing Materials

Imagine a material that possesses an innate ability to mend its own wounds, a substance that can rejuvenate itself to its original state. Like the regenerative power of nature itself, these materials can heal and restore functionality, showcasing a new magnitude of durability. From self-repairing polymers to regenerative metals, they contain intricate mechanisms and chemical reactions that activate when damage occurs.

To understand the full potential of this technology, consider concrete—one of the most ubiquitous materials in modern society. Over time, concrete degrades and one of the primary concerns is its susceptibility to cracking. Concrete is a brittle material, prone to developing cracks due to various factors[39]. Shrinkage, caused by the loss of moisture during the curing process, can lead to small, hairline cracks. Additionally, environmental factors such as temperature changes, freeze-thaw cycles, and chemical exposure can contribute to the formation of larger cracks. These cracks not only compromise the aesthetic appeal of concrete structures but also create pathways for water infiltration, leading to further deterioration. Small cracks, if left untreated, can grow over time, compromising the structure's strength and stability.

However, self-healing concrete can and does combat these issues[40,41]. Embedded within its composition are tiny capsules of healing agents or bacteria, patiently waiting to spring into action when damage occurs. When cracks form, these capsules release their contents, initiating a chemical reaction that fills the voids, restoring the material to its original integrity.

Steel and metals, commonly used in infrastructure, can also be self-healing[42,43]. Embedded within their alloyed composition are interstitial atoms or shape-memory alloys that possess the unique ability to reconfigure themselves when stimulated a certain way. Upon receiving damage, these components shift and rearrange, filling in cracks and restoring the metal's flexible strength.

This technology will help pave the way for the next generation of infrastructure that can withstand the test of time and nature a lot better. Imagine roads and runways that self-repair, ensuring uninterrupted operations and logistics. Envision fortifications that heal their battle scars, or a hospital building that can instantly heal damage from an unlucky lightning strike.

Picture vehicles crafted from self-healing metals, capable of autonomously repairing themselves after collisions or impact. Envision self-healing exoskeletons that protect and augment the abilities of the wearer, repairing themselves after overexertion. In the future, the application of self-healing materials will expand to everything, from coatings and ceramics to electronics and optics.

Superconducting Materials

Another type of material that is positioned to become an

essential part of future tech is superconducting materials. These materials have been of considerable interest due to their unique properties and potential for groundbreaking applications.

Humanity has already developed superconducting materials. They are essential parts of MRI machines, particle accelerators, and quantum computers[44,45]. They can also be used in power grids, radio telescopes, radar systems, and even maglev trains.

Even though they are of paramount importance for the function of certain devices, there is still a limiting factor of current superconducting materials. They are required to maintain extremely cold temperatures to be superconductive. One of the goals of current scientific research is the development of superconducting materials at room temperature. This is because with current superconducting materials, if higher temperatures are reached, the behavior of electrons within the material is dominated by thermal energy, preventing superconductivity from occurring. The achievement of developing room-temperature superconducting materials would usher in an era of groundbreaking technologies[46,47].

Due to the extreme cold required for superconductivity to manifest, practical superconducting applications often involve the use of cryogenic systems. Liquid helium and liquid nitrogen are commonly used cryogens to cool superconducting materials to the necessary temperatures. This means that a material that is superconductive at room temperature would not require expensive and complex cryogenic cooling that results in bulky devices with expensive maintenance procedures.

Another likely result of room-temperature superconductivity is a revolution in computer architecture[47]. Superconducting materials could allow for digital devices that operate at incredible speeds without generating heat. The need for heat sinks and fans would be a thing of the past, leading to even smaller and thinner electronics. These materials could also lead to the development of more compact versions of devices like particle accelerators that currently cover enormous areas and require millions of dollars worth of equipment and staff.

Materials that are superconductive at room temperature could also usher in the development of power transmission lines that transport electricity over vast distances without any loss, dramatically improving the efficiency of power grids and facilitating the use of remote renewable energy sources.

Although there have been some recent disappointing claims about room-temperature superconductive materials like LK-99, which turned out to be false, there are still significant advancements being made.

Recently, a material known as *lanthanum decahydride* (LaH10) demonstrated the potential to achieve superconductivity near room temperature under high pressure conditions[48,49]. This material has set a new record by showcasing a superconducting transition temperature closer to room temperature, approximately at −23 °C or −10 °F, under high-pressure conditions.

The ability of LaH10 to exhibit superconductivity near room temperature, albeit under high pressure, is a remarkable stride towards the long-standing goal of finding room-temperature superconductors. It represents a substantial advance in the field and opens up exciting possibilities for further exploration and potential practical applications once the challenge of reducing the required pressure is overcome.

Thermophotovoltaic Cells

The concept of *thermophotovoltaic* (TPV) cells is simple, yet wonderfully effective: capture the thermal energy radiated by a heat source, convert it into light energy, and then transform that light energy into electrical power[50].

Today, these TPV cells are a masterclass in the conversion of energy. They operate in a similar way to the cells used in solar panels, except that instead of directly utilizing sunlight, they harness the energy from a heat radiated onto the cells. This allows them to function without the need for sunlight, thus offering the potential for round-the-clock power generation.

Though the concept of TPVs has been around since the 1960s, their practical implementation has been stymied by their low efficiency. However, the advent of materials like tungsten have sparked a resurgence of interest in TPV cells[51]. For example, researchers at MIT have developed a two-dimensional metallic dielectric photonic crystal that can improve the efficiency of TPVs by enhancing the emitter's ability to radiate energy[52,53].

The sheer versatility of thermophotovoltaic cells makes them ideal for a plethora of applications. In the domestic setting, the waste heat from cooking or heating could be converted into electricity by them, adding a new dimension to household energy efficiency. Similarly, in industries with high thermal outputs, like steel or glass manufacturing, TPV cells could be a game-changer, transforming wasted heat into valuable electricity and significantly reducing energy and production costs.

In remote or hazardous environments, where regular

maintenance is challenging, TPV generators could provide a reliable source of power. Whether it is powering research stations in Antarctica, providing electricity to off-grid settlements, or serving as dependable backup power sources, the possibilities are exciting.

Their potential in space exploration is also tantalizing. A spacecraft outfitted with thermophotovoltai cells could capture the body heat from cosmonauts or even the heat from the spacecraft's reentry into a planet's atmosphere[54]. Normally wasted, these heat sources could be stored and used to power the ship.

Thermophotovoltaic cells, therefore, have the potential to rewrite the rules of power generation. As we venture deeper into the future, these amazing cells may well become part of our everyday lives, silently generating electricity from the heat around us. Whether it is powering a remote outpost, an electric car, or a future starship propelling us into the cosmos, TPVs show promise of a future where every joule of thermal energy counts.

Auxetic Materials

Ordinarily, when you stretch a material, it narrows in the areas perpendicular to the applied force. Pull on a rubber band, for instance, and it will become thinner as it lengthens. Auxetic materials, on the other hand, possess a unique property known as a negative Poisson's ratio[55,56]. This means that when stretched, they actually become wider, and when compressed, they become thinner. It is as if you tugged on a rubber band and it decided to thicken rather than shrink in width.

But how can this be? How can we create materials that behave so oddly? The secret lies in the structure, auxetic materials are typically created by engineering their internal geometry. By manipulating the shape, size, and arrangement of the molecules within these materials, scientists can design them to exhibit this counter-intuitive behavior.

This peculiar property opens up a universe of fascinating possibilities. So much so that notable organizations including NASA, Yamaha, Toyota, and the United States Office of Naval Research are actively working on the development of novel auxetic materials[57].

Research has shown great potential in protective gear like helmets or body armor made from auxetic materials[58,59]. As the force from an impact or fall spreads over the material, it would become thicker and tougher instead of thinning out, providing an unprecedented level of protection.

From a medical standpoint, auxetic materials could be used to create more effective and comfortable casts that expand to accommodate swelling, or stents that widen to prevent the closure of an artery[60,61].

Auxetic materials have even shown potential to revolutionize the construction of mundane everyday items such as seat cushions[62]. The peculiar property of becoming denser when pressure is applied can lead to more comfortable, supportive seats that conform better to body shape.

In aerospace, auxetic foams could play a key role due to their ability to absorb energy efficiently[63]. They can also be utilized in light-weight sound and radar-absorbing materials which are crucial for aerospace applications[63].

From protective gear that becomes tougher on impact to revolutionary medical applications, auxetic materials stand poised to literally transform our world.

Piezoelectric Materials

Piezoelectricity, derived from the Greek word *piezein* meaning "to squeeze or press," is the electric charge that accumulates in certain solid materials in response to applied mechanical stress. This was first discovered in the 19th century by brothers Pierre and Jacques Curie when they found that certain crystals, including quartz, topaz, and sugar, generated an electric charge when compressed or deformed[64]. This discovery brought about the birth of the fascinating field of piezoelectricity.

But what exactly makes these materials so remarkable? At their core, piezoelectric materials have their atoms intricately arranged to respond to the vibrations that surround us. When pressure or stress is applied, these materials come alive, generating an electric charge. From self-powering devices that draw energy from their own vibrations to sensors that can detect the faintest anomaly, piezoelectric materials offer a gateway to a future where energy and information converge[65,66].

Imagine stepping onto a dance floor, where every twist, turn, and stomp of your feet produces not only rhythm and movement but also electricity. Piezoelectric tiles, when stressed by the impact of a footstep, generate electrical power that can be stored and used. Clubs in Europe have already harnessed this technology, using the energy produced by the dancers to power their light and sound systems, adding an entirely new dimension to the phrase "electric atmosphere"[67].

Now, let's scale this idea up. Envision bustling city

streets, teeming with people and cars, all generating power with every step and wheel rotation. Piezoelectric roads and sidewalks could harvest this untapped energy, providing a green power solution in the very heart of our urban jungles. The same principle can be applied to highways and railways, where the weight and movement of vehicles and trains can be used to generate electricity. This technology is already being tested in places like California, hinting at a future where our cities and roads are not just consumers, but also producers of energy[68]. This principle could even extend to air travel, with piezoelectric materials capturing the vibrations of an aircraft during flight[69].

On a more personal level, consider the humble wristwatch. Traditional watches require a power source, often a battery, which inevitably runs out and needs replacing. But what if the simple act of wearing a watch could power it indefinitely? Piezoelectric materials in the watch strap could convert the natural movements of your arm and wrist into electricity, keeping your watch running perpetually with use[70].

Beyond their energy-producing capabilities, piezoelectric materials also have potential in the realm of sensory technology[71,72]. In medical diagnostics, they can help detect pressure changes, enabling the monitoring of blood pressure, heart rate, and more. In the automotive industry, they can be used to detect impacts, triggering airbag deployment during a crash.

One prime piezoelectric material poised to cause monumental shifts in material science is *lead zirconate titanate* (PZT)[73,74]. At its core, PZT is a ceramic material composed of lead, zirconium, and titanium, carefully arranged in a crystalline structure.

The captivating properties of PZT are not limited to its ability to generate electrical charge. Its unique piezoelectric behavior extends to its capacity to undergo rapid and precise shape changes when subjected to electrical fields[75]. This makes PZT an ideal candidate for actuators and sensors, enabling intricate control and feedback mechanisms. Imagine agile drones capable of adjusting their wing shape mid-flight, adapting to changing environments with unparalleled efficiency.

Another promising piezoelectric material is *polyvinylidene fluoride* (PVDF)[76]. This versatile and resilient polymer holds the potential to reshape industrial applications with its enticing properties and remarkable adaptability. This is a material that possesses an inherent ability to withstand extreme conditions while remaining remarkably resilient. It's a polymer with an exceptional balance of strength and flexibility. PVDF can withstand harsh environments, including high temperatures, chemical exposure, and even radiation[76]. Its resilience and durability make it an ideal choice for outdoor and industrial applications, where materials must perform reliably in the face of adversity.

Imagine soldiers equipped with PVDF smart uniforms that adapt to their body movements, providing enhanced flexibility and comfort while maintaining protective qualities. PVDF's adaptability opens up a realm of possibilities for future military gear and equipment. As soldiers move and engage in combat, their actions generate vibrations and mechanical energy. PVDF can capture and convert these vibrations into usable electrical energy, powering sensors, communication devices, and wearable technologies[77,78]. Picture a soldier's backpack adorned with PVDF-based panels, silently harvesting the energy from their movements to charge essential equipment.

PVDF's versatility extends beyond its resilience and energy-harvesting capabilities. It can also be integrated with sensors and communication systems[79,80]. By embedding PVDF-based sensors into structures or vehicles that undergo stress, real-time data can be collected on various parameters like strain, temperature, and pressure. These sensors enable enhanced structural monitoring, improving safety and signal the need for maintenance.

Chapter References

1. Montes, S., & Maleki, H. (2020). Aerogels and their applications. *In Materials science*. https://www.sciencedirect.com/science/article/abs/pii/B9780128133576000152

2. Pacor Inc. (n.d.). The Advantages of Aerogel Insulation Compared to Other Types of Insulation. https://www.pacorinc.com/the-advantages-of-aerogel-insulation-compared-to-other-types-of-insulation/

3. McManus, D., & Kaushik, P. (2022, October 29). Aerogel Wonder Material: Climate-Resilient Buildings. *e-architect*. https://www.e-architect.com/articles/aerogel-wonder-material

4. Qi, Z., Huang, D., He, S., et al. (2013). Thermal Protective Performance of Aerogel Embedded Firefighter's Protective Clothing. *Journal of Engineered Fibers and Fabrics*, 8(2). https://doi.org/10.1177/155892501300800216

5. Du, Y., & Kim, H.-E. (2022). Research trends of the application of aerogel materials in clothing. *Fashion and Textiles*, 9, 23. https://doi.org/10.1186/s40691-022-00298-5

6. Edmondson, J. (2023, September 27). Growth Opportunities for Aerogels Outside the EV Market. *Electric Vehicles Research*. https://www.electricvehiclesresearch.com/articles/29901/growth-opportunities-for-aerogels-outside-the-ev-market

7. IDTechEx. (2021, September 23). EV Battery Packs Is the Major Application the Aerogel Industry Needed, Says IDTechEx. *CISION PR Newswire*. https://www.prnewswire.com/news-releases/ev-battery-packs-is-the-major-application-the-aerogel-industry-needed-says-idtechex-301383682.html

8. Baetens, R., Jelle, B. P., & Gustavsen, A. (2011). Aerogel insulation for building applications: A state-of-the-art review. *Energy and Buildings*, 43(4), 761-769. https://doi.org/10.1016/j.enbuild.2010.12.012

9. Thie, C., Quallen, S., Ibrahim, A., Xing, T., Johnson, B. (2023). Study of Energy Saving Using Silica Aerogel Insulation in a Residential Building. *Gels*, 9(2), 86. https://doi.org/10.3390/gels9020086

10. Turpen, A. (2017, January 29). Review: Oros' aerogel-insulated cold weather gear. *New Atlas*. https://newatlas.com/oros-nasa-aerogel/47573/

11. Williams, J. (2017, January 31). Staying Warm, Staying Fit with Help of Aerogel Insulated Apparel. *Aspen Aerogels*. https://www.aerogel.com/resources-library/staying-warm-staying-fit-with-help-of-aerogel-insulated-apparel/

12. NASA. (2011, July 28). Aerogels: Thinner, Lighter, Stronger. https://www.nasa.gov/aeronautics/aerogels-thinner-lighter-stronger/

13. Jones, S. M., & Sakamoto, J. (2011). Applications of Aerogels in Space Exploration. In M. Aegerter, N. Leventis, & M. Koebel (Eds.), Aerogels Handbook. *Advances in Sol-Gel Derived Materials and Technologies* (pp. 561-572). Springer. https://doi.org/10.1007/978-1-4419-7589-8_32

14. Papadopoulos, L. (2023, April 21). NASA engineers develop super-strong 3D printed alloy for aircraft and spacecraft parts. *Interesting Engineering*. https://interestingengineering.com/science/nasa-engineers-develop-super-strong-3d-printed-alloy-for-aircraft-and-spacecraft-parts

15. Smith, T. M., Kantzos, C. A., Zarkevich, N. A., Harder, B. J., Heczko, M., Gradl, P. R., Thompson, A. C., Mills, M. J., Gabb, T. P., & Lawson, J. W. (2023). A 3D printable alloy designed for extreme environments. *Nature*, 617, 513-518. https://www.nature.com/articles/s41586-023-05893-0

16. Aboulkhair, N. T., Simonelli, M., Parry, L., Ashcroft, I., Tuck, C., & Hague, R. (2019). 3D printing of Aluminium alloys: Additive Manufacturing of Aluminium alloys using selective laser melting. *Progress in Materials Science*, 106, 100578. https://doi.org/10.1016/j.pmatsci.2019.100578

17. E&T Editorial Staff. (2022, September 23). Method for 3D-printing strong stainless steel revealed with particle accelerator. *E&T Magazine*. https://eandt.theiet.org/content/articles/2022/09/large-particle-accelerator-reveals-method-for-3d-printing-strong-stainless-steel/

18. Buljak, V., & Ranzi, G. (2021). Shape memory alloys. In V. Buljak & G. Ranzi (Eds.), *Constitutive Modeling of Engineering Materials* (pp. 293-313). Academic Press. ISBN 9780128146965. https://doi.org/10.1016/B978-0-12-814696-5.00014-9

19. Andrianesis, K., & Tzes, A. (2015). Development and Control of a Multifunctional Prosthetic Hand with Shape Memory Alloy Actuators. *Journal of Intelligent and Robotic Systems: Theory and Applications*, 78(2), 257-289. https://doi.org/10.1007/s10846-014-0061-6

20. Kaplanoglu, E. (2012). Design of Shape Memory Alloy-Based and Tendon-Driven Actuated Fingers towards a Hybrid Anthropomorphic Prosthetic Hand. *International Journal of Advanced Robotic Systems*,

33

9(3). https://doi.org/10.5772/51276

21. Copaci, D., Arias, J., Moreno, L., & Blanco, D. (2022). Shape Memory Alloy (SMA)-Based Exoskeletons for Upper Limb Rehabilitation. *IntechOpen*. https://doi.org/10.5772/intechopen.101751

22. Riccio, A., Sellitto, A., Ameduri, S., Concilio, A., & Arena, M. (2021). Shape memory alloys (SMA) for automotive applications and challenges. In A. Concilio, V. Antonucci, F. Auricchio, L. Lecce, & E. Sacco (Eds.), *Shape Memory Alloy Engineering (Second Edition)* (pp. 785-808). Butterworth-Heinemann. ISBN 9780128192641. https://doi.org/10.1016/B978-0-12-819264-1.00024-8

23. Dunić, V. (2020). Shape memory alloys in the automotive industry: Overview, application, modeling. https://www.researchgate.net/publication/348018504_Shape_memory_alloys_in_automotive_industry_-_overview_application_modeling

24. Yang, Y., Wang, Y., Yao, T., & Feng, X. (2022). A flexible and smart shape memory alloy composite sheet based on efficient and bidirectional thermal management. *International Journal of Smart and Nano Materials*, 13(2), 315-329. https://doi.org/10.1080/19475411.2022.2076754

25. Kumar, N., & Dixit, A. (2019). Camouflage and Stealth Technology Based on Nanomaterials. *Nanotechnology for Defence Applications* (pp. 73-92). Springer, Cham. https://doi.org/10.1007/978-3-030-29880-7_5

26. Li, M., et al. (2020). Manipulating metals for adaptive thermal camouflage. *Science Advances*, 6, eaba3494. https://doi.org/10.1126/sciadv.aba3494

27. McCue, I. D., Valentino, G. M., Trigg, D. B., Lennon, A. M., Hebert, C. E., Seker, D. P., Nimer, S. M., Mastandrea, J. P., Trexler, M. M., & Storck, S. M. (2021). Controlled shape-morphing metallic components for deployable structures. *Materials & Design*, 208, 109935. https://doi.org/10.1016/j.matdes.2021.109935

28. Lan, X., Liu, L., Pan, C., Hou, G., Li, F., Liu, Z., Dai, W., Wang, L., Zhang, F., Sun, J., Yue, H., Liu, Y., Leng, J., Zhong, X., & Tang, Y. (2023). Smart Space Deployable Truss Based on Shape-Memory Releasing Mechanisms. *Journal of Spacecraft and Rockets*, 60(4). https://doi.org/10.2514/1.A35649

29. Greer, A. L. (2014). Metallic Glasses. In D. E. Laughlin & K. Hono (Eds.), *Physical Metallurgy (Fifth Edition)* (pp. 305-385). Elsevier. ISBN 9780444537706. https://doi.org/10.1016/B978-0-444-53770-6.00004-6

30. Dugdale, J. S., Pavuna, D., & Rhodes, P. (1985). Metallic glasses: Properties and applications. *Endeavour*, 9(2), 62-66. https://doi.org/10.1016/0160-9327(85)90038-9

31. Perkins, R. (2016, April 5). USC scientists follow the bouncing metallic glass. *USC Today*. https://today.usc.edu/follow-the-bouncing-metallic-glass/

32. Liao, G., Luan, C., Wang, Z., Liu, J., Yao, X., & Fu, J. (2021). Acoustic Metamaterials: A Review of Theories, Structures, Fabrication Approaches, and Applications. *Advanced Materials Technologies*, 6(2). https://doi.org/10.1002/admt.202000787

33. Choi, C., Bansal, S., Münzenrieder, N., & Subramanian, S. (2021). Fabricating and Assembling Acoustic Metamaterials and Phononic Crystals. *Advanced Engineering Materials*, 23, 2000988. https://doi.org/10.1002/adem.202000988

34. Cummer, S. A., Christensen, J., & Alù, A. (2016). Controlling sound with acoustic metamaterials. *Nature Reviews Materials*, 1, 16001. https://www.nature.com/articles/natrevmats20161

35. Kumar, S., & Lee, H. (2019). The Present and Future Role of Acoustic Metamaterials for Architectural and Urban Noise Mitigations. *Acoustics*, 3, 590-607. https://doi.org/10.3390/acoustics1030035

36. Gupta, A., Sharma, R., Thakur, A., & Gulia, P. (2023). Metamaterial foundation for seismic wave attenuation for low and wide frequency band. *Scientific Reports*, 13(2293). https://www.nature.com/articles/s41598-023-27678-1

37. Mizokami, K. (2019, October 3). How Metamaterials Could Lead to Invisible Tanks and Super-Stealthy Submarines. *Popular Mechanics*. https://www.popularmechanics.com/military/research/a29355374/metamaterials-stealth/

38. Crane, D. (2009, June 16). Will Future U.S. Military Submarines Be Invisible to Enemy Sonar Detection?: Enter Acoustic Metamaterial Cloaking Tech. *DefenseReview*. https://defensereview.com/title-will-future-us-military-submarines-utilize-an-acoustic-invisibility-cloak-to-defeat-sonar-detection/

39. ConcreteNetwork. (2020, April 22). Why Does Concrete Crack? How to Stop Cracking. https://www.concretenetwork.com/concrete/concrete_cracks/preventing_concrete_cracks.htm

40. Construction Placements. (2023, January 20; updated April 18). The use of bacteria to create self-healing concrete. https://www.

constructionplacements.com/use-of-bacteria-to-create-self-healing-concrete/

41. Nodehi, M., Ozbakkaloglu, T., & Gholampour, A. (2022). A systematic review of bacteria-based self-healing concrete: Biomineralization, mechanical, and durability properties. *Journal of Building Engineering*, 49, 104038. https://doi.org/10.1016/j.jobe.2022.104038

42. Bellah, M., Nosonovsky, M., & Rohatgi, P. (2023). Shape Memory Alloy Reinforced Self-Healing Metal Matrix Composites. *Applied Sciences*, 13(12), 6884. https://doi.org/10.3390/app13126884

43. Zhang, S., van Dijk, N., & van der Zwaag, S. (2020). A Review of Self-healing Metals: Fundamentals, Design Principles and Performance. *Acta Metallurgica Sinica (English Letters)*, 33, 1167–1179. https://doi.org/10.1007/s40195-020-01102-3

44. Ginsberg, D. M., Hosch, W. L., Liesangthem, G., Lotha, G., Rodriguez, E., Singh, S., & The Editors of Encyclopaedia Britannica. (2023, November 1). Superconductivity | Physics, Properties, & Applications. *Britannica*. https://www.britannica.com/science/superconductivity

45. Yakhmi, J. V. (2021). Superconducting Materials and Their Applications. *Institute of Physics Publishing*. https://doi.org/10.1088/978-0-7503-2256-0

46. Castelvecchi, D. (2023, September 1). How would room-temperature superconductors change science? *Nature*, 621, 18-19. https://doi.org/10.1038/d41586-023-02681-8

47. Pedram, M. (2023, March 28). Room-temperature superconductors could revolutionize electronics: An electrical engineer explains the material's potential. *The Conversation*. https://theconversation.com/room-temperature-superconductors-could-revolutionize-electronics-an-electrical-engineer-explains-the-materials-potential-201849

48. Drozdov, A. P., Kong, P. P., Minkov, V. S., et al. (2019). Superconductivity at 250 K in lanthanum hydride under high pressures. *Nature*, 569, 528–531. https://doi.org/10.1038/s41586-019-1201-8

49. Hong, F., Yang, L., Shan, P., Yang, P., Liu, Z., Sun, J., & Yin, Y. (2020). Superconductivity of Lanthanum Superhydride Investigated Using the Standard Four-Probe Configuration under High Pressures. *Chinese Physics Letters*, 37(10), 107401.https://doi.org/10.1088/0256-307X/37/10/107401

50. Gamel, M. M. A., Lee, H. J., Rashid, W. E. S. W. A., Ker, P. J., Yau, L. K., Hannan, M. A., & Jamaludin, M. Z. (2021). A Review on Thermophotovoltaic Cell and Its Applications in Energy Conversion: Issues and Recommendations. *Materials (Basel)*, 14(17), 4944. https://doi.org/10.3390/ma14174944

51. Celanovic, I., Jovanovic, N., & Kassakian, J. (2008). Two-dimensional tungsten photonic crystals as selective thermal emitters. *Applied Physics Letters*, 92(19), 193101. https://doi.org/10.1063/1.2927484

52. Sakakibara, R., Stelmakh, V., Chan, W. R., Geil, R. D., Krämer, S., Savas, T., Ghebrebrhan, M., Joannopoulos, J. D., Soljačić, M., & Čelanović, I. (2022). A high-performance, metallodielectric 2D photonic crystal for thermophotovoltaics. *Solar Energy Materials and Solar Cells*, 238, 111536. https://doi.org/10.1016/j.solmat.2021.111536

53. Sakakibara, R. (2021). High-performance metallo-dielectric photonic crystals: Design, fabrication, and testing of a practical emitter for portable thermophotovoltaic generators. *Massachusetts Institute of Technology*. https://dspace.mit.edu/handle/1721.1/139896

54. Datas, A., & Martí, A. (2017). Thermophotovoltaic energy in space applications: Review and future potential. *Solar Energy Materials and Solar Cells*, 161, 285-296. https://doi.org/10.1016/j.solmat.2016.12.007

55. Qin, G., & Qin, Z. (2020). Negative Poisson's ratio in two-dimensional honeycomb structures. *npj Computational Materials*, 6(51). https://doi.org/10.1038/s41524-020-0313-x

56. Yolcu, D. A., & Baba, B. O. (2022). Measurement of Poisson's ratio of the auxetic structure. *Measurement*, 204, 112040. https://doi.org/10.1016/j.measurement.2022.112040

57. Balan P, Mertens A. J, Bahubalendruni, M. V. A. R. (2023). Auxetic mechanical metamaterials and their futuristic developments: A state-of-art review. *Materials Today Communications*, 34, 105285. https://doi.org/10.1016/j.mtcomm.2022.105285

58. Underhill, Royale. (2014). Defense Applications of Auxetic Materials. https://www.researchgate.net/publication/263652141_Defense_Applications_of_Auxetic_Materials

59. Moroney, C., Alderson, A., Allen, T., Sanami, M., & Venkatraman, P. D. (2018). The Application of Auxetic Material for Protective Sports Apparel. *Proceedings*, 2(6), 251. https://doi.org/10.3390/proceedings2060251

60. Shirzad, M., Zolfagharian, A., Bodaghi, M., & Nam, S. Y. (2023). Auxetic metamaterials for bone-implanted medical devices: Recent advances and new perspectives. *European Journal of Mechanics - A/Solids*, 98, 104905. https://doi.org/10.1016/j.euromechsol.2022.104905

61. Lecina-Tejero, Ó., Pérez, M. Á., García-Gareta, E., & Borau, C. (2023). The rise of mechanical metamaterials: Auxetic constructs for skin wound healing. *Journal of Tissue Engineering*, 14. https://doi.org/10.1177/20417314231177838

62. Lowe, A., & Lakes, R. (2000). Negative Poisson's Ratio Foam as Seat Cushion Material. *Cellular Polymers*, 19. https://www.researchgate.net/publication/241282067_Negative_Poisson's_Ratio_Foam_as_Seat_Cushion_Material

63. Kim, J.-S., Mahato, M., Oh, J.-H., & Oh, I.-K. (2022). Multi-Purpose Auxetic Foam with Honeycomb Concave Micropattern for Sound and Shock Energy Absorbers. *Advanced Materials Interfaces*. https://doi.org/10.1002/admi.202202092

64. Piezo.com. (n.d.). History of Piezoelectricity. https://piezo.com/pages/history-of-piezoelectricity

65. Chandra Sekhar, B., Dhanalakshmi, B., Srinivasa Rao, B., Ramesh, S., Venkata Prasad, K., Subba Rao, P. S. V., & Parvatheeswara Rao, B. (2021). Piezoelectricity and Its Applications. *IntechOpen*. https://doi.org/10.5772/intechopen.96154

66. Zheng, H., Wang, Y., Liu, J., Wang, J., Yan, K., & Zhu, K. (2024). Recent advancements in the use of novel piezoelectric materials for piezocatalytic and piezo-photocatalytic applications. *Applied Catalysis B: Environmental*, 341, 123335. https://doi.org/10.1016/j.apcatb.2023.123335

67. Lahat, I. (2013, May 8). The Energy Groove: using the power of dance to create electricity. *FairPlanet*. https://www.fairplanet.org/story/the-energy-dance/

68. Sun, J-Q., Xu, T-B., & Yazdani, A. (2023). Ultra-High Power Density Roadway Piezoelectric Energy Harvesting System (Publication No. CEC-500-2023-036). *California Energy Commission*. https://www.energy.ca.gov/publications/2023/ultra-high-power-density-roadway-piezoelectric-energy-harvesting-system

69. Shah Alam, Md & Islam, Tanjemul & Rahman, Tajim Md Hasibur & Hasan, Mahmudul. (2015). *Power Harvesting from Aircraft Body using Piezoelectric Material*. 163-173. https://www.researchgate.net/publication/333203987_Power_Harvesting_from_Aircraft_Body_using_Piezoelectric_Material

70. Liu, Y., Khanbareh, H., Halim, M. A., Feeney, A., Zhang, X., Heidari, H., & Ghannam, R. (2021). Piezoelectric energy harvesting for self-powered wearable upper limb applications. *Advanced Materials Technologies*. https://doi.org/10.1002/nano.202000242

71. Wang, T. W., & Lin, S. F. (2020). Wearable Piezoelectric-Based System for Continuous Beat-to-Beat Blood Pressure Measurement. *Sensors (Basel)*, 20(3), 851. https://doi.org/10.3390/s20030851

72. Wang, Y., Yu, Y., Wei, X., & Narita, F. (2022). Self-Powered Wearable Piezoelectric Monitoring of Human Motion and Physiological Signals for the Postpandemic Era: A Review. *Advanced Materials Technologies*. https://doi.org/10.1002/admt.202200318

73. Neikov, O. D., Naboychenko, S. S., & Murashova, I. B. (2019). Production of Rare Metal Powders. In O. D. Neikov, S. S. Naboychenko, & N. A. Yefimov (Eds.), *Handbook of Non-Ferrous Metal Powders (Second Edition)* (pp. 757-829). Elsevier. ISBN 9780081005439. https://doi.org/10.1016/B978-0-08-100543-9.00024-5

74. Kimura, M., Ando, A., & Sakabe, Y. (2010). Lead zirconate titanate-based piezo-ceramics. In K. Uchino (Ed.), *Advanced Piezoelectric Materials* (pp. 89-110). Woodhead Publishing. ISBN 9781845695347. https://doi.org/10.1533/9781845699758.1.89

75. Zaszczyńska, A., Gradys, A., & Sajkiewicz, P. (2020). Progress in the Applications of Smart Piezoelectric Materials for Medical Devices. *Polymers (Basel)*, 12(11), 2754. https://doi.org/10.3390/polym12112754

76. *Material-Properties.org*. (n.d.). Polyvinylidene Fluoride (PVDF) | Formula, Properties & Application. https://material-properties.org/polyvinylidene-fluoride-pvdf/

77. Jiang, H., & Ao, H. (2022). Polyvinylidene Fluoride-Based Vibration Energy Harvester with Piezoelectric and Electromagnetic Mechanisms. *Energy Technology*, 10(12), 2200373. https://doi.org/10.1002/ente.202200373

78. Zhao, J., & You, Z. (2014). Models for 31-mode PVDF energy harvester for wearable applications. *Scientific World Journal*, 2014, 893496. https://doi.org/10.1155/2014/893496

79. Dange, E., Hamsa, R., Madhuri, M., et al. (2021). PVDF-based piezoelectric alarm system. *ISSS Journal of Micro Smart Systems*, 10, 83-86. https://doi.org/10.1007/s41683-021-00069-2

80. Guzman, E., et al. (2013). Survivability of integrated PVDF film sensors to accelerated ageing conditions in aeronautical/aerospace

structures. *Smart Materials and Structures*, 22(6), 065020. https://doi.org/10.1088/0964-1726/22/6/065020

Biomimetic Materials

In the grand narrative of innovation, there's a plot twist that consistently resurfaces: the realization that sometimes nature had it right all along. This is precisely the case with the rapidly emerging field of biomimetic materials, a realm of research that takes cues from the natural world to revolutionize our man-made one. From the graceful flight patterns of birds inspiring aerodynamic enhancements, to the uncanny water repellent and self-cleaning properties of lotus leaves, life on Earth has had millions of years to optimize solutions to a variety of challenges. Now it is humanity's turn to listen, learn, and leverage this wisdom in the creation of biomimetic materials. These materials echo the functionality, resilience, and efficiency of structures found in nature, charting a path forward that marries biological genius honed by nature over millions of years with human ingenuity.

The challenge in this field is decoding nature's blueprints and replicating its finest inventions. How can shark skin technology reduce bacterial growth in public spaces? What can we learn from spider silk to produce stronger, more durable textiles? Can the humble mussel inspire the adhesives of the future? These queries, once seemingly irrelevant, are now at the forefront of tangible and exciting progress.

Mussels

Dive beneath the ocean waves, and you'll discover a world of tenacious survivalists. Among the most remarkable are mussels, humble little creatures that harbor the secret to one of the future's most promising materials. Anchored securely to rocks, ship hulls, and even each other, these unassuming creatures weather the relentless force of the sea using an adhesive that's unlike any synthetic counterpart. This remarkable bond, resistant to the pounding surf and corrosive saltwater, has captivated scientists and material engineers across the globe[1,2].

The adhesive prowess of mussels comes from the *byssus*, a cluster of thread-like structures that mussels secrete to affix themselves to various surfaces[1]. Interestingly, these threads remain sturdy and flexible, even under the ocean's harshest conditions. The secret to this phenomenal underwater adhesive is a set of proteins rich in an amino acid called *L-DOPA*, which allows the formation of strong bonds with both organic and inorganic surfaces[1,3]. n

The potential of translating this mussel-inspired adhesive into synthetic form holds tantalizing implications across numerous sectors. Unlike many synthetic glues, which can dissolve or weaken when exposed to water, mussel-inspired adhesives could offer an unprecedented level of water-resistant bonding. This would be invaluable for industries such as marine construction, automotive manufacturing, and even medicine.

Picture ships and submarines that can undergo repairs directly in the water without needing to be hauled ashore, or cars equipped with components bound by adhesives that don't degrade in rain or snow.

Initial forays into creating such materials are already showing promise. Researchers have developed synthetic polymers mimicking the proteins rich in *L-DOPA* that are found in mussels, resulting in adhesives that can bond strongly to various surfaces and withstand wet environments[2,4]. These novel adhesives are not only robust but also eco-friendly, aligning with the increasing need for sustainability in material production.

In the realm of medicine, these mussel-inspired adhesives are already demonstrating their worth[5]. They offer the potential for more effective, less invasive treatments. Imagine surgical adhesives that work seamlessly in the wet environment of the human body, reducing the need for stitches and leading to faster, cleaner healing with less scarring. Imagine medical procedures that utilize biocompatible, water-resistant glues for sealing wounds or binding tissues, an innovation that would go beyond sutures and staples.

The future of electronics also stands to gain an advantage. Electronics often suffer from water damage, but with mussel-inspired adhesives, we could create next-level water-resistant seals for electronic components, safeguarding our devices from accidents and the elements.

The amazing prospects that mollusks like mussels show to future material science doesn't stop there, more magic lies within their shells. This amazing material is nacre or more commonly referred to as Mother of Pearl. This organic-inorganic composite material, found lining the inner shells of certain mollusks and the outer coating of pearls, has intrigued and inspired scientists, artisans, and engineers alike for centuries[6]. Now, as we stride boldly into the future, the unique structure and properties of nacre have the potential to revolutionize material science and engineering.

Nacre's ethereal iridescence, a spectacle to behold, belies the robustness and durability of its structure. The secret to this remarkable composite lies in its "brick and mortar" architecture. A layered arrangement of microscopic calcium carbonate tablets (the bricks) are held together by a thin layer of elastic biopolymers (the mortar)[7,8]. This hierarchical structure gives nacre a combination of strength, toughness, and resistance to fracture that far exceeds that of its constituent materials alone.

The potential applications of materials replicating the structure and properties of nacre are immense. For instance, imagine a future where our buildings and infrastructures are constructed with nacre-inspired materials. Such structures would not only exhibit exceptional resilience to natural disasters but could also incorporate the captivating iridescence of nacre, creating urban landscapes as enchanting as they are durable[9].

The world of protective gear and armor is another

domain where nacre-inspired materials can bring about a paradigm shift. The high impact resistance and energy absorption capacity of nacre can inform the design of advanced body armor and protective sports gear, safeguarding soldiers and athletes with a biomimetic shield that has evolved over millions of years[10].

Furthermore, nacre's intricate structure offers exciting possibilities in the realm of optoelectronics[11]. The characteristic iridescence of nacre arises from the diffraction and interference of light passing through its layered structure. By fabricating materials with a similar architecture, we can develop new classes of solar cells and sensitive optical sensors.

The development of nacre-inspired materials isn't just about borrowing designs from nature, it is also about embracing a more sustainable approach to materials science. Traditional production processes often involve high energy inputs and harmful emissions. In contrast, nacre is formed in the ocean, at ambient temperature and pressure, without any adverse impact on the environment. Thus, by studying and mimicking the process behind nacre's formation, we can stride towards a future of greener and more sustainable material production.

Sharks

The shark, an apex predator that has roamed the open oceans for millions of years, is born with something that could revolutionize future material design, its skin. Shark skin is a masterpiece of evolution, studded with tiny, tooth-like structures called *denticles*. These structures are composed of hard, enamel-like substances, each one precisely shaped and positioned to reduce drag and increase the shark's swimming speed. The denticles channel water more efficiently over the shark's body, reducing friction and making them more agile hunters. An equally significant feature is the denticles' ability to deter the growth of algae, barnacles, and other marine organisms that could slow the shark down by adding weight and further increasing drag.

The application of these evolutionary marvels into man-made materials is nothing short of revolutionary. By mimicking the structure of shark skin, engineers and scientists are designing surfaces that have the potential to enhance performance and efficiency across various sectors[12,13,14].

In the aviation industry, coatings inspired by shark skin are showing potential in dramatically reducing the aerodynamic drag on airplane surfaces, leading to significant fuel savings and reductions in emissions[15,16].

Imagine our airlines becoming as efficient as sharks, cutting through the air with lesser energy and lower environmental impact.

In the maritime domain, such surfaces on ships' hulls could reduce drag and the buildup of algae and microorganisms, leading to faster, more fuel-efficient vessels that require less frequent cleaning and maintenance[17,18]. This is not just a cost-saving measure, but a means to lessen the use of toxic anti-fouling coatings and substances on marine ecosystems.

In sports, athletes are already benefiting from clothing inspired by shark skin, which helps them cut through the air or water more efficiently. Swimsuits that mimic shark denticles became so effective that they were banned from competitive swimming events for giving wearers an unfair advantage[19,20].

Furthermore, materials based on shark skin are helping combat hospital-acquired infections[21]. With surfaces that mimic the micro-topography of shark skin, it is harder for bacteria to take hold, reducing the spread of bacteria in medical facilities[22,23].

Corals

In the grandeur of the world's oceans, no feature is perhaps as captivating as the coral reefs. These vibrant, living structures, crafted over millennia by tiny marine invertebrates known as *polyps*, stand as testament to nature's architectural prowess. As we gaze upon these remarkable underwater citadels, we find inspiration for the future of material science and engineering, gleaning valuable lessons from the humble coral.

Coral reefs are composed primarily of *calcium carbonate*, the same substance found in limestone and chalk. However, it is not the material itself that's extraordinary, but the process by which it is formed[24,25]. Each coral polyp excretes a hard, protective exoskeleton, layer upon layer, creating interconnected structures that are incredibly durable yet porous, allowing for water to flow and marine life to flourish.

What if we could mimic the coral's process to build structures in a more sustainable and efficient manner? The idea isn't as far-fetched as it sounds. Scientists and engineers are actively exploring biomimetic approaches to develop coral-inspired materials, aiming to recreate not only the form but also the function of these organic marvels[26,27].

For instance, consider the world of construction. Traditional methods of producing cement contribute significantly to global carbon emissions. There are environmentally friendly ways of producing cement being explored that is based on how corals build themselves[28,29]. One of these processes actually removes carbon dioxide, a greenhouse gas thought to cause climate change, from the air[28].

In healthcare, researchers are exploring coral-inspired materials for bone grafts. Given the structural similarity between corals and human bones, synthetic materials that mimic the structure of corals can serve as excellent scaffolds for bone regeneration[30,31]. This bio-inspired approach can potentially revolutionize treatments for bone-related injuries and diseases.

As corals face increasing threats from climate change and human activities, it is a bitter irony that these very creatures might hold the key to more sustainable and effective materials for our future. By studying and emulating the simple, yet profoundly effective strategies of the corals, we're not just finding innovative solutions for the present, we're nurturing a deeper connection with the natural world.

Spiders

Back on land, among the many uncanny marvels of nature that deserve our attention, the silk produced from the humble spider shows promise due to its unique properties. Few materials manage to encapsulate the paradox of being both delicate and incredibly strong, but this fantastic biomaterial does so with an elegance that gives credence to the years of evolutionary engineering behind it. This intricate balance of traits has sparked widespread fascination among scientists, leading to pioneering efforts to replicate its properties in the lab.

In nature, spider silk boasts a combination of tensile strength and elasticity that surpasses steel and rivals Kevlar, the synthetic material currently used in bulletproof vests[32]. Yet, it is incredibly lightweight and biodegradable, making it an ideal candidate for various applications across different fields.

Replicating the properties of spider silk isn't straightforward. Spiders are challenging to farm due to their territorial and cannibalistic tendencies. However, the dawn of genetic engineering and advancements in nanotechnology have brought us closer than ever to mass-producing similar materials.

One promising approach has been to insert the gene responsible for producing spider silk into other organisms such as bacteria, yeast, plants, and even goats[33,34,35].

Researchers from the University of Wyoming have developed a technique to incorporate spider silk-spinning genes into goats[36]. This enables the harvesting of silk protein, which is extracted from their milk. In this way, scientists have been able to produce proteins similar to spider silk, which can then be spun into fibers.

These spider-silk inspired materials are being explored for a myriad of applications. In the medical field, they could be used for sutures, tissue scaffolds, and drug delivery systems thanks to its biocompatibility, degradability, and minimal immune response[37,38].

The textile industry is also eyeing spider silk with interest. Imagine a future with clothes that are lightweight, breathable, strong, and biodegradable. Already, the first prototype garments made from biosynthetic spider silk have been debuted, and they offer a tantalizing glimpse into a more sustainable future for fashion[39,40].

In the military and aerospace sectors, ultra-strong fibers based on spider silk could provide innovative solutions for lightweight armor, parachutes, or aircraft construction materials[41,42]. Its impressive strength-to-weight ratio could lead to significant energy and cost savings.

Furthermore, the environmental benefits of these

materials cannot be overstated. In a world increasingly conscious of the impact of pollution and climate change, the shift towards more sustainable materials is a necessity. Being biodegradable and produced using less energy-intensive processes than many traditional materials gives these types of materials great potential for a sustainable future[43].

The Lotus Leaf

One of nature's most captivating marvels comes paradoxically from the seemingly simple lotus leaf. Revered in many cultures for its serene beauty, the lotus leaf is more than just a symbol of purity and enlightenment; it holds secrets that could transform the way we design materials in the future.

The surface of a lotus leaf is a masterclass in functional design, an epitome of the principle known as the *lotus effect*. Despite growing in muddy waters, lotus leaves always appear clean. The reason behind this intriguing phenomenon is the leaf's unique micro-architecture[44,45]. Tiny bumps on its surface trap air, preventing water and dirt from sticking to the leaf. Instead, water droplets roll off while taking dirt particles along with them, a phenomenon known as superhydrophobicity[44].

Replicating this lotus effect in man-made materials opens up fascinating possibilities. Imagine buildings that clean themselves when it rains, windshields that don't need wipers, or clothes that resist stains. The potential applications are vast and transformative. So far, we have developed paints, textiles, and other surfaces that mimic the self-cleaning properties of the lotus leaf[46,47,48]. These materials can repel water, dust, and other contaminants, reducing the need for cleaning and maintenance.

One of the most impressive realizations of this biomimetic principle is in the realm of architecture. Buildings inspired by the lotus effect are not just aesthetically pleasing, but also more sustainable. By reducing the need for chemical cleaners and frequent maintenance, these structures align with our growing need for more environment-friendly living solutions.

The superhydrophobic property of the lotus leaf also finds potential in the medical field. Surgical instruments and medical devices that resist bacterial adhesion can significantly reduce the risk of infections, leading to safer medical procedures.

In the realm of electronics, think about gadgets and devices that need to resist moisture damage, a persistent challenge in the industry. Materials inspired by the humble lotus leaf could provide a robust and durable solution, potentially increasing the lifespan of our everyday devices.

The world of energy is also taking note of the lotus effect. Researchers at Ben-Gurion University of the Negev have used the lotus effect to create a technique for removing dust from solar panels to maintain efficiency and light absorption[49]. This technique, inspired by the lotus effect, significantly outperformed traditional methods by removing 98% of dust particles compared to only 41% with hydrophilic smooth silicon-based wafers.

Chameleons

The chameleon's skin, renowned for its quick color-changing ability, has inspired research into tunable photonic materials. Chameleons can actively adjust the lattice of photonic crystals in their skin, thereby changing the way light reflects off and producing an array of different colors[50,51]. This phenomenon has implications for the development of responsive materials capable of real-time color change, a feature of interest in a variety of fields.

Recently, the chameleon skin's unique features inspired the creation of a system that can read glucose-levels in human bodily fluids without requiring any external energy source[52]. This system was made by embedding plasmonic silver nanocubes in a hydrogel network. When light hits the nanocubes, it creates a reaction that can be measured. This reaction is influenced by the presence of certain molecules, like glucose. This kind of system could be extremely beneficial for diabetics, who would no longer have to rely on powered devices or drawing blood to read their glucose levels.

The implication of this technology could extend to various other biosensing applications. This could include contributing to early disease detection and management, thereby potentially improving healthcare outcomes and reducing costs.

Geckos

In nature's endless source of inspiration, the nimble wall-climbing gecko has caught the attention of scientists and engineers. Their ability to effortlessly scale vertical surfaces and even dart across ceilings has intrigued the scientific community, prompting a closer look at their adhesion secrets.

Unlike the sticky residue of glue or tape, geckos rely on a phenomenon known as van der Waals forces for their acrobatic feats[53]. Named after the Dutch scientist who first proposed them, these forces arise due to the subtle electromagnetic interactions between molecules, and they are exceptionally weak. However, geckos have millions of tiny hairs on their feet called *setae* that amplify these forces[54]. When we consider that each foot can house up to half a million of these hairs, it's clear how geckos hold on tight to almost any surface.

Capturing this incredible capability, scientists have developed a synthetic material known as *geckskin*[55,56]. This material imitates the gecko's adhesive mechanism on a larger scale. It can stick to a wide range of surfaces, carry substantial loads, and be easily removed and reused without losing its stickiness or leaving a residue. It's able to stick to anything that's vaguely smooth, including glass, metal, drywall, and wood, and it even works on surfaces that are slightly curved.

The applications for geckskin are as broad as they are exciting. In the world of robotics, geckskin could empower robots with gecko-like climbing abilities, enabling them to navigate environments and carry out tasks previously unthinkable. This isn't purely theoretical, Stickybot is a real robotic gecko created by Stanford for this specific application[57]. Imagine a future where search-and-rescue robots deftly navigate rubble in disaster zones, or maintenance robots scamper up high-rises for window cleaning or structural repairs.

In the consumer electronics space, geckskin could revolutionize how we mount and display items. Forget about drilling holes or fumbling with sticky tape, a geckskin surface would allow a television to be effortlessly mounted on a wall and moved around as desired. The same goes for hanging pictures, installing speakers, or organizing tools in the garage.

The world of sports and athletic performance could reach a new level with geckskin. Shoes with geckskin tread could provide unrivaled grip and balance for athletes across a wide variety of sports. From the basketball courts where players pivot with split-second precision to the football field where catching a pass could make or break a game, geckskin's potential applications seem boundless.

Everyday items of our society could get an upgrade using geckskin technology. Golfers could reach unparalleled distance and accuracy with their geckskin golf clubs. Workers would have a new level of comfort handling geckskin tools or wearing geckskin gloves. Steering wheels and airplane controls wrapped with geckskin could be the difference between a near-miss and a tragic accident. The disabled and elderly of our society would gain new confidence using walking canes with geckskin handles or holding onto a guardrail wrapped in a geckskin layer. A distracted teenager could save themselves the disappointment of a cracked phone screen because their device slipped out of their hands.

The benefits of geckskin are obvious for the military. The prospect of troops being able to scale vertical surfaces, much like their reptilian inspiration, opens new tactical possibilities. This is already a reality, scientists and engineers at the Defense Advanced Research Projects Agency (DARPA) have already devised gecko-inspired paddles that recently helped a 218-pound man, lugging a 50-pound load, to scale and descend a 25-foot glass wall[58].

Chapter References

1. Li, Y., & Cao, Y. (2019). The molecular mechanisms underlying mussel adhesion. *Nanoscale Advances*, 1, 4246. https://doi.org/10.1039/C9NA00582J

2. Zhang, X., Liu, H., Yue, L., et al. (2020). Mussel-mimetic polymer underwater adhesives with l-Dopa functionality: influencing adhesion properties and simplified operation procedures. *Journal of Materials Science*, 55, 7981–7997. https://doi.org/10.1007/s10853-020-04572-z

3. Jaramillo, J., Rodriguez-Oliva, I., Abian, O., et al. (2020). Specific chemical incorporation of l-DOPA and functionalized l-DOPA-hyaluronic acid in Candida antarctica lipase: creating potential mussel-inspired bioadhesives. *SN Applied Sciences*, 2, 1731. https://doi.org/10.1007/s42452-020-03545-w

4. Mu, Y., Sun, Q., Li, B., & Wan, X. (2023). Advances in the Synthesis and Applications of Mussel-Inspired Polymers. *Polymer Reviews*, 63(1), 1-39. https://doi.org/10.1080/15583724.2022.2041032

5. Balkenende, D. W. R., Winkler, S. M., & Messersmith, P. B. (2019). Marine-Inspired Polymers in Medical Adhesion. *European Polymer Journal*, 116, 134-143. https://doi.org/10.1016/j.eurpolymj.2019.03.059

6. Gim, J., Schnitzer, N., Otter, L. M., et al. (2019). Nanoscale deformation mechanics reveal resilience in nacre of Pinna nobilis shell. *Nature Communications*, 10, 4822. https://doi.org/10.1038/s41467-019-12743-z

7. Yin, Z., et al. (2019). Impact-resistant nacre-like transparent materials. *Science*, 364, 1260-1263. https://doi.org/10.1126/science.aaw8988

8. Zhao, H., Yang, Z., & Guo, L. (2018). Nacre-inspired composites with different macroscopic dimensions: strategies for improved mechanical performance and applications. *NPG Asia Materials*, 10, 1-22. https://doi.org/10.1038/s41427-018-0009-6

9. Sharma, A., Shukla, N. K., Belarbi, M. O., Abbas, M., Garg, A., Li, L., Bhutto, J., & Bhatia, A. (2023). Bio-inspired nacre and helicoidal composites: From structure to mechanical applications. *Thin-Walled Structures*, 192, 111146. https://doi.org/10.1016/j.tws.2023.111146

10. Wang, L., Wang, B., Ziqiu, W., Huang, J., ... Gao, C., & Xu, Z. (2023).

Superior Strong and Tough Nacre-Inspired Materials by Interlayer. *Nano Letters*, 23(8), 3352–3361. https://doi.org/10.1021/acs.nanolett.3c00332

11. Madhav, D., Buffel, B., Moldenaers, P., Desplentere, F., & Vandeginste, V. (2023). A review of nacre-inspired materials: Chemistry, strengthening-deformation mechanism, synthesis, and applications. *Progress in Materials Science*, 139, 101168. https://doi.org/10.1016/j.pmatsci.2023.101168

12. Domel, A. G., Saadat, M., Weaver, J. C., Haj-Hariri, H., Bertoldi, K., & Lauder, G. V. (2018). Shark skin-inspired designs that improve aerodynamic performance. *Journal of The Royal Society Interface*, 15(139), 20170828. https://doi.org/10.1098/rsif.2017.0828

13. Gabler-Smith, M. K., & Lauder, G. V. (2022). Ridges and riblets: Shark skin surfaces versus biomimetic models. *Frontiers in Marine Science*, 9. https://doi.org/10.3389/fmars.2022.975062

14. Jo, W., Kang, H. S., Choi, J., Jung, J., Hyun, J., Kwon, J., ... & Kim, H.-T. (2021). Light-Designed Shark Skin-Mimetic Surfaces. *Nano Letters*, 21(13), 5500–5507. https://doi.org/10.1021/acs.nanolett.1c00436

15. Papadopoulos, L. (2022, December 25). This aircraft fuel-saving technology is based on the skin of sharks. *Interesting Engineering*. https://interestingengineering.com/innovation/aircraft-fuel-technology-skin-sharks

16. Whittle, N. (2019, May 13). Exciting New "Shark Skin" Technology To Cut Aircraft Fuel Usage. *Simple Flying*. https://simpleflying.com/shark-skin-paint-technology-aircraft/

17. Fu, Y. F., Yuan, C. Q., & Bai, X. Q. (2017). Marine drag reduction of shark skin inspired riblet surfaces. *Biosurface and Biotribology*, 3(1), 11-24. https://doi.org/10.1016/j.bsbt.2017.02.001

18. Bhushan, B. (2016). Shark-Skin Surface for Fluid-Drag Reduction in Turbulent Flow. *Biomimetics. Biological and Medical Physics, Biomedical Engineering*. Springer, Cham. https://doi.org/10.1007/978-3-319-28284-8_10

19. Smith, R. (2009, July 27). Swimsuit Banned as Technology Doping. *Symscape*. https://www.symscape.com/blog/swimsuit-banned-as-technology-doping

20. Nosowitz, D. (2012, July 26). Speedo's Super-Fast Sharkskin-Inspired Swimsuit Is Actually Nothing Like a Shark's Skin. *Popular Science*. https://www.popsci.com/technology/article/2012-07/speedos-super-fast-sharkskin-inspired-swimsuit-actually-nothing-sharks-skin/

21. Mann, E. E., Manna, D., Mettetal, M. R., et al. (2014). Surface micropattern limits bacterial contamination. *Antimicrobial Resistance & Infection Control*, 3, 28. https://doi.org/10.1186/2047-2994-3-28

22. Rettner, R. (2014, September 18). Shark Skin Inspires Hospital Superbug Battle. *Live Science*. https://www.livescience.com/47870-shark-skin-hospital-superbugs.html

23. Seegert, C., Ph.D. (2014, September 22). Shark Skin Inspires Antimicrobial Surfaces. *Med Device Online*. https://www.meddeviceonline.com/doc/shark-skin-inspires-antimicrobial-surfaces-0001

24. Lippsett, L. (2018, November 12). How Do Corals Build Their Skeletons? *WHOI*. https://www.whoi.edu/oceanus/feature/how-do-corals-build-their-skeletons/

25. How Reefs Are Made (n.d.). *Coral Reef Alliance*. https://coral.org/en/coral-reefs-101/how-reefs-are-made/

26. Yahia, L. H., Bayade, G., & Cirotteau, Y. (2021). Natural Coral as a Biomaterial Revisited. *American Journal of Biomedical Sciences & Research*, 13(6), AJBSR.MS.ID.001936. https://doi.org/10.34297/AJBSR.2021.13.001936

27. Green, D. W., Ben-Nissan, B., Yoon, K. S., Milthorpe, B., & Jung, H. S. (2017). Natural and Synthetic Coral Biomineralization for Human Bone Revitalization. *Trends in Biotechnology*, 35(1), 43-54. https://doi.org/10.1016/j.tibtech.2016.10.003

28. Salazar, J. (2012, April 27). Brent Constantz builds with cement like coral do. *EarthSky*. https://earthsky.org/human-world/brent-constantz-builds-cement-like-coral-do/

29. Gebru, K. A., Kidanemariam, T. G., & Gebretinsae, H. K. (2021). Bio-cement production using microbially induced calcite precipitation (MICP) method: A review. *Chemical Engineering Science*, 238, 116610. https://doi.org/10.1016/j.ces.2021.116610

30. Pountos, I., & Giannoudis, P. V. (2016). Is there a role of coral bone substitutes in bone repair? *Injury*, 47(12), 2606-2613. https://doi.org/10.1016/j.injury.2016.10.025

31. Fessenden, M. (2014, October 23). Sea Coral Makes Excellent Human Bone Grafts. *Smithsonian Magazine*. https://www.smithsonianmag.com/smart-news/sea-coral-makes-excellent-human-bone-grafts-180953121/

32. Matchar, E. (2017, July 26). New Artificial Spider Silk: Stronger Than Steel and 98 Percent Water. *Smithsonian Magazine*. https://www.smithsonianmag.com/innovation/new-artificial-spider-silk-stronger-steel-and-98-percent-water-180964176/

33. Kuta, S. (2023, October 17). Genetically Modified Silkworms Can Produce Spider Silk That's Stronger Than Kevlar. *Smithsonian Magazine*. https://www.smithsonianmag.com/smart-news/genetically-modified-silkworms-can-produce-spider-silk-thats-stronger-than-kevlar-180983090/

34. Whittall, D. R., Baker, K. V., Breitling, R., & Takano, E. (2021). Host Systems for the Production of Recombinant Spider Silk. *Trends in Biotechnology*, 39(6), 560-573. https://doi.org/10.1016/j.tibtech.2020.09.007

35. Xu, J., Dong, Q., Yu, Y., Niu, B., Ji, D., Li, M., … Tan, A. (2018). Mass spider silk production through targeted gene replacement in Bombyx mori. *Proceedings of the National Academy of Sciences*, 115(32), 8137-8142. https://doi.org/10.1073/pnas.1806805115

36. Zyga, L. (2010, May 31). Scientists breed goats to produce spider silk. *Phys.org*. https://phys.org/news/2010-05-scientists-goats-spider-silk.html

37. Salehi, S., Koeck, K., & Scheibel, T. (2020). Spider Silk for Tissue Engineering Applications. *Molecules*, 25(3), 737. https://doi.org/10.3390/molecules25030737

38. Bakhshandeh, B., Nateghi, S. S., Gazani, M. M., Dehghani, Z., & Mohammadzadeh, F. (2021). A review on advances in the applications of spider silk in biomedical issues. *International Journal of Biological Macromolecules*, 192, 258-271. https://doi.org/10.1016/j.ijbiomac.2021.09.201

39. Li, J., Jiang, B., Chang, X., Yu, H., Han, Y., & Zhang, F. (2023, April 14). Bi-terminal fusion of intrinsically-disordered mussel foot protein fragments boosts mechanical strength for protein fibers. *Nature Communications*. https://doi.org/10.1038/s41467-023-37563-0

40. StartUs Insights. (n.d.). 5 Top Synthetic Spider Silk Startups Impacting The Materials Industry. https://www.startus-insights.com/innovators-guide/5-top-synthetic-spider-silk-startups-impacting-the-materials-industry/

41. Lindner, D. (2018, August 6). Air Force Scientists Study Artificial Silk for Body Armor, Parachutes. U.S. Department of Defense. https://www.defense.gov/News/News-Stories/Article/Article/1594185/air-force-scientists-study-artificial-silk-for-body-armor-parachutes/

42. Rose, P. (2021, February 23). Spider silk research: From bone regeneration to bulletproof vests. MilitaryTimes. https://www.militarytimes.com/opinion/commentary/2021/02/23/spider-silk-research-from-bone-regeneration-to-bulletproof-vests/

43. Lefèvre, T., & Auger, M. (2016). Spider silk inspired materials and sustainability: perspective. *Materials Technology*, 31(7), 384-399. https://doi.org/10.1179/1753555715Y.0000000065

44. Ensikat, H. J., Ditsche-Kuru, P., Neinhuis, C., & Barthlott, W. (2011). Superhydrophobicity in perfection: the outstanding properties of the lotus leaf. *Beilstein Journal of Nanotechnology*, 2, 152-161. https://doi.org/10.3762/bjnano.2.19

45. Bhushan, B., Jung, Y. C., & Nosonovsky, M. (2010). Lotus Effect: Surfaces with Roughness-Induced Superhydrophobicity, Self-Cleaning, and Low Adhesion. In B. Bhushan (Ed.), *Springer Handbook of Nanotechnology* (pp. 1163-1188). Springer. https://doi.org/10.1007/978-3-642-02525-9_42

46. Collins, C. M., & Safiuddin, M. (2022). Lotus-Leaf-Inspired Biomimetic Coatings: Different Types, Key Properties, and Applications in Infrastructures. *Infrastructures*, 7(4), 46. https://doi.org/10.3390/infrastructures7040046

47. Sto SE & Co. KGaA. (2023). Lotusan: Self-cleaning exterior paint technology. https://www.sto.com/biomimetics/en/biomimetics/lotusan/index.html

48. Bangladesh Textile Today. (2010, July 1). A new approach optimizes lotus effect of soil repellent textiles. https://www.textiletoday.com.bd/a-new-approach-optimises-lotus-effect-of-soil-repellent-textiles

49. Heckenthaler, T., Sadhujan, S., Morgenstern, Y., Natarajan, P., Bashouti, M., & Kaufman, Y. (2019). Self-Cleaning Mechanism: Why Nanotexture and Hydrophobicity Matter. *Langmuir*, 35(48), 15526-15534. https://doi.org/10.1021/acs.langmuir.9b01874

50. Teyssier, J., Saenko, S. V., van der Marel, D., & Milinkovitch, M. C. (2015). Photonic crystals cause active color change in chameleons. *Nature Communications*, 6, 6368. https://doi.org/10.1038/ncomms7368

51. Service, R. F. (2015, March 10). The secret to chameleon color change: Tiny crystals. *Science*. https://www.science.org/content/article/secret-chameleon-color-change-tiny-crystals

52. Ziai, Y., Petronella, F., Rinoldi, C., et al. (2022). Chameleon-inspired multifunctional plasmonic nanoplatforms for biosensing applications.

NPG Asia Materials, 14, 18. https://doi.org/10.1038/s41427-022-00365-9

53. Van Der Waals and the Gecko. (n.d.). *NaturPhilosophie*. https://www.naturphilosophie.co.uk/van-der-waals-gecko/

54. Autumn, K., & Peattie, A. M. (2002). Mechanisms of Adhesion in Geckos. *Integrative and Comparative Biology*, 42(6), 1081-1090. https://doi.org/10.1093/icb/42.6.1081

55. University of Massachusetts Amherst. (2012, February 17). Super-Adhesive "Geckskin" Material Holds 700 Pounds. *SciTechDaily*. https://scitechdaily.com/super-adhesive-geckskin-material-holds-700-pounds/

56. Geckskin Fabric Mimics Gecko. (2014, November 1). *Apparel Resources*. https://apparelresources.com/business-news/sourcing/geckskin-fabric-mimics-gecko/

57. Ackerman, E. (2014, April 24). Gecko Adhesives: Moving From Robot Feet to Your Walls. *IEEE Spectrum*. https://spectrum.ieee.org/gecko-adhesives-moving-from-robot-feet-to-your-walls

58. Jontz, S. (2014, June 6). Gecko-Inspired DARPA Technology Helps Humans Scale Walls. *AFCEA Signal*. https://www.afcea.org/signal-media/gecko-inspired-darpa-technology-helps-humans-scale-walls

Nanomaterials

Throughout history, humanity has marveled at its own architectural prowess. From the Colosseum in Rome to the soaring heights of Dubai's Burj Khalifa, there exists an innate desire to touch the sky. Yet, no matter the zeniths we achieve, our ambitions never wane; they simply evolve. Dreams of space elevators and floating cities among the clouds, once relegated to the pages of science fiction, are edging closer to reality. At the heart of these aspirations lies our burgeoning proficiency in manipulating matter at the atomic and molecular scale. The dawn of nanomaterials heralds an era where we harness properties that transcend the boundaries of contemporary understanding, unlocking possibilities beyond our wildest imaginings.

Nanomaterials are often referred to as "two-dimensional materials"[1]. This is because they are substances that consist of a single to few layers of atoms. They exist almost entirely in just two dimensions: length and width. The concept might be hard to wrap your head around. After all, how can something be, effectively, one atom thick? Yet, they're very real, and they're starting to transform the world.

Two-dimensional materials are more than a scientific curiosity, they are a testament to the boldness of human curiosity and our ability to reshape the world at its most fundamental levels. As we continue to master the manufacture of these remarkable materials, we open doors to countless innovations.

Graphene

Leading the charge is *graphene*, the trailblazer among the two-dimensional materials. A single layer of carbon atoms arranged in a perfect honeycomb lattice, graphene defies the limitations of conventional materials[2]. With its exceptional conductivity, strength, and transparency, it promises a future of flexible electronics, ultra-fast computing, and groundbreaking energy storage solutions[2,3]. The possibilities seem limitless as graphene sets the stage for a technological revolution.

So, how does one go about creating this wondrous material? One of the initial methods developed was the *scotch tape method*, also known as *mechanical exfoliation*[4,5]. Here, a piece of scotch tape is used to peel layers off a chunk of graphite (which is essentially stacks of graphene). By repeatedly splitting the layers, scientists can isolate a single atomic layer of graphene. While this method was instrumental in the discovery of graphene, it is not very practical for large-scale production.

For more practical applications, methods such as *chemical vapor deposition* (CVD) have been developed[6,7]. In CVD, a substrate, often a metal, is exposed to one or more volatile precursors that react or decompose on the substrate's surface to yield the desired deposit. For graphene, a common precursor is methane, which is broken down at high temperatures. This gas breaks apart and the resulting tiny carbon atoms fall, sticking to the metal surface. What they leave behind is a super-thin, super-strong layer of graphene. The challenge here is removing the graphene layer without damaging it, a problem that scientists are continually finding new ways to solve.

Liquid-phase and electrochemical exfoliation are other techniques being developed[8,9]. These involve the immersion of bulk layered materials into liquids and using chemicals or electrical charges to separate the layers into individual, atom-thick sheets.

While having an incredible strength-to-weight ratio that far surpasses steel, graphene is also flexible and incredibly thin[10,11]. This means future architects could push the boundaries of design, creating structures that defy today's limitations. Flexible, lightweight, and resilient skyscrapers could reach higher into the sky than ever before, all while using less material and being able to withstand earthquakes and high winds that could topple conventional buildings[12,13]. Buildings so tall they pierce the clouds, yet remarkably lightweight, incredibly sturdy, and resistant to natural calamities. This might sound like science fiction, but with graphene, it could become a reality. The future might even see the construction of space elevators, a concept currently restricted by the lack of a material strong and light enough for the task. Graphene could potentially be the key to such monumental projects, creating a tether connecting the Earth and space, a literal stairway to the stars[14,15].

Beyond the vertical, graphene also offers potential in large-scale infrastructure projects. Consider bridges spanning distances currently impossible with conventional materials, or tunnels burrowing deep beneath the Earth or sea with unprecedented safety and stability. The utilization of graphene in cement and concrete significantly improves the durability and sustainability of infrastructure like buildings, dams, bridges, and roads due to its outstanding mechanical properties[16,17]. Graphene's resistance to corrosion also promises significantly longer lifespans for these structures, dramatically reducing maintenance and replacement costs[18].

Furthermore, graphene-infused materials could lead to houses that are more energy-efficient, safer, and capable of integrating advanced technologies[19]. Graphene's electrical conductivity could be leveraged to turn walls into light-emitting panels, eliminating the need for traditional lighting[20,21]. Solar cells, too, could be made more efficient with graphene, turning entire building exteriors into solar energy collectors[22,23].

Transportation, too, stands to be revolutionized with graphene. Envision train and subway systems enclosed in graphene tubes, capable of withstanding the pressures and stresses associated with transporting passengers or goods at super-high speeds. Aircraft made of graphene composites would be safer, a lot lighter, and more fuel efficient[24,25].

The immense strength of graphene also offers revolutionary implications for body armor[26]. Despite being as thin as a sheet of paper, it is about 200 times stronger than steel, making it one of the toughest materials known to man. This strength-to-weight ratio could give rise to new classes of armor, both for personnel and vehicles, that are lighter, more durable, and more protective than current solutions. Researchers are already exploring graphene composites for bullet-proof vests and vehicle armor that could withstand even the harshest combat scenarios[27,28].

The energy sector too, stands to be transformed by graphene because of the material's remarkable properties that make it ideal for improved batteries and capacitors[29,30]. These graphene-based power sources could offer significantly faster charging, greater energy densities, and longer lifespans compared to current batteries.

Graphene's outstanding electrical conductivity also presents exciting possibilities for communication systems[31,32]. Future communication devices, such as radios or satellite systems, could use graphene-based components for faster, more reliable, and secure data transmission. The material's thinness and flexibility also allow for the development of wearable communication devices, integrated directly into clothing[33].

All these characteristics make graphene an ideal material to build the future with. It's a material that could make our ambitious visions of space elevators and cities that reside amongst the clouds a reality. It's just a matter of time until the manufacturing of this material is practical at very large scales.

MXenes

Another type of material showing promise for future materials is known as *MXenes*. These are two-dimensional materials consisting of transition metal carbides or nitrides. These materials have a layered structure, similar to graphene, but with nearly 30 different types synthesized experimentally and many more predicted theoretically[34].

Why are these materials so promising? They're combined properties of excellent electric conductivity and high surface area hold great potential for the future of energy storage and conversion[35,36]. By facilitating higher energy and power densities, MXenes could significantly enhance the performance of batteries and supercapacitors.

MXenes also showcase superior hydrophilicity, which enhances the interaction between MXenes and aqueous environments, which is often crucial in electrocatalytic processes[37]. This gives these materials broad prospects as electrode material.

Furthermore, the chemical inertness and biocompatibility of MXenes gives them great potential for innovations in biomedical applications[38].

Boron Nitride Nanotubes

In the vast arena of nanomaterials, *boron nitride nanotubes* (BNNTs) are particularly promising. Imagine a tube as slender as an atom yet hundreds of times stronger than steel. It is a material where the atomic arrangement of boron and nitrogen creates a structure that defies convention. Like siblings to carbon nanotubes, BNNTs exhibit remarkable thermal and chemical stability, making them ideal for the harsh environments[39,40]. With their immense strength and lightweight nature, these microscopic marvels are primed to become intricate parts of future society.

Traditional materials struggle to dissipate heat efficiently, limiting the performance and longevity of equipment, this is where BNNTs make a difference. With their exceptional thermal conductivity, they have the potential to act as efficient heat sinks, preventing overheating and allowing for sustained performances in engines, electronics, and other mechanisms that transfer energy[41].

In the age of technology-driven warfare, electromagnetic interference poses a significant threat. From sophisticated communication systems to stealth operations, a reliable electromagnetic shield is paramount. Not only do BNNTs dissipate heat remarkably well, they also have a remarkable ability to absorb and dissipate electromagnetic radiation[42]. By incorporating BNNTs around vital equipment and electronics, they can serve a dual-purpose of dissipating heat of the components inside as well as establishing an invisible shield to offer protection against hostile electromagnetic attacks.

Chapter References

1. Baig, N. (2023). Two-dimensional nanomaterials: A critical review of recent progress, properties, applications, and future directions. *Composites Part A: Applied Science and Manufacturing*, 165, 107362. https://doi.org/10.1016/j.compositesa.2022.107362

2. Urade, A. R., Lahiri, I., & Suresh, K. S. (2023). Graphene Properties, Synthesis, and Applications: A Review. *JOM*, 75, 614-630. https://doi.org/10.1007/s11837-022-05505-8

3. Davies, E. (2023, October 23). Small Wonders. *Royal Society of Chemistry*. https://edu.rsc.org/feature/the-many-uses-of-nanomaterials/4018218.article

4. Moosa, A. A., & Abed, M. S. (2021). Graphene preparation and graphite exfoliation. *Turkish Journal of Chemistry*, 45(3), 493-519. https://doi.org/10.3906/kim-2101-19

5. Vestince, Mbayachi, Euphrem, Ndayiragije, Sammani, Thirasara, Taj, Sunaina, Mbuta, Elice, & Khan, Atta. (2021). Graphene synthesis, characterization and its applications: A review. *Results in Chemistry*, 3, 100163. https://doi.org/10.1016/j.rechem.2021.100163

6. Saeed, M., Alshammari, Y., Majeed, S. A., & Al-Nasrallah, E. (2020). Chemical Vapour Deposition of Graphene-Synthesis, Characterisation, and Applications: A Review. *Molecules*, 25(17), 3856. https://doi.org/10.3390/molecules25173856

7. Qing, F., Hou, Y., Stehle, R., & Li, X. (2019). Chemical vapor deposition synthesis of graphene films. *APL Materials*, 7(2), 020903. https://doi.org/10.1063/1.5078551

8. Amiri, A., Naraghi, M., Ahmadi, G., Soleymaniha, M., & Shanbedi, M. (2018). A review on liquid-phase exfoliation for scalable production of pure graphene, wrinkled, crumpled and functionalized graphene and challenges. *FlatChem*, 8, 40-71. https://doi.org/10.1016/j.flatc.2018.03.004

9. Sharma, V. (2017, November 15). Comparison Between Liquid Phase and Electrochemical Exfoliation of Graphite. *IncludeHelp*. https://www.includehelp.com/nanotechnology/comparison-between-liquid-phase-and-electrochemical-exfoliation-of-graphite.aspx

10. Hislop, M. (2017, January 12). MIT's 3D graphene material has

the world's best strength to weight ratio. *Designboom*. https://www. designboom.com/technology/mit-3d-graphene-material-01-11-2017/

11. Roos, D., & Henderson, A. (2023, September 29). How Graphene Could Change the World. *HowStuffWorks*. https://science.howstuffworks. com/innovation/new-inventions/graphene.htm

12. Souza, E. (2019, June 28). What is Graphene and How Can It Revolutionize Architecture? *ArchDaily*. https://www.archdaily.com/ 918953/what-is-graphene-and-how-can-it-revolutionize-architecture

13. Nanografi. (2019, August 23). Use of Graphene in Construction. https://nanografi.com/blog/use-of-graphene-in-construction/

14. Peterkin, Z. (2018, August 1). Space Elevator Technology and Graphene. *AZoM*. https://www.azom.com/article.aspx?ArticleID=16371

15. David, L. (2014, September 22). Space Elevator Advocates Take Lofty Look at Innovative Concepts. *Space.com*. https://www.space.com/ 27225-space-elevator-technology.html

16. Graphenea. (n.d.). Graphene Cement Enhancer Demonstrated in Large-Scale Construction Project. https://www.graphenea.com/blogs/ graphene-news/graphene-cement-enhancer-demonstrated-in-large-scale-construction-project

17. Asim, N., Badiei, M., Samsudin, N. A., Mohammad, M., Razali, H., Soltani, S., & Amin, N. (2022). Application of graphene-based materials in developing sustainable infrastructure: An overview. *Composites Part B: Engineering*, 245, 110188. https://doi.org/10.1016/j. compositesb.2022.110188

18. Frąckiewiczin, M. (2023, March 28). The Role of Graphene in Construction and Infrastructure. *TS2 Space*. https://ts2.space/en/the-role-of-graphene-in-construction-and-infrastructure/

19. Johnson, D. (2015, June 2). Graphene Heating System Dramatically Reduces Home Energy Costs. *IEEE Spectrum*. https:// spectrum.ieee.org/graphene-heating-system-dramatically-reduces-home-energy-costs

20. Junaid, M., Md Khir, M. H., Witjaksono, G., Ullah, Z., Tansu, N., Saheed, M. S. M., Kumar, P., Hing Wah, L., Magsi, S. A., & Siddiqui, M. A. (2020). A Review on Graphene-Based Light Emitting Functional Devices. *Molecules*, 25(18), 4217. https://doi.org/10.3390/molecules25184217

21. Zhang, H., Mischke, J., Mertin, W., & Bacher, G. (2022). Graphene as a Transparent Conductive Electrode in GaN-Based LEDs. *Materials*

(Basel), 15(6), 2203. https://doi.org/10.3390/ma15062203

22. Graphene Uses. (2020, April 21). Graphene Solar Panels: The Next Level Solar Cells. https://www.grapheneuses.org/graphene-solar-panels/

23. Chandler, D. L. (2020, June 5). Transparent graphene electrodes might lead to new generation of solar cells. *Massachusetts Institute of Technology.* https://news.mit.edu/2020/transparent-graphene-electrodes-solar-cells-0605

24. Nanografi. (2019, September 26). Graphene's Use in the Aerospace Industry. https://nanografi.com/blog/graphenes-use-in-the-aerospace-industry/

25. Stoker, L. (2013, March 17). Getting to grips with graphene: aviation's revolution? *Aerospace Technology.* https://www.aerospace-technology.com/features/featuregetting-to-grips-graphene-aviation-revolution/

26. Williams, M. (n.d.). Graphene Body Armor and Shielding. *HeroX.* https://www.herox.com/blog/154-graphene-body-armor-and-shielding

27. Schwandt, J. (2022, February 23). Great Graphene: Strong, Flexible Material Shows Military Promise. *Association of the United States Army.* https://www.ausa.org/articles/great-graphene-strong-flexible-material-shows-military-promise

28. Anthony, S. (2014, December 1). Graphene body armor: Twice the stopping power of Kevlar, at a fraction of the weight. *ExtremeTech.* https://www.extremetech.com/defense/195089-graphene-body-armor-twice-the-stopping-power-of-kevlar-at-a-fraction-of-the-weight

29. El-Kady, M., Shao, Y., & Kaner, R. (2016). Graphene for batteries, supercapacitors and beyond. *Nature Reviews Materials*, 1, 16033. https://doi.org/10.1038/natrevmats.2016.33

30. Brownson, D. A. C., Kampouris, D. K., & Banks, C. E. (2011). An overview of graphene in energy production and storage applications. *Journal of Power Sources*, 196(11), 4873-4885. https://doi.org/10.1016/j.jpowsour.2011.02.022

31. Han, S. J., Garcia, A., Oida, S., et al. (2014). Graphene radio frequency receiver integrated circuit. *Nature Communications*, 5, 3086. https://doi.org/10.1038/ncomms4086

32. Palacios, T., Hsu, A., & Wang, H. (2010). Applications of graphene devices in RF communications. *IEEE Communications Magazine*, 48(6), 122-128. http://hdl.handle.net/1721.1/61760

33. Huang, X., Leng, T., Zhu, M., et al. (2016). Highly Flexible and Conductive Printed Graphene for Wireless Wearable Communications Applications. *Scientific Reports*, 5, 18298. https://doi.org/10.1038/srep18298

34. Gao, L., Li, C., Huang, W., Mei, S., Lin, H., Ou, Q., Zhang, Y., Guo, J., Zhang, F., Xu, S., & Zhang, H. (2020). MXene/Polymer Membranes: Synthesis, Properties, and Emerging Applications. *Chemistry of Materials*, 32(5), 1703-1747. https://doi.org/10.1021/acs.chemmater.9b04408

35. De, S., Acharya, S., Sahoo, S., & Nayak, G. C. (2021). Current trends in MXene research: properties and applications. *Materials Chemistry Frontiers*. https://doi.org/10.1039/D1QM00556A

36. Li, X., Huang, Z., Shuck, C. E., et al. (2022). MXene chemistry, electrochemistry and energy storage applications. *Nature Reviews Chemistry*, 6, 389–404. https://doi.org/10.1038/s41570-022-00384-8

37. Bai, S., Yang, M., Jiang, J., et al. (2021). Recent advances of MXenes as electrocatalysts for hydrogen evolution reaction. *npj 2D Materials and Applications*, 5, 78. https://doi.org/10.1038/s41699-021-00259-4

38. Chen, L., Dai, X., Feng, W., & Chen, Y. (2022). *Biomedical Applications of MXenes: From Nanomedicine to Biomaterials. Accounts of Materials Research*, 3(8), 785-798. https://doi.org/10.1021/accountsmr.2c00025

39. Lu, Y., Zhao, R., Wang, L., & E, S. (2023). Boron nitride nanotubes and nanosheets: Their basic properties, synthesis, and some of applications. *Diamond and Related Materials*, 136, 109978. https://doi.org/10.1016/j.diamond.2023.109978

40. Kim, J. H., Pham, T. V., Hwang, J. H., et al. (2018). Boron nitride nanotubes: Synthesis and applications. *Nano Convergence*, 5, 17. https://doi.org/10.1186/s40580-018-0149-y

41. Dolbec, R. (n.d.). Boron Nitride Nanotubes: Properties, Synthesis and Applications. *Millipore Sigma*. https://www.sigmaaldrich.com/US/en/technical-documents/technical-article/materials-science-and-engineering/microelectronics-and-nanoelectronics/boron-nitride-nanotubes

42. Zhan, Y., Lago, E., Santillo, C., Del Rio Castillo, A. E. E., Hao, S., Buonocore, G., Chen, Z., Xia, H., Lavorgna, M., & Bonaccorso, F. (2020). An anisotropic layer-by-layer carbon nanotube/boron nitride/rubber composite and its application in electromagnetic shielding. *Nanoscale*, 12(14), 7782-7791. https://doi.org/10.1039/C9NR10672C

Advanced Nuclear Technology

The origins of us harnessing the power of the atom can be traced back to the 1930s, where pioneers like Lise Meitner, Enrico Fermi, and J. Robert Oppenheimer grappled with the enigmatic properties of the atom[1]. In the shadows of world wars, they paved the way for the first nuclear chain reaction and revealed the immense energy residing in uranium and plutonium[2].

In the subsequent decades, the gargantuan power of the atom was tamed for peaceful use, propelling us into the atomic age[3]. Nuclear power plants sprung up around the world, promising a cornucopia of clean, reliable, and nearly limitless energy[4]. Despite the tragedies of Chernobyl and Fukushima, nuclear power has remained a mainstay in our energy grids, owing to its impressive efficiency and low carbon emissions[5]. At the present, current technological advancements are paving new ways of utilizing this technology[6].

Nuclear Sterling Engine

In the exciting world of mechanical engineering and power production, there's an innovative piece of technology making a resurgence: the *Stirling engine*. Named after its inventor, Robert Stirling, this device was first patented in 1816 as a safer alternative to steam engines[7]. But in the high-tech context of the 21st century, it has taken on a new persona: the nuclear Stirling engine.

To understand nuclear Stirling engines, one must first understand the basic principles of a Stirling engine. In its simplest form, a Stirling engine operates on a cycle of heating and cooling gas, often air or helium, to convert thermal energy into mechanical work. When the gas is heated, it expands, pushing a piston. When it is cooled, it contracts, pulling the piston back. This movement of the piston can be used to do useful work, like turning a generator to produce electricity[9,10].

In a nuclear Stirling engine, the heat comes from a nuclear reactor. The reactor's heat can be used directly to heat the gas in the Stirling engine, creating a high-temperature differential that drives the engine[11]. The cooling phase can be achieved passively with radiators, or actively with a coolant like water or helium. Because Stirling engines are externally heated, they can run on virtually any heat source, including nuclear[9].

These engines have great potential in remote, off-grid locations where refueling is challenging or impossible. They could provide a reliable, continuous power supply for research stations in the Arctic, communication equipment on remote mountaintops, or automated weather stations in the middle of the ocean[11].

In the future, large-scale nuclear Stirling power plants could serve as a clean, efficient alternative to traditional nuclear power plants. Instead of using nuclear heat to generate steam and drive turbines, these power plants would use nuclear heat to drive Stirling engines, simplifying the power generation process and reducing the risk of dangerous high-pressure steam leaks[9].

Even though they could have useful applications here on land, they also show great potential for use in space exploration. In terms of development and real-world examples, NASA is a frontrunner[13,16]. NASA is developing a small fission reactor called Kilopower that can generate a continuous output of 10 kilowatts of electricity for at least

10 years, which is sufficient to power several average American households[14]. This reactor will use Stirling engines to convert heat from uranium fission into mechanical power.

In addition, the NASA Glenn Research Center has been supporting the development of high-efficiency Stirling power converters for potential use in Radioisotope Power Systems for space missions[15]. These converters can potentially reduce the amount of plutonium fuel required by a factor of four while maintaining long life and high reliability. Two units have each accumulated over 103,000 hours of operation without performance degradation.

Small Modular Reactors

Of the many recent advances in nuclear power technology, *small modular reactors* (SMRs) are one of the most exciting[18]. Small modular reactors, as the name suggests, are nuclear power plants compact enough to be assembled off-site and delivered in parts, yet mighty enough to generate hundreds of megawatts of electricity[19]. They're modular in design, meaning that additional reactors can be added as necessary to increase capacity. By contrast, traditional nuclear power plants are mammoth structures with large single reactors, necessitating on-site construction and immense capital investment.

These portable reactors operate on the same principles as their larger counterparts, splitting atomic nuclei to release energy in the form of heat, which then produces steam to drive electricity-generating turbines. The differences lie in the design. SMRs utilize advanced cooling techniques and passive safety systems that rely on natural phenomena like convection, eliminating the need for active, powered cooling mechanisms[20]. This makes SMRs inherently safer and less vulnerable to accidents.

Current developments in portable reactors are nothing short of remarkable. NuScale Power, a leading player in the field, has received regulatory approval in the United States for its SMR design, a major step towards commercial deployment[21]. NuScale's design involves up to 12 individual modules, each capable of producing 77 megawatts of electricity, fitting neatly into a containment vessel approximately one twentieth the size of a conventional reactor.

Meanwhile, Rolls-Royce in the United Kingdom is designing its own modular reactor, aiming to produce a fleet of reactors by the late 2020s[22,23]. China, Russia, and Canada are also at various stages of developing small nuclear reactors, underscoring the global recognition of the potential with such technology[25,26,27].

But the potential applications of SMRs extend far beyond conventional power generation. Their compact size and modularity make them ideal for remote locations with limited infrastructure. Imagine powering Arctic research stations, isolated mining operations, or off-grid communities with clean, reliable, and scalable energy[28,29].

In the realm of desalination, SMRs could be instrumental in addressing global water scarcity. A nuclear-powered desalination process could provide fresh water to arid regions without contributing to greenhouse gas emissions[30]. Similarly, the high-temperature steam generated by SMRs could be used in hydrogen production, advancing the quest for clean, sustainable fuels[30,31].

In the realm of space exploration, nuclear power holds tremendous promise. NASA's Perseverance rover, currently exploring Mars, is powered by a *radioisotope thermoelectric generator* (RTG), a testament to the utility of nuclear energy in the harshest of environments[32,33,34,35]. Future manned missions to Mars and beyond may depend on nuclear propulsion for speedy and efficient travel, while nuclear-powered habitats could allow humans to sustain life in the most remote corners of our solar system[39,41,42,43]. NASA's Kilopower project envisions using small nuclear reactors for powering habitats and equipment on the

Moon, Mars, and beyond. These tiny reactors could function where solar power falls short, providing a steady and reliable power source for long-duration space missions[35].

Radiation Waste Management

One of the biggest downsides to current nuclear power is that it produces radioactive waste. This waste is awful for the environment and is expensive to deal with. A lot of this radioactive waste ends up buried underground or in concrete bunkers and has to be monitored[42,43,44].

There is a new type of nuclear reactor that can help deal with this toxic waste[46,47]. Sometimes referred to as *advanced fast reactors*, these reactors are designed to consume the radioactive waste produced by traditional nuclear reactors. By using fast neutrons to induce fission, these reactors can reduce the volume and radioactivity of nuclear waste.

Similarly, there is a process called *transmutation* that can be used to make radiated waste less toxic by converting long-lived radioactive isotopes into shorter-living or stable isotopes. By using particle accelerators or specialized reactors, transmutation can change the atomic nuclei of radioactive elements, potentially reducing the time waste remains hazardous[48,49,50,51].

There are also efforts being made to deal with irradiated water. A new method has been developed at MIT for reducing the volume of contaminated water from nuclear power plants, which could significantly improve the management of radioactive waste[52]. This method involves a process called *shock electrodialysis*, which uses an electric field to generate a deionization shockwave in the water. This shockwave pushes the charged particles, or ions, to one side of a tube filled with charged porous material, allowing for the concentrated stream of contaminants to be separated from the rest of the water.

The shock electrodialysis process was initially developed as a general method of removing salt from water, but the team has now focused on this specific application for nuclear power plants[52]. The method could be particularly useful for routine cleanup and could also make a significant difference in dealing with extreme cases, such as the contaminated water at the Fukushima Daiichi power plant in Japan.

Another promising process is *vitrification*. This involves mixing high-level radioactive waste with molten glass, which then solidifies, trapping the waste in a stable form[53]. Once solidified, these glass logs can be stored more safely and are less likely to leach into the environment.

Although these processes are effective, the most elegant solution for dealing with nuclear waste might be what is called *bioremediation*. This process deals with how to use biological organisms, primarily microorganisms, to degrade, transform, or immobilize radioactive waste. For example, a bacterium known as *Geobacter sulfurreducens* can reduce uranium from a soluble form (U+6) to an insoluble form (U+4). Theoretically, this could be used to extract uranium from the groundwater to prevent it from spreading[55,56,57].

Fungi are also showing potential for bioremediation. *Rhizopus arrhizus* is a fungal species known to bioaccumulate uranium and other heavy metals. Fungi, due to their mycelial network, can often access contaminants in places that bacteria cannot[58.59,60]. There are also various algae species like *Chlorella vulgaris* and *Spirulina* that have demonstrated an ability to absorb radionuclides from contaminated waters[61,62,63]. Using one or a combination of these methods, humanity can rid itself of one of the biggest drawbacks to nuclear power.

Nuclear Propulsion

In the enthralling realm of future technology, nuclear propulsion holds a tantalizing promise. A concept that is gradually being molded into reality, changing our expectations of travel across the celestial expanse[64].

Nuclear propulsion, as the name suggests, leverages the enormous energy released in nuclear reactions to power engines and systems. Whether it is heating a propellant to high temperatures in a nuclear thermal rocket or creating charged particles for a nuclear electric engine, the basic premise remains the same: harnessing nuclear energy to create propulsion[65].

One form of this is *nuclear thermal propulsion*. Unlike a conventional chemical rocket, which burns fuel and an oxidizer to create hot gases for thrust, a nuclear thermal propulsion system employs a nuclear reactor[66]. This reactor runs on hydrogen—a gas with the lowest molecular weight, making it an ideal propellant for this method. Instead of producing electricity, the reactor's primary function is to generate immense heat. The hydrogen propellant is circulated through the reactor core, where it becomes super-heated and pressurized. The heated hydrogen is then expelled, generating thrust far more efficiently than traditional rocket propulsion.

The development of nuclear thermal propulsion technology is far from fictional. NASA is actively researching this area, with projects such as The Nuclear Thermal Propulsion Project, which is working on creating a functional nuclear thermal engine that could significantly reduce the duration of manned Mars missions. The proposition is a travel time of only three months, half of what the most powerful chemical rockets can achieve[67].

Similarly, DARPA is in the process of developing a nuclear thermal propulsion system for the *Demonstration Rocket for Agile Cislunar Operations* (DRACO) program. Initiated in 2020, the program's aim is to demonstrate a nuclear thermal propulsion system that can operate in cislunar space, the region of space between the Earth and the Moon[68,69,70].

Chapter References

1. Rhodes, R. (1986). *The Making of the Atomic Bomb*. Simon & Schuster.

2. Krige, J. (1987). *The Birth of the Bomb: The Untold Story of Britain's Part in the Weapon That Changed the World*. Zed Books.

3. Goldschmidt, B. (1990). *Atomic Rivals*. Rutgers University Press.

4. Walker, J. S. (2004). *Three Mile Island: A Nuclear Crisis in Historical Perspective*. University of California Press.

5. Findlay, T. (2011). Nuclear energy and global governance: Ensuring safety, security, and non-proliferation. *Routledge*. https://www.routledge.com/Nuclear-Energy-and-Global-Governance-Ensuring-Safety-Security-and-Non-proliferation/Findlay/p/book/9780415532488

6. Nuttall, W. J., & Ince, D. M. (2017). *Nuclear Re-Envisioned: The Next Wave of Innovation in the Nuclear Industry*. Cambridge University Press.

7. Encyclopedia Britannica (2023, June 2). Robert Stirling. https://www.britannica.com/biography/Robert-Stirling

8. Mechanical Engineering Tools. (2004). *MIT OpenCourseWare*. https://ocw.mit.edu/courses/2-670-mechanical-engineering-tools-january-iap-2004/pages/study-materials/

9. Stroski, P. N. (2020, June 16). Stirling engine: What is it and how it works? *Electrical e-Library.com*. https://www.electricalelibrary.com/en/2020/06/16/stirling-engine-what-is-it-and-how-it-works/

10. Nice, K. (2021, February 9). How Stirling Engines Work. *HowStuffWorks*. https://auto.howstuffworks.com/stirling-engine.htm

11. Qi, Y., Sun, D., & Zhang, J. (2023). Numerical study on a nuclear-powered Stirling system for space power generation. *Applied Thermal Engineering*, 233, 121140. https://doi.org/10.1016/j.applthermaleng.2023.121140

12. Nguyen, T. (2020, May 15). Why NASA thinks nuclear reactors could supply power for human colonies in space. *Chemical & Engineering News*. https://cen.acs.org/energy/nuclear-power/NASA-thinks-nuclear-reactors-supply/98/i19

13. National Academies of Sciences, Engineering, and Medicine. (2021). *Space nuclear propulsion for human Mars exploration*. The

National Academies Press. https://doi.org/10.17226/25977

14. Dickinson, D. (2018, January 23). NASA Unveils New Power Source for Space Exploration. *Sky & Telescope*. https://skyandtelescope.org/astronomy-news/nasa-unveils-new-nuclear-power-source-future-exploration/

15. NASA Science Editorial Team. (2018, April 16). High-Efficiency Stirling Convertor Demonstrates Long-Term Performance. *NASA*. https://science.nasa.gov/science-research/science-enabling-technology/technology-highlights/high-efficiency-stirling-convertor-demonstrates-long-term-performance/

16. NASA. (n.d.). Powering Missions to Deep Space in a New Way https://www.nasa.gov/centers/glenn/technology/stirling_prt.htm

17. Chan, J., Wood, J. G., & Schreiber, J. G. (2007). Development of Advanced Stirling Radioisotope Generator for Space Exploration. *AIP Conference Proceedings*, 880, 615–623. https://doi.org/10.1063/1.2437500

18. International Atomic Energy Agency. (2022). Advances in Small Modular Reactor Technology Developments. https://aris.iaea.org/Publications/SMR_booklet_2022.pdf

19. Hussein, E. M. A. (2020). Emerging small modular nuclear power reactors: A critical review. Physics Open, 5, 100038. https://doi.org/10.1016/j.physo.2020.100038

20. Frontiers. (n.d.). Advances in Small Modular Reactors. https://www.frontiersin.org/research-topics/52454/advances-in-small-modular-reactors

21. NRC Certifies First U.S. Small Modular Reactor Design. (2023, January 20). Department of Energy. https://www.energy.gov/ne/articles/nrc-certifies-first-us-small-modular-reactor-design

22. Rolls-Royce Small Modular Reactors. (n.d.). Rolls-Royce. https://www.rolls-royce.com/innovation/small-modular-reactors.aspx

23. Kua, I. (2022, April 19). Rolls-Royce expecting UK approval for mini nuclear reactor by mid-2024. *Reuters*. https://www.reuters.com/business/energy/rolls-royce-expecting-uk-approval-mini-nuclear-reactor-by-mid-2024-2022-04-19/

24. Wang, B. (2023, October 9). New Nuclear Reactor Technology is Being Developed. NextBigFuture.com. https://www.nextbigfuture.com/2023/10/new-nuclear-reactor-technology-is-being-developed.html

25. Institute for Energy Research. (2023, October 12). Texas and the UK Look to Small Modular Nuclear Reactors, but China is Ahead. https://www.instituteforenergyresearch.org/nuclear/texas-and-the-uk-look-to-small-modular-nuclear-reactors-but-china-is-ahead/

26. Cohen, A. (2019, April 25). China Enters Global Tech Race for Small Modular Nuclear Reactors. *Forbes*. https://www.forbes.com/sites/arielcohen/2019/04/25/china-enters-global-tech-race-for-small-modular-nuclear-reactors/

27. Natural Resources Canada. (n.d.). Canada's Small Nuclear Reactor Action Plan. https://natural-resources.canada.ca/our-natural-resources/energy-sources-distribution/nuclear-energy-uranium/canadas-small-nuclear-reactor-action-plan/21183

28. Microreactors. (n.d.). Idaho National Laboratory. https://inl.gov/trending-topics/microreactors/

29. Small Modular Reactors. (n.d.). Small Modular Reactors (SMRs): Applications and Opportunities. https://small-modular-reactors.org/smr-applications/

30. Small Modular Reactors. (n.d.). Small Modular Reactors (SMRs) and Hydrogen Production. https://small-modular-reactors.org/smr-hydrogen-production/

31. NuScale Power. (2023, May 31). NuScale Enhances Case for Small Modular Reactor Applications in Major Industrial Processes. https://www.nuscalepower.com/en/news/press-releases/2023/nuscale-enhances-case-for-small-modular-reactor-applications-in-major-industrial-processes

32. NASA. (n.d.). Power Source - Mars 2020 Mission Perseverance Rover. https://mars.nasa.gov/mars2020/spacecraft/rover/electrical-power/

33. NASA Jet Propulsion Laboratory. (2020, July 8). Rover Power Source. https://www.jpl.nasa.gov/images/pia23981-rover-power-source

34. NASA. (n.d.). Rover Summary. https://mars.nasa.gov/mars2020/spacecraft/rover/power/

35. Idaho National Laboratory. (n.d.). INL Powers Mars Perseverance Rover. https://inl.gov/mars-2020/

36. NASA. (n.d.). Space Nuclear Propulsion. https://www.nasa.gov/tdm/space-nuclear-propulsion/

37. Jackson, G. (2020, November 17). Nuclear Propulsion for Manned Mars Missions. *Chicago Society for Space Studies*. https://www.chicagospace.org/nuclear-propulsion-for-manned-mars-missions/

38. Hall, L. (2018, May 25). Nuclear Thermal Propulsion: Game Changing Technology for Deep Space Exploration. *NASA*. https://www.nasa.gov/directorates/stmd/tech-demo-missions-program/nuclear-thermal-propulsion-game-changing-technology-for-deep-space-exploration/

39. Mohon, L. (2017, December 12). Kilopower. *NASA*. https://www.nasa.gov/directorates/spacetech/kilopower

40. NASA Glenn Research Center. (n.d.). Fission Surface Power (FSP) / Kilopower. https://www1.grc.nasa.gov/research-and-engineering/thermal-energy-conversion/kilopower/

41. NASA. (n.d.). Fission Surface Power. https://www.nasa.gov/tdm/fission-surface-power/

42. World Nuclear Association. (2022, January). Radioactive Waste Management | Nuclear Waste Disposal. https://world-nuclear.org/information-library/nuclear-fuel-cycle/nuclear-wastes/radioactive-waste-management.aspx

43. World Nuclear Association. (2023, January). Storage and Disposal of Radioactive Waste. https://world-nuclear.org/information-library/nuclear-fuel-cycle/nuclear-waste/storage-and-disposal-of-radioactive-waste.aspx

44. U.S. Energy Information Administration. (n.d.). Nuclear power and the environment. https://www.eia.gov/energyexplained/nuclear/nuclear-power-and-the-environment.php

45. Jacoby, M. (2020, March 30). As nuclear waste piles up, scientists seek the best long-term storage solutions. *Chemical & Engineering News*. https://cen.acs.org/environment/pollution/nuclear-waste-pilesscientists-seek-best/98/i12

46. Houten, M. (2023, April 11). Fast Breeder Reactors: A solution for nuclear waste or an eternal empty promise? *Innovation Origins*. https://innovationorigins.com/en/fast-breeder-reactors-a-solution-for-nuclear-waste-or-an-eternal-empty-promise/

47. Kaiser, P., Rickwood, P., & Experts from the IAEA Department of Nuclear Energy. (2013, March 1). Fast Reactors Provide Sustainable Nuclear Power for "Thousands of Years". *IAEA*. https://www.iaea.org/newscenter/news/fast-reactors-provide-sustainable-nuclear-power-

thousands-years

48. Nuclear Energy Agency. (n.d.). Transmutation of Radioactive Waste. https://www.oecd-nea.org/trw/

49. Federal Office for the Safety of Nuclear Waste Management. (2021, March 10). Transmutation of high-level radioactive waste. https://www.base.bund.de/EN/ns/ni-germany/transmutation/transmutation.html

50. Salvatores, M., & Palmiotti, G. (2011). Radioactive waste partitioning and transmutation within advanced fuel cycles: Achievements and challenges. *Progress in Particle and Nuclear Physics*, 66(1), 144-166. https://doi.org/10.1016/j.ppnp.2010.10.001

51. Ray, J. (2011, March 11). Accelerator Transmutation of Waste. *Stanford University*. http://large.stanford.edu/courses/2011/ph241/ray2/

52. Alkhadra, M., Bazant, M., et al. (2019, December 19). A new way to remove contaminants from nuclear wastewater. *Massachusetts Institute of Technology*. https://news.mit.edu/2019/remove-contaminants-nuclear-plant-wastewater-1219

53. International Atomic Energy Agency. (n.d.). Taking a Closer Look at Vitrification: How the IAEA Helps Countries Immobilize Radioactive Waste. https://www.iaea.org/newscenter/news/taking-a-closer-look-at-vitrification-how-the-iaea-helps-countries-utilize-advanced-immobilization-technologies

54. Patel, R., Mugunthan, J., Singh, P., Mukherjee, S., & Koka, R. (2022). Microbial bioremediation and biodegradation of radioactive waste contaminated sites. In J. A. Malik (Ed.), *Microbes and Microbial Biotechnology for Green Remediation* (pp. 733-746). Elsevier. https://doi.org/10.1016/B978-0-323-90452-0.00044-X

55. Prakash, D., Gabani, P., Chandel, A. K., Ronen, Z., & Singh, O. V. (2013). Bioremediation: A genuine technology to remediate radionuclides from the environment. *Microbial Biotechnology*, 6(4), 349-360. https://doi.org/10.1111/1751-7915.12059

56. Acevedo, A. J., Rosario, E., Toranzos, G., & Cabrera, C. (2023, August 13). Electrochemical bioremediation of uranium (VI) using Geobacter sulfurreducens on a boron-doped diamond electrode surface. *ACS Fall 2023, American Chemical Society*. https://acs.digitellinc.com/products/view/571825

57. Cologgi, D. L., Speers, A. M., Bullard, B. A., Kelly, S. D., & Reguera, G. (2014). Enhanced uranium immobilization and reduction by Geobacter

sulfurreducens biofilms. *Applied and Environmental Microbiology*, 80(21), 6638-6646. https://doi.org/10.1128/AEM.02289-14

58. Tsezos, M., & Volesky, B. (1982). The mechanism of uranium biosorption by Rhizopus arrhizus. *Biotechnology and Bioengineering*, 24(2), 385-401. https://doi.org/10.1002/bit.260240211

59. Tsezos, M. (1983). The role of chitin in uranium adsorption by R. arrhizus. *Biotechnology and Bioengineering*, 25(8), 2025-2040. https://doi.org/10.1002/bit.260250812

60. Stein, J. (2016, March 5). Fungal Nuclear Remediation. *Stanford University*. http://large.stanford.edu/courses/2016/ph241/stein1/

61. Sayadi, M. H., Rashki, O., & Shahri, E. (2019). Application of modified Spirulina platensis and Chlorella vulgaris powder on the adsorption of heavy metals from aqueous solutions. *Journal of Environmental Chemical Engineering*, 7(3), 103169. https://doi.org/10.1016/j.jece.2019.103169

62. Yadav, M., Kumar, V., Sandal, N., et al. (2022). Quantitative evaluation of Chlorella vulgaris for removal of toxic metals from the body. *Journal of Applied Phycology*, 34, 2743–2754. https://doi.org/10.1007/s10811-021-02640-8

63. Knoji. (2011, March 14). Chlorella and Spirulina Protects Your Health from Radiation. https://knoji.com/article/chlorella-and-spirulina-protects-your-health-from-radiation-exposure/

64. Rawlins, S. B., & Thomas, L. D. (2022). Feasibility of Low-Enriched Uranium Fueled Nuclear Thermal Propulsion in the Low-Thrust Region Below 16klbf. *Annals of Nuclear Energy*, 179, 109368. https://doi.org/10.1016/j.anucene.2022.109368

65. Hall, L. (2018, May 25). Nuclear Thermal Propulsion: Game Changing Technology for Deep Space Exploration. *NASA*. https://www.nasa.gov/directorates/stmd/tech-demo-missions-program/nuclear-thermal-propulsion-game-changing-technology-for-deep-space-exploration/

66. NASA Announces Nuclear Thermal Propulsion Reactor Concept Awards. (2021, July 13). *NASA*. https://www.nasa.gov/news-release/nasa-announces-nuclear-thermal-propulsion-reactor-concept-awards/

67. Houts, M., Mitchell, D., Kim, T., Borowski, S., Power, K., Scott, J., Belvin, A., & Clement, S. (2015, July 27). NASA's Nuclear Thermal Propulsion Project. Paper presented at the Nuclear and Emerging Technologies for Space 2015 (NETS), Albuquerque, NM. NASA Technical

Reports Server. https://ntrs.nasa.gov/citations/20150016484

68. Dodson, T. (n.d.). Demonstration Rocket for Agile Cislunar Operations. *DARPA*. https://www.darpa.mil/program/demonstration-rocket-for-agile-cislunar-operations

69. DARPA. (2023, January 24). DARPA, NASA Collaborate on Nuclear Thermal Rocket Engine. https://www.darpa.mil/news-events/2023-01-24

70. DARPA. (2021, April 12). DARPA Selects Performers for Phase 1 of Demonstration Rocket for Agile Cislunar Operations (DRACO) Program. https://www.darpa.mil/news-events/2021-04-12

Photonics

Photonics, as the name suggests, revolves around the study and manipulation of light. It is the science behind our devices' screens, fiber-optics, imaging systems, and a host of other technologies. Similar to electronics, which is concerned with electrons and their interactions, photonics deals with photons and their behavior. Photonics harnesses the properties of light itself to transmit, manipulate, and store information[1].

If you've ever used the internet or made a long-distance call, you've already experienced the power of photonics. Fiber-optic cables, which use light to transmit information across vast distances at the speed of light, have been the backbone of our telecommunications network for decades[2,3,4,5]. Yet, this is just the tip of the proverbial iceberg when it comes to applications using photonic technology. Sophisticated metamaterials and advanced manufacturing techniques are paving the way for new innovative applications in this field[6,7,8,9]. One thing is apparent, the future looks bright with photonics.

Negative Refraction Optics

Today, the field of optics is witnessing a revolution thanks to advanced optics capable of negative refraction. To understand negative refraction, we must first address the nature of light. When light passes from one medium to another, such as from air into water, it changes speed and direction in a process known as refraction. This effect is responsible for common optical phenomena like the illusion of a bent straw in a glass of water or the splitting of white light into a rainbow of colors by a prism. The degree of this bending is determined by the material's refractive index. Most natural materials have a positive refractive index, causing light to bend in a particular direction[10].

But what if a material could cause light to bend in the opposite direction? Enter the realm of *negative refraction*. In the early 2000s, researchers created the first rudimentary metamaterials capable of negative refraction, bending microwaves in the "wrong" direction[11,12]. This monumental achievement ignited a firestorm of research into negative refraction optics and brought forth the promise of some quite extraordinary possibilities.

Imagine, for instance, a lens that overcomes the diffraction limit that has long constrained conventional optics. This limit, based on the wavelength of light, restricts the finest details that a lens can resolve. However, an optical lens made from a negatively refracting metamaterial can surpass this limit. This would allow the imaging of objects and structures smaller than the wavelength of light, something considered impossible with conventional optics[10].

This breakthrough could lead to various other improvements and breakthroughs in a wide range of fields. One of the most obvious fields that would benefit is microscopy. The ability to focus light beyond its diffraction limit would greatly enhance nanoscale imaging and microscopy[13,14]. Researchers could examine biological cells, molecules, and nanostructures with unprecedented clarity and detail. In the field of semiconductor manufacturing, these technologies could enable smaller sizes and higher resolution in chip fabrication, leading to more powerful and efficient electronic devices[15,16,17,18]. Even solar energy would benefit from these technologies. Concentrating sunlight onto small solar cells using negative-refraction optics and metamaterials could improve the efficiency of solar energy capture, making solar power more viable and cost-effective. Moreover, negative refraction could lead to revolutionary advancements in telecommunications. Telecommunication networks based on optical fibers rely on the positive refraction of light[19,20,21,22]. Introducing materials with negative refraction could enable new types of optical components or systems, perhaps making our communication systems even faster and more efficient[23,24].

Improving our communication systems and devices is just scratching the surface of what is possible with this technology. One of the most impressive applications would be functioning "invisibility cloaks." By guiding light waves around an object, much like water flowing around a stone in a stream, an object could be rendered invisible to an observer. While true invisibility cloaks are not yet available, early stage cloaking experiments using negative refraction have already been demonstrated in the lab[23,25,26].

Imagine a battlefield where tanks, jets, and soldiers move unseen and undetected much like the alien from the movie *Predator*. The military advantage of such invisibility cloaks is undeniable. Entire platoons could advance with the stealth of a shadow, and fighter jets could strike without ever being spotted.

But the promise of invisibility extends far beyond the theatre of war. Surgeons could operate with tools that, while invisible, work with precision. Such invisibility technology could revolutionize minimally invasive surgeries. Surgeons would not be hindered by the sight of their tools, allowing for an unobstructed view of the procedure at hand.

Nature, in its untamed beauty, is often disturbed by the very presence of those who seek to study it. With this cloaking technology, wildlife researchers could become mere whispers in the wind, observing animals in their most candid moments, undisturbed and unaltered by human presence.

Our everyday interaction with devices and objects could completely change. Imagine using computers and phones with completely transparent screens. Your living room could transform at a command, with walls becoming transparent to let in the natural light, and letting the dweller enjoy the majestic outside view while remaining comfortable inside.

Additionally, the mastering of negative refraction optics is an important step for the development of photonic circuits[27]. This in return is a necessary step that bring us closer to photonic computers.

Photonic Crystals

Imagine a structure that can manipulate light as easily as a sculptor shapes clay. This is possible with *photonic crystals*, a class of materials that may very well revolutionize technology as we know it[28]. As we look towards the future, these materials offer a tantalizing glimpse into a world where our interaction with light takes on a whole new dimension.

Photonic crystals are not like the shiny gemstones one might imagine. Rather, they are nano-structured materials capable of controlling and manipulating the flow of light[28,29,30]. In simple terms, they can allow certain colors (wavelengths of light) to pass while blocking others. Much like how semiconductors control the movement of electrons, photonic crystals control the flow of photons, giving us an unprecedented tool to harness and manipulate light.

The magic of these materials lies in their periodic structure, which causes interference patterns in light that interact with them, leading to phenomena such as reflection, refraction, and diffraction. It is this periodic structure that provides photonic crystals with the ability to manipulate light in ways that no other material can[31,32].

From ultra-efficient solar cells, through faster and more

powerful optical computers, to materials that change color at will, the possibilities are as endless as they are exciting[33,34,35,36]. Photonic crystals could be the foundation to usher in a new age of technological advancements, redefining industries ranging from telecommunications and computing to energy, medicine, and defense.

Advanced Solar Power

Harnessing the sun's energy is an age-old concept, from the myth of Icarus to the design of sunrooms in Roman villas[36,37,38,39]. Solar panels are a common sight today, from rooftops to fields, and even on Mars rovers. However, the science and technology of solar energy are far from reaching their pinnacle. The solar revolution is just getting started.

At its core, solar technology converts sunlight into electricity using semiconducting materials, usually silicon. Traditional silicon solar cells have already become much more efficient and cost-effective over the past decades[40]. However, the silicon cells have an efficiency ceiling around 30%[41,42]. To make more significant leaps, scientists are experimenting with advanced solar technologies that could redefine the way we think about solar energy.

Perovskite solar cells are a relatively new entrant in this field and are creating quite a stir. These materials, named for the crystal structure they share with a mineral discovered in the Ural Mountains, offer excellent light absorption and charge transportation properties. Plus, they're potentially cheaper and easier to manufacture than silicon-based cells[43,44,45,46]. From a average efficiency of around 4% in 2009, perovskite solar cells have achieved efficiencies over 25% in just a decade, rivaling the performance of conventional silicon cells.

An Oxford-based company, Oxford PV, is a pioneer in the commercialization of perovskite technology. They are developing perovskite-silicon tandem cells, a technology that layers a perovskite cell on a silicon one to utilize a broader spectrum of sunlight, potentially breaking the efficiency ceiling imposed on traditional silicon cells[47,48,49,50].

Another advanced solar technology making waves is *quantum dot solar cells*. Quantum dots, tiny semiconductor particles only a few nanometers wide, can be tuned to absorb different parts of the solar spectrum by changing their size. This adjustability and their potential for multiple electron generation per photon absorbed open the door for ultra-high efficiencies, potentially over 60%[51,52].

Canadian company QD Solar is leading the charge in

this field. They're developing solar cells which use quantum dots to harness the infrared light that silicon cells cannot, again, aiming to beat the efficiency limit of silicon-based solar technology[53].

Applications for these advanced solar technologies are vast and varied. Rooftop solar installations could generate more power from a smaller area, making solar energy viable even in dense, urban environments. With increased efficiency and potentially lower costs, vast solar farms could become an even more attractive proposition for utilities[54,55].

On a smaller scale, think about electric vehicles with advanced solar cells incorporated into their design, adding substantial range and reducing dependency on charging infrastructure. In remote or disaster-hit areas, high-efficiency, portable solar devices could provide critical power.

From a broader perspective, advanced solar photovoltaics could play a significant role in a future sustainable energy mix, accelerating the transition away from fossil fuels. They could facilitate the electrification of various sectors, from transportation to heating, helping reduce global carbon emissions.

There is another form of extracting energy from light

that might leave solar photovoltaics obsolete, *artificial photosynthesis*. This technique aims to mimic natural photosynthesis to convert sunlight into energy-rich fuels, often in the form of hydrogen or hydrocarbons. While the concept has been around for several decades, recent advances in materials science and chemistry have brought this futuristic idea closer to reality.

At the heart of artificial photosynthesis is a group of materials known as *photoelectrochemical cells*. When these materials are exposed to sunlight, they trigger chemical reactions that split water into hydrogen and oxygen, or transform carbon dioxide into useful hydrocarbons[56,57]. The key challenge is finding materials that can efficiently and stably facilitate these reactions under sunlight, something that many researchers worldwide are working to achieve.

Take the Joint Center for Artificial Photosynthesis, for instance. This research collaboration between multiple US institutions, including the California Institute of Technology and the Lawrence Berkeley National Laboratory, is one of the leading research efforts in artificial photosynthesis. They have developed several prototype systems that use sunlight to split water or reduce carbon dioxide[58,59].

In Japan, researchers from the University of Tokyo have

developed a photoelectrode that can harvest 85% of visible light, converting it into hydrogen energy with 60% efficiency[60]. This is a remarkable step forward in harnessing solar energy for fuel production.

The fuels generated through this process, known as "solar fuels," could be used in a wide range of applications. Hydrogen, a clean-burning fuel, could be used in everything from cars to power plants. Hydrocarbons could serve as the feedstock for the chemical industry, reducing our dependency on fossil fuels.

Imagine a future where buildings are coated with materials that absorb sunlight and carbon dioxide to produce fuel and oxygen, effectively turning our cities into energy-producing, air-cleaning ecosystems. Or consider the implications for space travel, where long-duration missions could produce their fuel, reducing the payload and costs associated with carrying fuel from Earth.

Free-Electron Lasers

A notable development in the field of photonics is *free-electron lasers* (FELs). Unlike traditional lasers that rely on a medium like a crystal, gas, or semiconductor to produce light, FELs generate intense beams of light by accelerating electrons to nearly the speed of light along a magnetic field[61]. The result is a laser beam with a wavelength that can be tuned across a wide range, from microwaves to X-rays[62]. This allows FELs to adapt their output for different effects and applications.

To grasp the inner workings of a free-electron laser, let's first take a look at how a regular laser functions. In standard lasers, light is emitted when excited electrons in a medium like a crystal or a gas drop to a lower energy state. However, a free-electron laser doesn't use a traditional medium. Instead, it uses a beam of rapid, "free" electrons traveling through a magnetic structure called an *undulator*[63].

In an undulator, alternating magnets push the electrons side to side, causing them to move in a sinusoidal path. This wiggling action forces the electrons to emit light. Moreover, the wavelength of the emitted light can be adjusted depending on the energy of the electrons and the undulator's magnetic field strength[64].

Instead of confining electrons to atoms or molecules, free-electron lasers liberate them, allowing these particles to emit light of almost any wavelength. They represent a shift from the conventional, opening up a multitude of possibilities, from advanced imaging to laser weaponry and even the potential for laser-driven particle accelerators[65,66].

One of the most renowned real-world examples of an operational free-electron laser is the Linac Coherent Light Source (LCLS) at Stanford's SLAC National Accelerator Laboratory. This facility generates ultra-short, ultra-bright pulses of X-ray light that scientists use to investigate the atomic and molecular world, revolutionizing our understanding of matter[67].

Another example is the European XFEL based in Germany. This facility offers an unprecedented intensity of X-ray light for myriad scientific applications, including capturing detailed snapshots of viruses and biomolecules, investigating the extreme conditions of the Earth's interior, or decoding the atomic details of new materials[68].

Due to their ability to produce incredibly short and intense pulses, FELs can be used to study the world at the atomic level and even quantum mechanics[69,70]. This can be used to reveal how chemical reactions unfold in real-time[71]. They can also be used to analyze the vibrational modes of specific isotopes in complex materials, shedding light on intricate details of their behavior[72]. Additionally, FELs can produce conditions not readily achievable in laboratories, allowing scientists to study states of matter that exist in extreme conditions, such as the interiors of large planets or during certain astrophysical events[73,74].

The energy sector could also benefit from this laser technology. These lasers could be used to drive novel forms of nuclear fusion, potentially providing a clean and abundant source of power.

In addition, free-electron lasers could transform manufacturing, as they can be used to make extremely precise cuts and modifications in materials at a microscopic scale, facilitating the creation of advanced nano-scale components and devices.

Optical Tweezers

Out of the many exciting developments in photonics, *optical tweezers* are one of the most fantastical. Optical tweezers, or *optical traps* as they are often called, work on a principle that seems borrowed from a *Star Trek* episode. Here, a focused laser beam is used to trap and manipulate tiny particles, as small as a single atom, in three dimensions[75]. Light, contrary to our everyday experiences, exerts a force when it hits an object. This phenomenon, known as *radiation pressure*, is the principle behind the functioning of optical tweezers[76,77].

But how do optical tweezers really work? The answer lies in the property of refraction. When the highly focused laser beam of an optical tweezer hits a small refractive particle, the light is bent or refracted[78]. This change in direction imparts a small force on the particle, pushing it back towards the center of the beam where the light intensity is highest[79]. This effect creates a "trap," hence the name optical trap.

Since their inception in the 1980s by Arthur Ashkin of Bell Labs, who won the 2018 Nobel Prize in Physics for this work[80], optical tweezers have become an indispensable tool in several fields[81,82]. One of their most prominent applications has been in biology, where they are used to study and manipulate living cells[83]. Scientists can isolate a single cell, or even a part of it, and hold it for observation[84]. Optical tweezers can also measure minute forces, such as those generated by *molecular motors*. These are tiny machines inside our cells that do work[85].

But the journey of optical tweezers doesn't end there. Fast forward to today, and researchers are pushing the capabilities of optical tweezers even further. A real-world example is the use of "holographic" optical tweezers. Here, using the principles of holography, a single laser beam can be split into multiple independent traps, allowing simultaneous manipulation of multiple particles[86,87].

Now, let's cast our gaze to the future, where optical tweezers promise even more amazing applications. With continuing advancements in light manipulation, we may see the emergence of optical tweezers in surgery. Surgeons could use this technology to manipulate cells or small biological structures with unmatched precision, all without physically touching the patient.

The technology behind optical tweezers might also open the door for laser-based repair systems similar to *laser cladding*. This technique, also known as laser additive manufacturing, is a process that uses lasers to deposit materials onto a substrate to form a fully dense, adhered layer. This is achieved by simultaneously feeding a stream of powdered material into the path of a high-powered laser beam, which melts the powder and the substrate surface, resulting in a coating that is fused to the substrate[88,89].

Moreover, in the realm of quantum computing, optical tweezers could play a vital role. They might be used to organize and manipulate atoms or other *qubits* (quantum bits), providing a basis for quantum information processing.

Tractor Beams

As a staple in the treasury of space operas and interstellar adventures, it refers to a focused beam of energy that can draw objects towards its source. Imagine a light beam with an uncanny ability of pulling instead of just illuminating. The concept has tantalized and inspired many creative minds.

So, what exactly is a *tractor beam*? A tractor beam, in theory, is a form of directed energy that manipulates objects from a distance. It is a staple of science fiction technology that allows spaceships to grab, tow, or capture other objects without physical contact. This might sound impossible, but in recent years, the line between science fiction and reality has started to blur.

In order to understand the science behind tractor beam technology there has to be understanding about what laser propulsion is. Laser propulsion is a method of moving an object by shining a laser on it. That's right, a beam of focused, amplified light provides the push[90]. Light has no mass but it does carry momentum. When a light photon hits an object, it imparts a small force onto it[91,92]. A single photon's impact is minuscule, but a laser beam would contain enormous numbers of photons. Collectively, they can generate a significant thrust, especially in the frictionless vacuum of space[93].

The intriguing thing about laser propulsion is that the energy source (the laser) remains separate from the spacecraft. This is a radical departure from conventional rocket propulsion, where the vehicle carries its fuel and expels it to generate thrust.

Now, you might be wondering, how far has this technology come? Well, it is no longer in the realm of pure theory. In 2019, scientists at the California Institute of Technology demonstrated a form of laser propulsion, known as *photonic propulsion*, with a tiny, lightweight prototype. The so-called "lightcraft" was levitated and propelled by laser beams in a vacuum chamber[94]. This marked a promising advance in the field, but scaling up this technology for larger, practical spacecraft is still a work in progress.

Another example of this principle is in a 2015 research study from the University of Bristol. They successfully demonstrated a new method of levitation using lasers, known as *acoustic levitation*. Rather than relying solely on the momentum transfer from the photons, this method uses lasers to create a resonant acoustic field that can trap and levitate small particles[95,96].

So how does this translate into tractor beam technology? The vital clue lies in light's momentum. In laser propulsion, photons "push" an object away. Theoretically, if we could manipulate light's momentum in a way that it could "pull" instead of "push," we would have the basis for a real-life tractor beam.

Recent experiments by scientists from the Australian National University have made this possibility closer to reality. They used a hollow laser beam to transfer angular momentum to tiny glass particles suspended in air, effectively drawing the particles towards the laser source. Voila! We have pulling with light, the core mechanism of a tractor beam[97,98].

Of course, the jump from manipulating tiny particles to larger, practical objects is a challenge, but the science behind it has been proven. Picture a spaceship deploying a laser-based tractor beam to gently pull in space debris or malfunctioning satellites. Spacecraft could use tractor beams for docking procedures, eliminating the risk of physical collisions and making resource extraction from asteroids a reality.

The world of logistics and manufacturing will be empowered by tractor beams. Warehouse robots could use tractor beams to lift and move goods, making the processes faster, safer, and more efficient. In assembly lines, tractor beams could handle delicate parts that could be damaged by physical contact, making production smoother and less prone to errors.

In the entertainment industry, tractor beams could open new dimensions of virtual reality and gaming experiences. Imagine physically interacting with light projections, feeling the simulated environment's texture and shapes, transforming virtual reality into a truly tactile experience.

Finally, the world of art and design could see a revolution with tractor beams. Artists could create dynamic, moving sculptures with floating elements, controlled by nothing but light. Architects and designers could use the technology to model 3D structures in real-time, allowing clients to see and feel their designs come to life.

Photonic Computing

Imagine a device where data isn't processed by the motion of electrons, as it is in traditional computers, but by the ultra-fast movement of light. This shift from electron-based to photon-based processing could catapult computing into a new era of speed, efficiency, and capability.

Electrons, which form the core of traditional computing, aren't the speediest of particles. Even in the fastest processors, the speed of electrical signals is significantly slower than the speed of light because electrons carry mass while photons do not. By harnessing the sheer velocity of photons, *photonic computers* have a substantial speed advantage over traditional machines. In theory, these computers would not only process information faster, but they would also communicate faster between the different computer components, significantly reducing latency, and without the heat buildup that currently limits the size and speed of electronic chips[99].

But how does a photonic computer work? The idea is to harness the unique properties of light. Just as electronic circuits control the flow of electrons, *photonic circuits* control the flow of photons. Photons can be generated with lasers, guided with fiber-optic cables, and manipulated with various optical elements. The information is carried in the light waves themselves using their frequency, phase, and polarization to differentiate the data.

Though the field of photonic computing is still emerging, there are already some exciting real-world examples that hint at its future potential. For instance, researchers at MIT have developed a photonic chip that can perform complex mathematical computations in a fraction of the time it would take a traditional electronic chip[99].

Meanwhile, at the University of Oxford, a team has built a prototype photonic computer that can solve certain problems much faster than its electronic counterparts[100,101]. Companies like IBM and Intel are already investing heavily in the development of photonic computing technology, a sure sign that it is being taken seriously in the world of information technology[102,103].

As for the future, the potential applications of photonic computing are dizzying. We could see the rise of ultra-high-speed internet services, powered by light-speed computations. Big data analytics, machine learning, and artificial intelligence could all be supercharged, allowing for real-time data processing on a massive scale.

Chapter References

1. Synopsys. (n.d.). What is Photonics and How Does it Work? https://www.synopsys.com/glossary/what-is-photonics.html

2. Cisco Press. (2004, April 23). A Brief History of Fiber-Optic Communications. https://www.ciscopress.com/articles/article.asp?p=170740

3. V1 Fiber. (2020, February 19). The History of Fiber Optics. https://v1fiber.com/the-history-of-fiber-optics/

4. Agrawal, G.P. (2016). Optical Communication: Its History and Recent Progress. In: Al-Amri, M., El-Gomati, M., Zubairy, M. (eds) *Optics in Our Time*. Springer. https://doi.org/10.1007/978-3-319-31903-2_8

5. Encyclopedia Britannica. (2023, October 20). fiber optics. https://www.britannica.com/science/fiber-optics

6. Coffey, V. C. (2019, January). The Dawn of New Optics: Emerging Metamaterials. *Photonics Spectra*. https://www.photonics.com/Articles/The_Dawn_of_New_Optics_Emerging_Metamaterials/a64154

7. Laine, E. (2021, August 10). Metamaterials research challenges fundamental limits in photonics. *Cornell Chronicle*. https://news.cornell.edu/stories/2021/08/metamaterials-research-challenges-fundamental-limits-photonics

8. Halir, R., et al. (2022). Silicon Photonics: Advanced Metamaterials and Sensors. *2022 Photonics North (PN)*. Niagara Falls, ON, Canada. https://doi.org/10.1109/PN56061.2022.9908316

9. Mascolo, D., Petrone, I., Pascale, E., Pisco, M., & Cutolo, A. (2011). Production Technologies for Manufacturing of Metamaterials and Photonic Crystals. *Selected Topics In Photonic Crystals And Metamaterials* (pp. 505-532). https://doi.org/10.1142/9789814355193_0018

10. Physics World. (2003, May 1). The Reality of Negative Refraction. https://physicsworld.com/a/the-reality-of-negative-refraction/

11. Than, K. (2007, April 1). The Magic of Metamaterials. *Duke Magazine*. https://alumni.duke.edu/magazine/articles/magic-metamaterials

12. Valentine, J., Zhang, S., Zentgraf, T., et al. (2008). Three-dimensional optical metamaterial with a negative refractive index.

Nature, 455, 376–379. https://doi.org/10.1038/nature07247

13. Zhang, X., Liu, Z. (2008). Superlenses to overcome the diffraction limit. *Nature Materials*, 7, 435–441. https://doi.org/10.1038/nmat2141

14. Wen, Y., Wang, K., & Kuang, D. (2019). Improvement of telescope resolution using a diffractive phase modulator. *Scientific Reports*, 9, 3475. https://doi.org/10.1038/s41598-019-39804-z

15. Kong, W., Liu, L., Wang, C., Pu, M., Gao, P., Liu, K., Luo, Y., Jin, Q., Zhao, C., & Luo, X. (2022). A planar ultraviolet objective lens for optical axis free imaging nanolithography by employing optical negative refraction. *Nanoscale Advances*, 4(8), 2011-2017. https://doi.org/10.1039/D1NA00883H

16. Rahman, M. S., & Al Sayem, A. (2016). Broad angle negative refraction in lossless all dielectric or semiconductor based asymmetric anisotropic metamaterial. *Journal of Optics*, 18(1), 015101. https://doi.org/10.1088/2040-8978/18/1/015101

17. Radovanović, J., Ramović, S., Daničić, A., et al. (2012). Negative refraction in semiconductor metamaterials based on quantum cascade laser design for the mid-IR and THz spectral range. *Applied Physics A*, 109, 763–768. https://doi.org/10.1007/s00339-012-7343-2

18. Hoffman, A. J., Alekseyev, L., Howard, S. S., Franz, K. J., Wasserman, D., Podolskiy, V. A., & Gmachl, C. (2007). Negative refraction in semiconductor metamaterials. *Nature Materials*, 6(12), 946-950. https://doi.org/10.1038/nmat2033

19. Chourasiya, S. (2021, January). Optical Fiber | Optical Fiber Communication | Working Principle | Types and Applications. *M-Physics Tutorial*. https://www.mphysicstutorial.com/2021/01/optical-fiber-communication-working-principle-types-and-applications.html

20. Weir, M. (2021, March 17). What Is Fiber Optics? Here's What You Need to Know. *Business Insider*. https://www.businessinsider.com/guides/tech/fiber-optic

21. Rao, R. (2020). Optical communication systems serve as the backbone of today's technologies. *MRS Bulletin*, 45(12), 1056-1057. https://doi.org/10.1557/mrs.2020.319

22. FS Community. (2021, December 22). The Advantages and Disadvantages of Optical Fiber. https://community.fs.com/blog/the-advantages-and-disadvantages-of-optical-fibers.html

23. Harutyunyan, H., Beams, R., & Novotny, L. (2013). Controllable

optical negative refraction and phase conjugation in graphite thin films. *Nature Physics*, 9, 423–425. https://doi.org/10.1038/nphys2618

24. California Institute of Technology. (2007, March 23). Cloaking Device Breakthrough? Negative Refraction Of Visible Light Demonstrated. *ScienceDaily*. https://www.sciencedaily.com/releases/2007/03/070322132145.htm

25. Savage, N. (2008, August 1). Metamaterials Breakthrough Brings Invisibility Closer. *IEEE Spectrum*. https://spectrum.ieee.org/metamaterials-breakthrough-brings-invisibility-closer

26. Wong, Zi, Wang, Yuan, O'Brien, Kevin, Rho, Junsuk, Yin, Xiaobo, Zhang, Shuang, Fang, Nicholas, Yen, Ta-Jen, & Zhang, Xiang. (2017). Optical and acoustic metamaterials: Superlens, negative refractive index and invisibility cloak. *Journal of Optics*, 19, 084007. https://doi.org/10.1088/2040-8986/aa7a1f

27. California Institute of Technology. (2022, January 28). Nano-architected material refracts light backward; an important step toward creating photonic circuits. *Phys.org*. https://phys.org/news/2022-01-nano-architected-material-refracts-important-photonic.html

28. Gamma Editorial Team. (2022, July 1). The Properties and Applications of Photonic Crystals. *Gamma Scientific*. https://gamma-sci.com/the-properties-and-applications-of-photonic-crystals/

29. Butt, M.A., Khonina, S.N., & Kazanskiy, N.L. (2021). Recent advances in photonic crystal optical devices: A review. *Optics & Laser Technology*, 142, 107265. https://doi.org/10.1016/j.optlastec.2021.107265

30. Taylor-Smith, Kerry. (2022, August 13). Properties and Applications of Photonic Crystals. *AZoOptics*. https://www.azooptics.com/Article.aspx?ArticleID=1467

31. Zhu, K., Fang, C., Pu, M., Song, J., Wang, D., & Zhou, X. (2023). Recent advances in photonic crystal with unique structural colors: A review. *Journal of Materials Science & Technology*, 141, 78-99. https://doi.org/10.1016/j.jmst.2022.08.044

32. Ruda, H., & Matsuura, N. (2019). Properties and Applications of Photonic Crystals. *Optical Properties of Materials and Their Applications* (pp. 251-268). https://doi.org/10.1002/9781119506003.ch9

33. Taylor-Smith, K. (2018, November 2). Properties and Applications of Photonic Crystals. *AZoOptics*. https://www.azooptics.com/Article.aspx?ArticleID=1467

34. Gamma Scientific. (2022, July 1). The Properties and Applications of Photonic Crystals. https://gamma-sci.com/2022/07/01/the-properties-and-applications-of-photonic-crystals/

35. Inoue, S. (2013). Photonic Crystals: Manipulating Light with Periodic Structures. In Aoyagi, Y., Kajikawa, K. (Eds.), *Optical Properties of Advanced Materials* (Springer Series in Materials Science, Vol. 168). Springer. https://doi.org/10.1007/978-3-642-33527-3_2

36. Fan, S., Mekis, A., Johnson, S. G., & Joannopoulos, J. D. (2001). Manipulating light with photonic crystals. *AIP Conference Proceedings*, 560(1), 57–76. https://doi.org/10.1063/1.1372716

37. Perlin, J. (2014, January 6). Let It Shine: Solar Energy in Ancient Rome. *Mother Earth News*. https://www.motherearthnews.com/sustainable-living/renewable-energy/solar-energy-in-ancient-rome-zbcz1401/

38. Richardson, L. (2023, April 26). Solar history: Timeline & invention of solar panels. *EnergySage*. https://www.energysage.com/about-clean-energy/solar/the-history-and-invention-of-solar-panel-technology/

39. Chu, E., & Tarazano, D. L. (n.d.). A Brief History of Solar Panels. *Smithsonian Magazine*. https://www.smithsonianmag.com/sponsored/brief-history-solar-panels-180972006/

40. Matasci, S. (2022, February 8). How solar panel cost and efficiency have changed over time. *EnergySage*. https://www.energysage.com/solar/solar-panel-efficiency-cost-over-time/

41. Green, M. A. (2009). The path to 25% silicon solar cell efficiency: History of silicon cell evolution. *Progress in Photovoltaics: Research and Applications*, 17, 183-189. https://doi.org/10.1002/pip.892

42. Andreani, L. C., Bozzola, A., Kowalczewski, P., Liscidini, M., & Redorici, L. (2019). Silicon solar cells: Toward the efficiency limits. *Advances in Physics: X*, 4(1). https://doi.org/10.1080/23746149.2018.1548305

43. Nair, S., Patel, S. B., & Gohel, J. V. (2020). Recent trends in efficiency-stability improvement in perovskite solar cells. Materials Today Energy, 17, 100449. https://doi.org/10.1016/j.mtener.2020.100449

44. Roy, P., Ghosh, A., Barclay, F., Khare, A., & Cuce, E. (2022). Perovskite Solar Cells: A Review of the Recent Advances. *Coatings*, 12(8), 1089. https://doi.org/10.3390/coatings12081089

45. Zhang, H., Ji, X., Yao, H., Fan, Q., Yu, B., & Li, J. (2022). Review on

efficiency improvement effort of perovskite solar cell. *Solar Energy*, 233, 421-434. https://doi.org/10.1016/j.solener.2022.01.060

46. Shi, Z., & Jayatissa, A. H. (2018). Perovskites-Based Solar Cells: A Review of Recent Progress, Materials and Processing Methods. *Materials*, 11(5), 729. https://doi.org/10.3390/ma11050729

47. Kumagai, J. (2019, January 4). Power From Commercial Perovskite Solar Cells Is Coming Soon. *IEEE Spectrum*. https://spectrum. ieee.org/power-from-commercial-perovskite-solar-cells-is-coming-soon

48. Fu, F., Li, J., Yang, T. C.-J., Liang, H., Faes, A., Jeangros, Q., Ballif, C., Hou, Y. (2022). Monolithic Perovskite-Silicon Tandem Solar Cells: From the Lab to Fab?. *Advanced Materials*, 34, 2106540. https://doi.org/ 10.1002/adma.202106540

49. PV Magazine. (2023, May 24). Oxford PV sets 28.6% efficiency record for full-size tandem cell. https://www.pv-magazine.com/ 2023/05/24/oxford-pv-sets-28-6-efficiency-record-for-full-size-tandem-cell/

50. Extance, A. (2014, September 30). Tandem cells speed route to perovskite commercialization. *Optics.org*. https://optics.org/news/ 5/9/53

51. Nozik, A. J. (2002). Quantum dot solar cells. *Physica E: Low-dimensional Systems and Nanostructures*, 14(1–2), 115-120. https://doi. org/10.1016/S1386-9477(02)00374-0.

52. Salama, H. (2022). Quantum Dot Solar cells. *arXiv*. https://arxiv. org/abs/2211.06898

53. Business Wire. (2023, February 14). QD Solar reports on highly efficient perovskite solar cells developed for large-scale manufacturing. https://www.businesswire.com/news/home/20230214005803/en/QD-Solar-reports-on-highly-efficient-perovskite-solar-cells-developed-for-large-scale-manufacturing

54. Edwards, R. (n.d.). Rooftop Solar vs. Solar Farms: Which Is Best for You? *Solar Power Authority*. https://www.solarpowerauthority.com/ rooftop-solar-vs-solar-farms/

55. National Renewable Energy Laboratory. (n.d.). Photovoltaic Applications. https://www.nrel.gov/pv/applications.html

56. Ng, A. Y. R., Boruah, B., Chin, K. F., Modak, J. M., & Soo, H. S. (2020). *ChemNanoMat*, 6, 185. https://onlinelibrary.wiley.com/doi/abs/ 10.1002/cnma.201900616

57. Andreiadis, E. S., Chavarot-Kerlidou, M., Fontecave, M., & Artero, V. (2011). Artificial photosynthesis: from molecular catalysts for light-driven water splitting to photoelectrochemical cells. *Photochemical & Photobiological Sciences*, 87(5), 946-964. https://doi.org/10.1111/j.1751-1097.2011.00966.x

58. Moseman, A. (2020, August 7). Converting Sunlight into Fuels. *Caltech Magazine*. https://magazine.caltech.edu/post/converting-sunlight-into-fuels

59. Svitil, K. (2015, April 30). JCAP receives a 5-year, $75M funding renewal. *Caltech Magazine*. https://www.caltech.edu/about/news/jcap-receives-5-year-75m-funding-renewal-46671

60. Hokkaido University. (2018, September 10). Photoelectrode that can harvest 85 percent of visible light. *Phys.org*. https://phys.org/news/2018-09-photoelectrode-harvest-percent-visible.html

61. Carbajo, S. (2020). Free Electron Lasers: The Biggest and Brightest Light Sources. *Research Outreach*. https://doi.org/10.32907/RO-118-162165

62. Critchley, L. (2022, November 07). Underlying Principles of a Free-Electron Laser. *AZoOptics*. https://www.azooptics.com/Article.aspx?ArticleID=1737

63. Paschotta, R. (2008). Free electron lasers. *Encyclopedia of Laser Physics and Technology*. Wiley-VCH. ISBN 978-3-527-40828-3. https://www.rp-photonics.com/free_electron_lasers.html

64. Sundermier, A. (2022, September 30). Explainer: What is an X-ray free-electron laser? *SLAC National Accelerator Laboratory*. https://www6.slac.stanford.edu/research/slac-science-explained/xfels

65. Socol, Y. (2013). High-power free-electron lasers—technology and future applications. *Optics & Laser Technology*, 46, 111-126. https://doi.org/10.1016/j.optlastec.2012.06.040

66. O'Shea, P. G., & Freund, H. P. (2001). Free-electron lasers: Status and applications. *Science*, 292, 1853-1858. https://doi.org/10.1126/science.1055718

67. SLAC National Accelerator Laboratory. (2023, September 18). SLAC fires up the world's most powerful X-ray laser: LCLS-II ushers in a new era of science. https://www6.slac.stanford.edu/news/2023-09-18-slac-fires-worlds-most-powerful-x-ray-laser-lcls-ii-ushers-new-era-science

68. European XFEL. (n.d.). The European X-Ray Free-Electron Laser. https://www.xfel.eu/

69. Berkowitz, R. (2023, October 17). Intense X Rays Can Free Bound Electrons. *APS Physics*. https://physics.aps.org/articles/v16/s142

70. Debus, A., et al. (2019, April 15). Realizing quantum free-electron lasers: a critical analysis of experimental challenges and theoretical limits. *Physica Scripta*, 94(074001). https://doi.org/10.1088/1402-4896/aaf951

71. Moshammer, R., & Schnorr, K. (2016). Molecular physics and gas-phase chemistry with free-electron lasers. In E. Jaeschke, S. Khan, J. Schneider, & J. Hastings (Eds.), *Synchrotron Light Sources and Free-Electron Lasers*. Springer. https://doi.org/10.1007/978-3-319-14394-1_26

72. Can, K., Zahra, M., Paolo, G. P., Antonello, A., Illya, D., Dario, G., Rosaria, M., Giovanni, M., Michele, O., Domenico, P., Andrea, P., Vittoria, P., Bruno, P., Andrea, R., Marcel, R., Paolo, R., & Luca, S. (2022). Multi-Pass Free Electron Laser Assisted Spectral and Imaging Applications in the Terahertz/Far-IR Range Using the Future Superconducting Electron Source BriXSinO. *Frontiers in Physics*, 10. https://doi.org/10.3389/fphy.2022.725901

73. Ren, S., Shi, Y., van den Berg, Q. Y., et al. (2023). Non-thermal evolution of dense plasmas driven by intense x-ray fields. *Communications Physics*, 6, 99. https://doi.org/10.1038/s42005-023-01216-x

74. Bencivenga, F., Principi, E., Giangrisostomi, E., Battistoni, A., Cucini, R., Danailov, M. B., Demidovich, A., Di Cicco, A., D'Amico, F., Di Fonzo, S., Filipponi, A., Gessini, A., Gunnella, R., Hatada, K., Kurdi, N., Mahne, N., Mincigrucci, R., Raimondi, L., Svetina, C., Zangrando, M., & Masciovecchio, C. (2015). Matter under extreme conditions probed by a seeded free-electron-laser. *AIP Conference Proceedings*, 1673(1), 020001. https://doi.org/10.1063/1.4928255

75. Block Lab. (n.d.). Optical Tweezers. Stanford University. https://blocklab.stanford.edu/optical_tweezers.html

76. Nieminen, T. A., du Preez-Wilkinson, N., Stilgoe, A. B., Loke, V. L. Y. , Bui, A. A. M., & Rubinsztein-Dunlop, H. (2014). Optical tweezers: Theory and modeling. *Journal of Quantitative Spectroscopy and Radiative Transfer*, 146, 59-80. https://doi.org/10.1016/j.jqsrt.2014.04.003

77. Zaltron, A., Merano, M., Mistura, G., & Cojoc, D. (2020). Optical tweezers in single-molecule experiments. *European Physical Journal Plus*, 135, 896. https://doi.org/10.1140/epjp/s13360-020-00907-6

78. LUMICKS. (n.d.). What Are Optical Tweezers? https://lumicks.com/knowledge/what-are-optical-tweezers/

79. Ashkin, A., Dziedzic, J. M., Bjorkholm, J. E., & Chu, S. (1986). Observation of a single-beam gradient force optical trap for dielectric particles. *Optics Letters*, 11(5), 288-290. https://doi.org/10.1364/OL.11.000288

80. Nobel Prize Outreach AB. (2023). Arthur Ashkin – Facts – 2018. *NobelPrize.org*. https://www.nobelprize.org/prizes/physics/2018/ashkin/facts/

81. Polimeno, P., Magazzù, A., Iatì, M. A., Patti, F., Saija, R., Degli Esposti Boschi, C., Donato, M. G., Gucciardi, P. G., Jones, P. H., Volpe, G., & Maragò, O. M. (2018). Optical tweezers and their applications. *Journal of Quantitative Spectroscopy and Radiative Transfer*, 218, 131-150. https://doi.org/10.1016/j.jqsrt.2018.07.013

82. Lenton, I. C. D., Scott, E. K., Rubinsztein-Dunlop, H., & Favre-Bulle, I. A. (2020). Optical Tweezers Exploring Neuroscience. *Frontiers in Bioengineering and Biotechnology*, 8. https://doi.org/10.3389/fbioe.2020.602797

83. Favre-Bulle, I. A., & Scott, E. K. (2022). Optical tweezers across scales in cell biology. *Trends in Cell Biology*, 32(11), 932-946. https://doi.org/10.1016/j.tcb.2022.05.001

84. Keloth, A., Anderson, O., Risbridger, D., & Paterson, L. (2018). Single Cell Isolation Using Optical Tweezers. *Micromachines (Basel)*, 9(9), 434. https://doi.org/10.3390/mi9090434

85. Nicholas, M. P., Rao, L., & Gennerich, A. (2014). An Improved Optical Tweezers Assay for Measuring the Force Generation of Single Kinesin Molecules. In D. Sharp (Ed.), *Mitosis* (pp. 155-170). Humana Press. https://doi.org/10.1007/978-1-4939-0329-0_10

86. Padgett, M., & Di Leonardo, R. (2011). Holographic optical tweezers and their relevance to lab on chip devices. *Lab on a Chip*, 11(7), 1196-1205. https://doi.org/10.1039/C0LC00526F

87. Chen, H-C., & Cheng, C-J. (2022). Holographic Optical Tweezers: Techniques and Biomedical Applications. *Applied Sciences*, 12(20), 10244. https://doi.org/10.3390/app122010244

88. Li, J., Chen, Z., Liu, Y., Kollipara, P. S., Feng, Y., Zhang, Z., & Zheng, Y. (2021). Opto-refrigerative tweezers. *Science Advances*, 7(26), eabh1101. https://doi.org/10.1126/sciadv.abh1101

89. TWI Ltd. (n.d.). What is Laser Cladding Technology? https://www.twi-global.com/technical-knowledge/faqs/what-is-laser-cladding

90. Bonsor, K. (1970, January 1.). How Light Propulsion Will Work. *HowStuffWorks*. https://science.howstuffworks.com/light-propulsion.htm

91. The Naked Scientists. (2012, July 17). How can photons impart momentum to objects? https://www.thenakedscientists.com/articles/questions/how-can-photons-impart-momentum-objects

92. The Naked Scientists. (2016, October 24). How can photons impart momentum to objects? https://www.thenakedscientists.com/articles/questions/how-can-photons-impart-momentum-objects

93. Levchenko, I., Bazaka, K., Mazouffre, S., et al. (2018). Prospects and physical mechanisms for photonic space propulsion. *Nature Photon*, 12, 649–657. https://doi.org/10.1038/s41566-018-0280-7

94. Ilic, O., & Atwater, H. A. (2019). Self-stabilizing photonic levitation and propulsion of nanostructured macroscopic objects. *Nature Photonics*, 13, 289–295. https://doi.org/10.1038/s41566-019-0373-y

95. Gohd, C. (2018, January 22). Could we levitate humans with the world's most powerful acoustic tractor beam? *Futurism*. https://futurism.com/could-levitate-humans-worlds-most-powerful-acoustic-tractor-beam

96. Barnes, A. C., Drinkwater, B. W., & Marzo, A. (2017). TinyLev: A multi-emitter single-axis acoustic levitator. *Review of Scientific Instruments*, 88. https://doi.org/10.1063/1.4989995

97. Shvedov, V., Davoyan, A., Hnatovsky, C., & Rode, A. V. (2014). A long-range polarization-controlled optical tractor beam. *Nature Photon*, 8(11), 846–850. https://doi.org/10.1038/nphoton.2014.242

98. Dickerson, K. (2014, October 23). Real-life tractor beam pulls in particles. *Live Science*. https://www.livescience.com/48414-tractor-beam-pulls-in-particles.html

99. Shipps, A. (2023, September 11). System combines light and electrons to unlock faster, greener computing. *Massachusetts Institute of Technology*. https://news.mit.edu/2023/system-combines-light-electrons-unlock-faster-greener-computing-0911

100. Feldmann, J., Youngblood, N., Li, X., & Bhaskaran, H. (2021, January 11). Light-carrying chips advance machine learning. *University of Oxford*. https://www.ox.ac.uk/news/2021-01-11-light-carrying-chips-advance-machine-learning?ref=image

101. Lee, J. S., Bhaskaran, H. (2022, June 16). Researchers develop the world's first ultra-fast photonic computing processor using polarisation. *University of Oxford.* https://www.ox.ac.uk/news/2022-06-16-researchers-develop-worlds-first-ultra-fast-photonic-computing-processor-using

102. Smolaks, M. (2015, May 13). IBM reports success of silicon photonics project. *Data Center Dynamics.* https://www.datacenterdynamics.com/en/news/ibm-reports-success-of-silicon-photonics-project/

103. Business Wire. (2022, June 28). Intel Labs announces integrated photonics research advancement. https://www.businesswire.com/news/home/20220628005468/en/Intel-Labs-Announces-Integrated-Photonics-Research-Advancement

Plasma Technology

Once seen as an exotic state of matter only found in the heart of stars or the ephemeral tail of a comet, *plasma* has been just outside humanity's grasp for much of its history. Increasingly, plasma is being harnessed and re-created in laboratories across the globe and is showing extraordinary promise in revolutionizing our society and way of life. Whether its limitless clean energy or innovative forms of propulsion, we are poised for a future with this obscure form of matter.

Laser-Induced Plasma Filaments

Imagine a world where communication travels without a

trace, where environmental sensors reach the granularity of pinpointing a droplet's pH before it hits the ground, and where pollutants in our atmosphere are neutralized mid-air. This may sound impossible, but with the advancements in *laser-induced plasma filaments* (LIPFs), these scenarios inch closer to reality.

LIPFs are a phenomenon where a high-intensity laser beam can create a plasma filament in the atmosphere. This plasma filament can serve as a sort of guide for other laser beams, effectively allowing lasers to "bend" around obstacles[1,2]. The harnessing of this phenomenon point to exciting applications.

Traditionally, laser-based communication (free-space optical communication) has a drawback: its vulnerability to atmospheric conditions. Fog, rain, and dust can scatter and absorb the laser beams, disrupting the communication link. However, these plasma filaments, due to their self-guided nature, can maintain a consistent beam through adverse atmospheric conditions. This makes them a potential avenue for reliable and stealthy laser communication[3].

This type of technology could also be used to help save regions from droughts and barren conditions. Researchers have already demonstrated the ability to use this technology for cloud seeding[4]. ionized filaments generated by ultra-short laser pulses can induce water-cloud condensation in the atmosphere, even when it is not fully saturated with moisture. The mechanisms behind this include photo-oxidative chemistry and electrostatic effects, which could potentially be used to influence or trigger precipitation.

Additionally, satellite internet that is often lamented because of its slow speeds, could use plasma filaments to provide internet that is many times better than their current capabilities[5,6].

There is currently a technique used to analyze material composition that is called *laser-induced breakdown spectroscopy* (LIBS). This relies on lasers to ionize a sample and then analyze the emitted light spectrum to determine the composition of material and environmental samples[7,8]. With LIPFs, there's potential to perform such analysis remotely. Imagine drones or space probes equipped with LIPF technology that can assess the quality of elements and environments from a safe distance[9,10].

Similarly, there's ongoing research into how LIPFs can be used to neutralize pollutants in the air. By creating plasma filaments, it is possible to induce chemical reactions that can transform pollutants into less harmful compounds[11]. Given the current trajectory of global pollution, this application could provide cities with a tool to improve air quality, benefiting public health.

Plasma in Warfare

The mere idea of a "plasma weapon" evokes images of brilliant arcs of searing energy, potent enough to disintegrate anything in their path. But beyond the realms of science fiction and fantasy, what exactly is plasma weaponry, and could it really exist?

Plasma is essentially a hot soup of free-moving ions and electrons. Its properties are quite unique, as it responds to and generates electric and magnetic fields along with the ability to conduct electricity. Natural examples include lightning and the aurora borealis, while man-made plasma can be found in fluorescent lights and plasma cutting torches.

Plasma weaponry would harness this high-energy state of matter to inflict damage. You would need to generate a high-energy plasma, contain it long enough to prevent dissipation, and then accurately direct it towards your target. This is where reality becomes a little more complicated than science fiction.

As of 2023, despite significant advances in plasma technology, we haven't yet developed a practical or deployable plasma weapon. The closest we have come is the development of *plasma torches* used in industry for cutting and welding. These devices generate a stream of plasma directed at the material to be cut, melting it quickly and efficiently. However, they work at a close range, and the plasma dissipates quickly into the air, making them unsuitable for use as a weapon.

The key lies in containment and control. You would need to generate a high-energy plasma, contain it long enough to prevent dissipation, and then accurately direct it towards your target. This is where reality becomes a little more complicated than science fiction. All of this would require a considerable amount of energy, not to mention a way of controlling the plasma bolt's direction and ensuring it doesn't dissipate before reaching its target.

Although plasma blasters are unlikely in the near future, there are other more realistic uses. The use of plasma shields in the future could be an extremely effective defense against future offensive weaponry. Theoretically, a high-energy plasma shield could absorb, dissipate, or even reflect energy-based attacks such as lasers or other forms of directed energy. This could be accomplished by using powerful electromagnetic fields to contain and shape the plasma, similar to how it is done in experimental nuclear fusion reactors[12]. The electromagnetic field could, in theory, be adjusted dynamically to counter incoming threats, providing a flexible, responsive shield. These plasma shields would be extremely effective to protect sensitive electronic equipment from the harmful effects of an electromagnetic pulse (EMP)[13,14].

On a micro level, plasma has been shown to be effective in neutralizing certain biological agents, including some pathogens[15]. Plasma could potentially be used to neutralize biological weapons or sanitize areas that always need to be sterile like surgery rooms[16].

Furthermore, there are practical uses for plasma in defense. Using high-energy lasers to ionize the air and create a localized cloud of plasma, this cloud could potentially reflect radar waves, giving the illusion of a physical object where there is none, thus creating a false radar signature[17]. These plasma clouds could also absorb or scatter electromagnetic radiation, potentially making them useful for electronic countermeasures and anti-radar technology[18]. A system based on this concept could theoretically provide a range of deceptive capabilities, from making an object appear larger, smaller, or in a different location, to completely cloaking it from radar detection.

The usefulness of such systems in warfare is obvious, assault operations or a squad of bombers approaching an area could be faked using false radar signatures, while the actual location of friendly forces are rendered invisible to the enemy's radar.

Fusion Power

When it comes to the future of power and drive systems, there's a radiant gem that has teased scientists and engineers for decades—*fusion power*. This incredible technology, the very same process that fuels the stars in the universe, could become humanity's ultimate power source.

Fusion requires a high-speed collision of two light atoms, such as hydrogen isotopes. When heated to extreme temperatures (millions of degrees Celsius), these isotopes in a plasma state overcome their natural repulsion (both are positive charges) and collide[19]. The collision is so forceful that the two nuclei fuse together, creating a heavier helium atom and a free neutron[20]. This process also releases a tremendous amount of energy, nearly four million times more potent than burning coal, oil or gas and four times as powerful as nuclear fission[20].

The allure of fusion is profound. Picture an energy source that is practically limitless, relying on hydrogen isotopes like deuterium and tritium, which we can extract from seawater and lithium[21]. It produces no greenhouse gases and, unlike its cousin, nuclear fission, it generates no long-lived radioactive waste[20]. Also, fusion reactions are inherently safe because if something goes wrong, the process quickly fizzles out.

Despite these irresistible benefits, harnessing the power of the stars is an incredibly challenging feat. For fusion to occur, we must create conditions akin to those found in the sun's core, which means superheating hydrogen gas to millions of degrees, forming a plasma. This plasma then needs to be compressed and confined long enough for fusion to occur.

An important milestone for fusion power was reached not too long ago. On December 5, 2022, history was made. At 1 p.m. Pacific time, the Department of Energy's Lawrence Livermore National Laboratory fired the world's most energetic lasers to turn hydrogen into helium. The process required an input of 2 MJ of energy, and resulted in the output of just over 3 MJ[23]. This is a tremendous breakthrough considering that up until now, all attempts at fusion energy has output less energy than input[23].

The future of fusion power could make even miniaturized nuclear reactors obsolete. Imagine a world powered by fusion reactors. Using the efficiency from this recent experiment, a future fusion-powered car would be able to use 1 gram of fuel to go over 350,000 miles! This newly achieved efficiency could also mean that 1 gram of fuel could theoretically power around 3,520 average homes for an entire year.

Fusion Propulsion

On a more futuristic note, fusion reactors could even propel spacecraft. This isn't as far-fetched as it sounds, the concept of *fusion propulsion* has been studied since the early days of space exploration. *Project Daedalus*, a study conducted by the British Interplanetary Society in the 1970s, proposed a fusion-propelled interstellar spacecraft that could reach nearby star systems within a human lifetime[24]. Although we are still far from realizing this vision, it provides a tantalizing glimpse into the potential of fusion propulsion. Fusion-powered rockets could potentially reduce the travel time to Mars from months to weeks, opening up the solar system for human exploration[25]. But what exactly is fusion propulsion and how does it work?

Fusion propulsion is a form of spacecraft propulsion that uses nuclear fusion reactions to generate thrust. The beauty of fusion propulsion lies in its efficiency and power. Compared to traditional chemical rockets, fusion engines can produce significantly more thrust per unit of propellant. This means spacecraft equipped with fusion engines could potentially reach much higher speeds, drastically reducing the travel time to distant planets and moons[26,27].

That being said, developing a fusion propulsion system is no easy task. It is akin to miniaturizing a star and taming its power for our use. Despite these challenges, real-world advancements are bringing fusion propulsion closer to reality.

For instance, the *Direct Fusion Drive* project, a collaboration between Princeton Satellite Systems and Princeton University, is making steady progress[28]. This project combines fusion and electric propulsion technologies, and its research has received funding from NASA's *Innovative Advanced Concepts* program. The goal is to produce a propulsion system that can cut travel time to Saturn to just two years[29].

The advantages of fusion propulsion go beyond speed. The vast energy output of a fusion reaction could also be harnessed to power everything from life support systems to scientific instruments. In essence, a fusion-powered spacecraft could be a self-contained, mobile outpost, capable of extended missions to the farthest reaches of our solar system and beyond.

Fusion-based propulsion might also be realized through what is referred to as a *magnetohydrodynamic* (MHD) drive. Imagine a world where ships glide through water with no visible means of propulsion, no wake, and no sound. Picture spacecraft darting through the cosmos in every direction without any rockets or thrusters, defying conventional rocket science.

An MHD drive harnesses the principles of magnetohydrodynamics, the study of the behavior of electrically conductive fluids in magnetic fields. To comprehend how MHD drives work, we first need to understand plasma. In plasma, the intense heat has provided enough energy for atoms to be stripped of their electrons, resulting in a soup of free electrons and ions (atoms that have lost or gained electrons). This gives plasma some unique properties, such as being electrically conductive and being affected by magnetic fields. MHD drives work by sending an electric current through this plasma, creating a magnetic field. By interacting with a secondary magnetic field, the plasma experiences a force known as Lorentz force, which propels it in a specific direction[30,31]. In simpler terms, think of an MHD drive as a boat engine without any moving parts, where the water is the plasma and the paddle is the magnetic field.

Unlike traditional propulsion systems, MHD drives don't rely on propellers or turbines. These mechanical components not only produce noise but are also prone to wear and tear. In contrast, the absence of moving parts in MHD drives makes them virtually silent and not restricted to a specific direction.The absence of mechanical friction also suggests that MHD drives could theoretically boast longer operational lifetimes and lower maintenance needs.

Furthermore, MHD drives could achieve higher speeds than conventional propellers. They work by directly accelerating the surrounding fluid, which allows for potentially higher thrust and more efficient operation at high speeds. This characteristic could revolutionize propulsion across air, sea, and space.

MHD drives' fascinating characteristics offers a multitude of exciting applications, from silent and swift seafaring vessels to revolutionary space propulsion[32].

In maritime applications, the advent of MHD drive technology could see the rise of virtually silent ships and submarines[31]. These vessels would be faster and more efficient, with the potential to reduce the maritime industry's environmental impact. Their reduced noise could mitigate harm to marine life, often distressed by the underwater cacophony produced by traditional shipping.

Perhaps the most awe-inspiring applications lie beyond our planet. In space, where the concepts of "up" and "down" have no meaning, the omnidirectional thrust capabilities of MHD drives could allow for precise maneuvering. Their potential for high speeds could significantly cut down interplanetary travel times, and the absence of mechanical parts reduces the risk of catastrophic failures, making space travel safer.

Even more remarkably, MHD drives could enable spacecraft to "scoop" ionized gas from the interstellar medium or a planet's atmosphere and use it as fuel[32]. This concept, known as "air-breathing," could allow for long-duration space missions without the need to carry vast quantities of fuel onboard[32]. Imagine a spacecraft that can go near a star when it begins to run low on fuel and extract plasma directly from it, obtaining all the fuel it needs in a few seconds.

Chapter References

1. Skrodzki, P. J., Burger, M., & Jovanovic, I. (2017). Transition of Femtosecond-Filament-Solid Interactions from Single to Multiple Filament Regime. *Scientific Reports*, 7, 12740. https://doi.org/10.1038/s41598-017-13188-4

2. Kautz, E. J., Phillips, M. C., & Harilal, S. S. (2021). Laser-induced fluorescence of filament-produced plasmas. *Journal of Applied Physics*, 130(20), 203302. https://doi.org/10.1063/5.0065240

3. Hening, A., Wayne, D., Lovern, M., & Lasher, M. (2014). Applications of laser-induced filaments for optical communication links. *Proceedings of SPIE* (Vol. 9224, p. 92240J). https://doi.org/10.1117/12.2063559

4. Rohwetter, P., Kasparian, J., Wöste, L., & Wolf, J.-P. (2010). Laser-induced water condensation in air. *Nature Photonics*, 4(7), 451–456. https://doi.org/10.1038/nphoton.2010.115

5. Yan, B., Liu, H., Li, C., Jiang, X., Li, X., Hou, J., Zhang, H., Lin, W., Liu, B., & Liu, J. (2020). Laser-filamentation-assisted 1.25 Gb/s video communication under harsh conditions. *Optics & Laser Technology*, 131, 106391. https://doi.org/10.1016/j.optlastec.2020.106391.

6. Martialay, M. L. (2020, November 10). Transmitting Data From Space to Earth With Laser Filaments. *Rensselaer Polytechnic Institute*. https://news.rpi.edu/content/2020/11/10/pulsed-light-clears-path-through-atmosphere-second-beam-information

7. Legnaioli, S., Campanella, B., Poggialini, F., Pagnotta, S., Harith, M. A., Abdel-Salam, Z. A., & Palleschi, V. (2020). Industrial applications of laser-induced breakdown spectroscopy: A review. *Analytical Methods*, 12(8), 1014-1029. https://doi.org/10.1039/C9AY02728A

8. Thermo Fisher Scientific. (n.d.). How Does LIBS Work? https://www.thermofisher.com/us/en/home/industrial/spectroscopy-elemental-isotope-analysis/portable-analysis-material-id/industrial-elemental-radiation-solutions/how-does-libs-work.html

9. Rohwetter, Ph., Stelmaszczyk, K., Wöste, L., Ackermann, R., Méjean, G., Salmon, E., Kasparian, J., Yu, J., & Wolf, J.-P. (2005). Filament-induced remote surface ablation for long-range laser-induced breakdown spectroscopy operation. *Spectrochimica Acta Part B: Atomic Spectroscopy*, 60(7-8), 1025-1033. https://doi.org/10.1016/j.sab.2005.03.017.

10. Kautz, E. J., Yeak, J., Bernacki, B. E., Phillips, M. C., & Harilal, S. S.

(2020). Expansion dynamics and chemistry evolution in ultrafast laser filament-produced plasmas. *Physical Chemistry Chemical Physics*, 22(16), 8304-8314. https://doi.org/10.1039/d0cp00078g

11. Jiang, J., Xie, N., Jiang, Y., Han, J., Feng, G., Shi, Z., & He, C. (2022). Rapid photodegradation of methylene blue by laser-induced plasma. *RSC Advances*, 12, 21056-21065. https://doi.org/10.1039/D2RA03633A

12. Hsu, J. (2013, April 19). Plasma ring experiment offers new path for fusion power. *IEEE Spectrum*. https://spectrum.ieee.org/plasma-ring-experiment-offers-new-path-for-fusion-power

13. Wenz, J. (2015, March 23). Boeing is working on a real-life force field. *Popular Mechanics*. https://www.popularmechanics.com/military/research/a14683/boeing-patent-plasma-shield/

14. Ding, Y., Bai, B., Li, X., Niu, G., & Liu, Y. (2023). Research on EM Shielding Mechanism of the Plasma-Sheath-Covered Target. *IEEE Transactions on Plasma Science*, 51(3), 632-640. https://doi.org/10.1109/TPS.2022.3217096

15. Shaw, P., Kumar, N., Kwak, H. S., Park, J. H., Uhm, H. S., Bogaerts, A., Choi, E. H., & Attri, P. (2018). Bacterial inactivation by plasma treated water enhanced by reactive nitrogen species. *Scientific reports*, 8(1), 11268. https://doi.org/10.1038/s41598-018-29549-6

16. Choi, E.H., Uhm, H.S. & Kaushik, N.K. Plasma bioscience and its application to medicine. *AAPPS Bull*. 31, 10 (2021). https://doi.org/10.1007/s43673-021-00012-5

17. Hambling, D. (2020, May 11). U.S. Navy laser creates plasma 'UFOs'. *Forbes*. https://www.forbes.com/sites/davidhambling/2020/05/11/us-navy-laser-creates-plasma-ufos/?sh=63395c0f10741

18. Wendorf, M. (2021, November 5). Stealth plasma could challenge 75 years of air defense strategy. *Interesting Engineering*. https://interestingengineering.com/innovation/stealth-plasma-could-challenge-75-years-of-air-defense-strategy

19. Barbarino, M. (2023, August 3). What is nuclear fusion? *IAEA*. https://www.iaea.org/newscenter/news/what-is-nuclear-fusion

20. Department of Energy. (2021, April 1). Fission and Fusion: What is the difference? https://www.energy.gov/ne/articles/fission-and-fusion-what-difference

21. Gates, S. (2023, February). Researchers make hydrogen from

seawater without pre-treatment. *RMIT University News*. https://www.rmit.edu.au/news/all-news/2023/feb/hydrogen-seawater

22. Gillam, W. (2022, November 2). Originating from UW research, Zap Energy is on its way to making sustainable energy from nuclear fusion a practical reality. *UW Department of Electrical & Computer Engineering*. https://www.ans.org/news/article-4575/breakeven-breakthrough-at-the-national-ignition-facility/

23. Lawrence Livermore National Laboratory. (2022, December 14). Lawrence Livermore National Laboratory achieves fusion ignition.https://www.llnl.gov/archive/news/lawrence-livermore-national-laboratory-achieves-fusion-ignition

24. Tackett, S. (2013, March 27). Nuclear Pulse Propulsion: Gateway to the Stars. *ANS Nuclear Cafe*. https://www.ans.org/news/article-1294/nuclear-pulse-propulsion-gateway-to-the-stars/

25. Space.com Staff. (2013, April 10). Nuclear Fusion Rocket Could Reach Mars in 30 Days. *Space.com*. https://www.space.com/20609-nuclear-fusion-rocket-mars.html

26. Bonsor, K. (n.d.). Flying on Fusion Power - How Fusion Propulsion Will Work. *HowStuffWorks*. https://science.howstuffworks.com/fusion-propulsion2.htm

27. Cuthrell, S. (2023, July 31). Nuclear Fusion Engine Designed to Speed Space Flight Starts Construction. *EE Power*. https://eepower.com/news/nuclear-fusion-engine-designed-to-speed-space-flight-starts-construction/

28. Paluszek, M., Price, A., Koniaris, Z., Galea, C., Thomas, S., Cohen, S., & Stutz, R. (2023). Nuclear fusion powered Titan aircraft. *Acta Astronautica*, 210, 82-94. https://doi.org/10.1016/j.actaastro.2023.04.029

29. Hall, L. (2017, April 6). Fusion-Enabled Pluto Orbiter and Lander. *NASA*. https://www.nasa.gov/general/fusion-enabled-pluto-orbiter-and-lander/

30. Mizokami, K. (2023, June 2). How the Pentagon Could Make Magnet-Powered Subs Like 'Red October' a Reality. *Popular Mechanics*. https://www.popularmechanics.com/military/navy-ships/a44067238/mhd-drive-technology-submarines/

31. Neukart, F. (2023). Magnetic Fusion Plasma Drive. https://ar5iv.org/abs/2309.11524

32. Martin, J. A. (1998). Magnetohydrodynamic propulsion using on-board sources. *AIP Conference Proceedings*, 420, 985–990. https://doi.org/10.1063/1.54903

Holographic Technologies

There are few things as iconic as the hologram message R2-D2 carries of Princess Leia asking for help. Far from mere trickery, this technology involves complex science and sophisticated techniques to manifest 3D images that can be viewed from different angles, just like real objects. But how does this miraculous technology work, and what other marvel applications does it offer in the future?

In essence, a hologram is a physical structure that diffracts light into an image. The term *holography* comes from the Greek words *holos* (whole) and *graphe* (writing), fittingly expressing its ability to display a complete 3D picture. When a laser beam illuminates a hologram, it reconstructs the light field reflected from the original object when the hologram was created. Unlike a regular photograph, which captures a two-dimensional representation, a hologram recreates the 3D light field, enabling us to see an object from various perspectives as if it were actually present[1,2].

There are techniques currently used that look like holograms, but are really just optical illusions. One of these techniques is called *Pepper's ghost* and has been around since the 19th century. Popularized by Henry Pepper, this technique is used in theaters and haunted house attractions, as well as in some modern holographic displays. The technique produces transparent or "ghostly" images that appear to be on stage or within a room[3,4]. An updated version of this concept was combined with high-definition video projection and used at Coachella in 2012, culminating in a performance by a Tupac Shakur "hologram"[5,6]. More advanced systems can create volumetric images using intersecting light beams, but these can be complex and limited in terms of viewing angles[7,8].

Now, we're on the brink of breakthroughs that could make interactive, high-resolution holography a common feature of our daily lives[9,10]. Companies are developing prototype displays for smartphones and other devices that can project 3D holographic images[10]. Meanwhile, scientists are exploring photopolymers and nanophotonic optical elements to create true, full-color holograms[11].

Holography would bridge the gap between the physical and digital worlds like never before. While we're still in the early days, the holographic revolution is gathering pace. From enhancing how we work, learn, and play to redefining art, entertainment, and personal communication, holography holds the promise to illuminate our future in dazzling three dimensions.

Holograms

What does the future look like when we infuse it with the magic of holography? In communication, holographic technology could revolutionize how we connect with each other. Picture this: you're sitting in your living room, and before you materializes a three-dimensional image of your loved one who resides miles away. This is not a pixelated projection on a flat screen, but a full-bodied, dynamic representation so vivid and lifelike you can perceive the subtle changes in their facial expression, their body language, and even the clothes they are wearing. Such communication would transcend the boundaries of traditional audio-visual communication. This is not just talking, it is feeling, connecting, and interacting as if you were in the same room.

In the world of business, holography promises a

seismic shift. The future corporate meeting is not a collection of faces on a screen but an immersive holographic experience that captures the nuances of in-person interactions. Think about executives from global branches convening in a shared virtual boardroom, debating each other and making decisions as if they were physically present.

But these will not just be 3D images, they will have a texture and feel. The tantalizing blend of holography and haptic technology is a burgeoning field that promises to revolutionize our interaction with the digital world[12,13,14]. This fusion of technologies is ushering in a new era of communication that surpasses visual and auditory feedback, making way for an immersive experience where virtual objects can be touched, felt, and manipulated.

Haptic feedback, the use of touch to communicate with users, adds an extra dimension to our interaction with technology. From feeling the gentle vibration of a smartphone to the intricate force feedback in VR gaming, haptic technology has come a long way. However, combining it with holography elevates it to a whole new level of user experience.

Imagine walking into your living room and calling up a holographic screen to read the morning news. With a wave of your hand, you navigate through the headlines, feeling a gentle buzz under your fingertips as they skim the edges of the "buttons." The immersive experience extends beyond visual stimuli, making you feel as if you are physically interacting with the information.

On a grander scale, *haptic holography* can revolutionize fields like medicine and education[15]. Medical students, for instance, could practice complex surgeries on holographic humans that not only look, but also feel real. The haptic feedback would allow them to experience the tension of tissues, the resistance of bone, providing a training experience that's indistinguishable from reality.

Holographic Mapping

Holographic mapping would bring a whole new level of depth and detail over our current 2D digital maps. Everything from education and medicine, to surveying and probing would benefit from holographic mapping[16].

This technology has the potential to revolutionize military command and control, blurring the line between the strategic and tactical spheres and providing an unparalleled level of situational awareness. Rather than merely depicting static terrain and markers, these maps can reflect the fluid, chaotic nature of modern warfare in real-time, showcasing moving units, changing weather conditions, and unfolding events.

Imagine a battlefield viewed in three dimensions with multiple layers of information superimposed. Commanders can visualize troop movements in real-time, complete with an instant analysis of terrain and visibility. They can observe a bird's-eye view of an ongoing operation, or zoom in to inspect a specific location, down to the smallest detail.

Through integrated *sensor fusion*, holographic maps can display a wealth of data collected from satellites, drones, and ground units, allowing commanders to understand the battlefield's complexity better[17,18]. Imagine seeing heat signatures from hidden enemy encampments, tracking the progress of friendly forces through a dense forest, or predicting an adversary's movements based on their historical patterns, all on a 3D map.

These maps aren't limited to surface data. The holographic nature of the map allows for a volumetric depiction of the environment. As such, information on subterranean features like tunnels or bunkers, or the airspace above the battlefield, complete with flying drones and aircraft, can be visualized simultaneously. Commanders could manipulate the map, rotate it, dissect it layer by layer, from the bedrock to the stratosphere, providing a comprehensive understanding of the battlefield.

The impact of these maps extends beyond strategy. By visualizing the field, these maps can enhance communication between the command center and field units. Information that would have been hard to convey through words alone. Things like terrain features, enemy positions, and recommended routes could be shared visually a lot more efficiently than 2D maps and would help reduce misunderstanding and friendly fire.

As the technology advances, these maps could incorporate virtual and augmented reality features. Commanders could step into the map, walking through a virtual version of the battlefield, or overlay the holographic data onto the real world, melding the digital and the physical for an unparalleled view of the conflict.

In conclusion, the future battlefield will be a place of intense data, a space where every piece of information holds potential tactical value. Holographic maps, integrated with cutting-edge technology, will provide commanders with the ability to view, understand, and manipulate this data like never before, fundamentally transforming the way battles are fought and won.

Holographic Entertainment

In the realm of entertainment, the possibilities are mind-boggling. Imagine watching sports where the players run, jump, and score right on your coffee table. Haptic holography could redefine gaming, creating immersive worlds where players can feel the grip of a sword, the tension of a bowstring, or the cold metal of a spaceship control panel. In movies, viewers could feel the splash of ocean waves or the gust of a stormy wind, bridging the gap between audience and story, making cinema a truly immersive experience. 3D holographic cinema would make viewers feel as if they are inside the movie, witnessing the events firsthand. The characters could walk around them, making eye contact, and talking directly to them. Viewers might even be able to influence the storyline through their actions, leading to an entirely personalized movie experience.

Consider music concerts, the epitome of live entertainment. Artists would be able to perform for global audiences without ever leaving their studios. Simultaneous holographic concerts could be held in stadiums worldwide, where fans will revel in a 3D, life-like performance. The holographic performers could move around the stage, interact with the crowd, and even shake hands with their fans.

And the magic doesn't stop there. With advancements in artificial intelligence, holographic performers could interact with their audience in real-time. They could respond to cheers, alter their performance based on audience reactions, and even answer fan questions during the performance.

The concept of mortality could be forever altered by holography. Imagine a world where the loss of an artist doesn't signify the end of their performances. The holographic avatars of artists could continue to give performances long after their passing. From Elvis Presley to Prince, fans could once again experience the electrifying performances of music's legends. They could even release "new" music, with AI technology generating songs in their unique style[19].

Holographic Shopping and Advertising

In a world not far from now, holography and haptic feedback technologies will revolutionize the way we shop and engage with advertisements[20,21]. They will not only transform our purchasing processes but also redefine the nature of advertising, turning it from an often-ignored necessity into an immersive, interactive, and enjoyable experience.

Picture this: You walk past a high-end fashion store, and instead of traditional mannequins behind a glass pane, a life-sized holographic fashion show unfolds before your eyes. The models strut down the runway, showcasing the latest collections, and you can rotate, zoom in, and view the garments from any angle you wish. With AI this advertising will become extremely personalized, brands and stores will be able to create and show holographic recreations of potential buyers as they walk by with the brand's specific clothing. The shopping experience would go beyond a visual spectacle. Thanks to haptic feedback technology, you will be able to feel the smoothness of silk, the softness of cashmere, and the rugged texture of denim.

In a similar vein, shopping for furniture and home items could transform into a magical experience. Instead of just imagining how a piece would look in your home, holographic projections could place a 3D model of the furniture in your actual living space. You could walk around it, inspect it from all angles, and even feel the texture of its upholstery or the hardness of its wooden surface.

Grocery shopping will also evolve. When looking for fresh produce, holographic displays could provide information about the origin of the fruits and vegetables, their nutritional value, and even suggest recipes. For packaged products, instead of reading labels, holograms could visually break down the ingredients, providing an in-depth understanding of what you're buying.

Instead of static billboards or intrusive pop-up ads, the future will see advertisements as interactive holographic experiences[20,21]. A sneaker ad, for example, could include a holographic basketball player dunking right in front of you, landing and showcasing the sneakers. You could inspect the shoes from all angles, change their color, size, and even feel the texture of their material. Interactive holographic ads for movies could include engaging mini-games related to the film's plot. Car ads will offer a virtual test drive right from your living room.

Holographic Training & Education

Consider a biology class, where instead of studying textbook diagrams of the human heart, students observe a 3D holographic heart, pulsating right in front of them. They could rotate it, dissect it layer by layer, view it from different angles, and gain an in-depth understanding of its workings. Haptic feedback could let them touch and feel the differences in texture between various tissues. Even the sensation of a heartbeat could be replicated, turning learning from passive to experiential.

Haptic holography could bring abstract concepts to life, enabling students to feel the force of gravity or the pressure of a gas. The tactile engagement would make learning interactive, memorable, and fun. History lessons could recreate crucial events, allowing students to walk alongside historical figures, witness historical events firsthand, and gain an emotional understanding of the past. In Physics, understanding abstract concepts could become simpler. Students could virtually manipulate forces, feel the tug of gravity, and observe its effects on various objects. Chemistry students could interact with 3D models of molecules, rotate them, break and form bonds, creating a tangible comprehension of chemical reactions.

Imagine a scenario where a cadet walks into a military training room. At the heart of the room is a pulsating holographic battlefield, a 1:1 scale replica of a real-world terrain. It is not a video game, but a highly advanced holographic simulation capable of emulating real-world combat situations with an uncanny degree of detail. This holographic battlefield provides a virtual yet palpable environment that accurately depicts the sounds, sights, and dynamics of a live combat zone.

With the additional layer of haptic feedback, the

simulation comes alive. As the soldier maneuvers through the terrain, the sensation of trudging through mud, climbing a rock face, or even the recoil of a weapon will be simulated. Not just a visual spectacle, the trainee can feel the weight of their gear, the rush of wind as they parachute down, the heat of an explosion. The line between reality and simulation blurs, providing an intense, multi-sensory training experience that prepares them for real combat scenarios.

For pilot training, these technologies will prove equally transformative. Traditional flight simulators, although effective, are limited by physical constraints and fail to provide a fully immersive experience. With holographic cockpits, a pilot could train for any aircraft type without needing a physical simulator for each. The cockpit instrumentation can be programmed to mimic any aircraft's controls, allowing the pilot to familiarize themselves with various models.

Haptic feedback will allow the trainee to feel the aircraft's response, providing tactile cues as they manipulate the throttle, ailerons, or rudder. It could simulate the vibrations during takeoff, the feedback on the control stick, even the subtle changes in pressure and temperature. It is not just about flight mechanics; emergencies, such as engine failure or loss of hydraulic pressure, can be safely rehearsed, ensuring pilots are ready to handle any situation.

In both military and pilot training, these technologies can adapt to provide personalized learning experiences. The system can monitor the trainee's performance, identify areas of improvement, and adjust the training scenarios accordingly. This data-driven approach ensures that the training is comprehensive and that the trainee is fully prepared for their role.

While the primary goal of these technologies is to enhance training and increase safety, they also represent significant cost savings. With virtual simulations replacing physical training environments and equipment, maintenance, repairs, and upgrades will become far more manageable and less costly.

Holographic Designing

The biggest impact of future holographic technology will be how it allows us to view and interact with the world around us, not just each other. Imagine the architect of the future, not bound by the static blueprints of old but free to walk through an ethereal replica of their design. As they wander through their creation, their holographic blueprint enables them to perceive their project from all angles.

They can zoom in to examine the texture of the walls, scrutinize the sheen on the floor tiles, and even study the sway of the structure in a virtual breeze.

This transformative technology goes beyond mere visualization. Architects can reach out and manipulate their designs with simple gestures, stretching a wall here, shrinking a window there. They can examine their structures under various lighting conditions, test the acoustics of a concert hall with a virtual orchestra, or observe how pedestrian traffic flows through a public plaza. The experience is immersive, intuitive, and inspiring, a fusion of the physical and digital that reshapes the creative process.

Similarly, the possibilities for engineers are boundless. Structural engineers can put their designs through rigorous virtual stress tests long before any material is molded or any foundation is laid. They can simulate extreme weather conditions, earthquake tremors, and even decades of wear and tear, adjusting and optimizing their designs in response to these holographic trials.

The potential for prototyping is remarkable. The holographic engine enables engineers to assemble, disassemble, tweak, and optimize components in a virtual space. This capacity accelerates the design iteration process and saves costs by minimizing the need for physical prototypes. Engineers can collaborate in shared holographic spaces, each contributing from their own unique perspective, no matter their geographic location.

For designers, holography expands the canvas on which they create. Industrial designers can model new products, rotate them in 3D space, dissect them layer by layer, and scrutinize every detail. Interior designers can experiment with different decor elements, rearranging furniture, changing color palettes, or swapping out flooring materials with a wave of their hand. Fashion designers can even drape their virtual models in holographic fabrics, observing how different materials flow and fold in real time.

Holographic Art

Picture yourself stepping into an art gallery, but this gallery is unlike any you've ever seen before. There are no physical canvases or sculptures, but instead, holographic projectors scattered around a seemingly empty space. As you enter, a spectrum of colors dances into existence, forming vibrant sculptures that float in mid-air. They shift and change as you move around, casting light and shadows that seem almost tangible. You reach out, and the holograms respond to your touch, reshaping themselves, their colors ebbing and flowing with your movements. This is an interactive holographic art exhibition, a playground of light, color, and motion[22,23].

In this holographic realm, the boundary between the artist and the viewer becomes permeable. Artists might create pieces that change and evolve based on the viewer's emotions, detected via biometric sensors. Picture a holographic sculpture that beats in sync with your heart or a virtual landscape that changes from day to night, from sunshine to rain, reflecting your mood.

Consider the potential for immersive storytelling within these interactive spaces. Artists could weave narratives that envelop viewers, allowing them to not only observe the story but also become a part of it. A holographic reimagining of Van Gogh's Starry Night could let you stroll through the rolling hills and under the swirling stars.

Holographic art could also take public art to new dimensions. Imagine city spaces brought to life with massive, animated murals visible only with the right lens or device. Public squares could be home to monumental holographic statues that commemorate events, not as static reminders of the past, but as vibrant, interactive pieces that connect people with history in a dynamic, personal way.

Furthermore, with the advent of mixed reality devices, holographic art will not be confined to galleries or public spaces. Artists could create personalized, immersive pieces that exist within the home or workplace. You could start your day under a holographic sunrise, fill your living room with a surreal, shifting sculpture, or dine under a canopy of virtual stars.

The future of holographic art offers endless possibilities, pushing the boundaries of creativity and transforming passive viewers into active participants. Through holography, art can become a living and interactive entity, not confined by the laws of physics or the limitations of traditional materials. It promises a future where art is not just seen, but experienced, touched, and altered.

Holographic Data Storage

In our increasingly digital world, the amount of data we generate is growing at an explosive rate. From high-resolution images to 4K videos, complex simulations to extensive databases, the demand for efficient and compact data storage solutions is at an all-time high. This is where the interplay between theoretical physics and technology becomes fascinatingly relevant. The *holographic principle* could pave the way for revolutionary advancements in data storage technology[24,25,26].

The holographic principle originates from the enigmatic realms of black holes and string theory, positing that all the information within a volume of space can be fully described by data on the boundary of that space[27,28]. Imagine a 3D object being represented entirely by information on a 2D surface, much like how a hologram card creates a 3D image from a flat surface. This principle challenges the conventional notions of dimensions and information storage, offering a thought-provoking model for encoding voluminous data on a minimal surface.

Now, you might wonder, how does this abstract concept from theoretical physics relate to the practical world of data storage technologies? Well, *holographic data storage*, a technology already under development, is the bridge connecting this principle to tangible applications[29,30].

Holographic data storage is a technique that utilizes light to store information. It leverages the interference pattern of laser light to store data throughout the volume of a photosensitive optical material, rather than just on the surface. This enables a level of data density and speed of retrieval that is orders of magnitude greater than conventional optical or magnetic storage methods.

However, the holographic principle could take this idea even further. Inspired by this principle, researchers are exploring novel ways to increase the data density of storage mediums. The holographic principle suggests the potential for encoding the information of a 3D volume onto a 2D surface, a concept analogous to compressing data without losing the inherent information. Applying this to data storage could revolutionize the way we store and retrieve data, allowing us to store even larger amounts of data in smaller spaces and at higher speeds.

Beyond mere data density, the holographic principle also carries implications for data integrity and error correction. Just like a holographic image retains the entire image even when part of the hologram is damaged, data stored using principles inspired by the holographic model could have a high level of redundancy. This means that even if part of the data is lost or corrupted, the original information can still be fully or partially retrieved.

Chapter References

1. Wilson, T. V. (2023, August 30). How holograms work. *HowStuffWorks*. https://science.howstuffworks.com/hologram.htm

2. Helmenstine, A. M. (2019, March 2). Introduction to holography. *ThoughtCo*. https://www.thoughtco.com/how-holograms-work-4153109

3. Christopher, B. (2016, January 11). Explaining the Pepper's Ghost Illusion with Ray Optics. *COMSOL*.https://www.comsol.com/blogs/explaining-the-peppers-ghost-illusion-with-ray-optics/

4. Museum of Modern Art. (n.d.). Pepper's Ghost. https://www.moma.org/collection/terms/peppers-ghost

5. Wagstaff, K. (2012, April 16). The technology behind the Tupac hologram at Coachella. *TIME*. https://techland.time.com/2012/04/16/the-science-behind-the-tupac-hologram-at-coachella/

6. Thier, D. (2012, April 17). Tupac "Hologram" wasn't a hologram at all. *Forbes*.https://www.forbes.com/sites/davidthier/2012/04/17/tupac-hologram-wasnt-a-hologram-at-all/

7. Queensland University of Technology. (2022, June 6). Intersecting light beams key in transformative 3D printer potential. *Phys.org*. https://phys.org/news/2022-06-intersecting-key-3d-printer-potential.html

8. Sudo, T., Morishima, H., Osaka, T., & Taniguchi, N. (2000). 3D display using intersection of light beams. *Stereoscopic Displays and Virtual Reality Systems VII* (Vol. 3957, pp. 3 May 2000). *SPIE*. https://doi.org/10.1117/12.384445

9. Choi, C. Q. (2020, November 10). Thin holographic video display for mobile phones. *IEEE Spectrum*. https://spectrum.ieee.org/holovideo-phones

10. hah, K. (2020, November 10). Watch Samsung's prototype holographic video screen in action. *New Scientist*. https://www.newscientist.com/article/2259406-watch-samsungs-prototype-holographic-video-screen-in-action/

11. Piao, M.-L., Wu, H.-Y., & Kim, N. (2014). Development of full-color holographic optical element recorded on aspherical substrate with photopolymer. *Proceedings of SPIE - The International Society for Optical Engineering*, 9296. https://doi.org/10.1117/12.2071753

12. Romanus, T., Frish, S., Maksymenko, M., Frier, W., Corenthy, L., &

Georgiou, O. (2019). Mid-air haptic bio-holograms in mixed reality. *2019 IEEE International Symposium on Mixed and Augmented Reality Adjunct (ISMAR-Adjunct)* (pp. 348-352). IEEE. https://doi.org/10.1109/ISMAR-Adjunct.2019.00-14

13. University of Glasgow. (2021, September 2). Tactile holograms are a touch of future tech. *TechXplore.* https://techxplore.com/news/2021-09-tactile-holograms-future-tech.html

14. Georgiou, O., Martinez, J., Abdouni, A., & Harwood, A. (2022). Mid-air Haptic Texture Exploration in VR. *2022 IEEE Conference on Virtual Reality and 3D User Interfaces Abstracts and Workshops (VRW)* (pp. 964-965). Christchurch, New Zealand. https://doi.org/10.1109/VRW55335.2022.00333

15. Gani, A., Pickering, O., Ellis, C., Sabri, O., & Pucher, P. (2022). Impact of haptic feedback on surgical training outcomes: A Randomised Controlled Trial of haptic versus non-haptic immersive virtual reality training. *Annals of Medicine and Surgery (London)*, 83, 104734. https://doi.org/10.1016/j.amsu.2022.104734

16. Jha, D. K. (2019, May 23). How holograms revolutionize the education system and the world nowadays. *eLearning Industry.* https://elearningindustry.com/holograms-revolutionize-education-system-world-nowadays

17. Nabors, R. (2018, April 19). Integrated sensors: The critical element in future complex environment warfare. *Mad Scientist Laboratory.* https://madsciblog.tradoc.army.mil/46-integrated-sensors-the-critical-element-in-future-complex-environment-warfare/

18. Keller, J. (2008, November 1). Joining sensors through data fusion. *Military Aerospace.* https://www.militaryaerospace.com/communications/article/16706739/joining-sensors-through-data-fusion

19. Matthews, J., & Nairn, A. (2023, June 1). Holograms and AI can bring performers back from the dead – but will the fans keep buying it? *The Conversation.* https://theconversation.com/holograms-and-ai-can-bring-performers-back-from-the-dead-but-will-the-fans-keep-buying-it-202431

20. van Hooijdonk, R. (2020, February 28). Holographic technology is the future of advertising in an era of ad-blockers. *Richard van Hooijdonk Blog.* https://blog.richardvanhooijdonk.com/en/holographic-technology-is-the-future-of-advertising-in-an-era-of-ad-blockers/

21. Tohana, L. (2020, September 23). Advantages of Holograms and What It Means for the Future of Marketing. *Future of Marketing Institute.* https://futureofmarketinginstitute.com/advantages-of-holograms-and-

what-it-means-for-the-future-of-marketing/

22. Mariola, D. (Producer & Director). (2000). Interactive Art: The New Age of Holography. *PBS Western Reserve*. https://www.pbswesternreserve.org/luminus/interactive-art-the-new-age-of-holography/

23. Terras, R. (2017, June 5). Five surprising ways holograms are revolutionising the world. *The Conversation*. https://theconversation.com/five-surprising-ways-holograms-are-revolutionising-the-world-77886

24. Ruan, H. (2014). Recent advances in holographic data storage. *Frontiers of Optoelectronics*, 7, 450–466. https://doi.org/10.1007/s12200-014-0458-7

25. Zhu, J., Zou, F., Wang, L., Lu, X., & Zhao, S. (2023). Multiplexing Perfect Optical Vortex for Holographic Data Storage. *Photonics*, 10(7), 720. https://doi.org/10.3390/photonics10070720.

26. Psaltis, D., & Burr, G. W. (1998). Holographic data storage. *Computer*, 31(2), 52-60. https://doi.org/10.1109/2.652917

27. Thorlacius, L. (2004). Black Holes and the Holographic Principle. https://arxiv.org/abs/hep-th/0404098

28. Bigatti, D., Susskind, L. (2000). The Holographic Principle. In: Thorlacius, L., Jonsson, T. (eds) M-Theory and Quantum Geometry. *NATO Science Series*, vol 556. Springer, Dordrecht. https://doi.org/10.1007/978-94-011-4303-5_4

29. Curtis, K., Dhar, L., Hill, A., Wilson, W., & Ayres, M. (2010). *Holographic Data Storage: From Theory to Practical Systems*. Wiley. ISBN: 978-0-470-74962-3

30. Timucin, D. A., Downie, J. D., & Norvig, P. (2000, January 2). Holographic Optical Data Storage. *NASA Ames Research Center; Corning, Inc.* https://ntrs.nasa.gov/citations/20010071572

Neuroscience

Imagine being able to control a computer or drone using nothing but your thoughts, or having the ability to instantly download skills into your brain, much like in the movie *The Matrix*. While this might sound like science fiction, it is rapidly becoming a reality through the astonishing developments with neural interfaces and *brain-computer interfaces* (BCIs)[1,2,3].

In essence, BCIs read your brain activity to turn your thoughts, in neurological terms, into action[1]. This cutting-edge technology is not only expanding our understanding of how the brain works but is also set to revolutionize numerous aspects of human life.

The underlying principle of BCIs is quite fascinating.

Our brains are essentially biological computers, with about 86 billion neurons transmitting signals through intricate networks[4]. These signals, known as brainwaves, are patterns of electrical activity that can be measured using *electroencephalography* (EEG). BCIs tap into these brainwaves, interpreting them into actionable commands.

There are two main types of BCIs: invasive and non-invasive. Invasive BCIs involve implanting electrodes directly into the brain to record neural activity, thus providing high-resolution data. On the other hand, non-invasive BCIs use sensors placed on the surface of the scalp, avoiding the risks associated with surgery[5]. While non-invasive BCIs offer lower resolution than their invasive counterparts, advancements in signal processing and machine learning are increasingly overcoming this limitation.

BCIs are also revolutionizing the way we interact with technology. In 2020, a startup named Neurable showcased a prototype of the world's first brain-controlled virtual reality game[6,7]. To play the game, users wear a VR headset equipped with multiple electroencephalography sensors that capture brain activity. The system uses machine learning algorithms to interpret these signals and translate them into game commands, creating an immersive and intuitive gaming experience.

Perhaps the most ambitious and futuristic of all current BCI endeavors is Elon Musk's Neuralink. The company aims to implant flexible "threads" into the brain to create a high-bandwidth interface with machines[8,9]. Although still in the early stages, Musk envisions a future where people can control devices, access information, or communicate telepathically using just their thoughts.

These examples are just the tip of the iceberg. From helping locked-in patients communicate, aiding in stroke rehabilitation, to even potentially decoding dreams, BCIs are on the brink of changing lives in unprecedented ways.

Cybernetic Devices

The ability to interact and provide input to computers with mere thought is going to revolutionize society and the way we interact with devices. Consider, for instance, the future of communication. In the age of texting, tweeting, and emailing, communication is about the manipulation of devices. But what if you could compose a message or an email just by thinking about it? BCIs could bring about a new age of communication, bypassing the physical confines and turning every thought into a potential message to the world.

Imagine the transformation in the realm of entertainment and gaming. BCIs could bring video games and virtual reality to an entirely new level, providing an immersive experience that goes beyond the visual and auditory, enabling players to engage with digital worlds directly with their thoughts[10,11].

Think about the possibilities in the field of art and design. Artists could "think" their creations into existence, bypassing the need for a physical medium. Designers could visualize and create complex designs, using thoughts alone, revolutionizing the way we create and innovate.

The world of work would not remain untouched either. BCIs could redefine productivity, where thought-controlled machinery and software would lead to efficiency and safety, especially in high-risk industries like construction or mining[2]. Moreover, the technology would open up a new world of opportunities for those with physical disabilities.

Even our interactions with everyday devices like smartphones, home automation systems, and cars would change drastically. As BCIs become more advanced and accessible, we could potentially live in smart homes or drive smart cars that respond not to our voice commands or touch but our thoughts, creating an environment that is more responsive and personalized than ever before[12,13].

Neuroprosthetics

Consider the traditional prosthetic limb: functional, but lacking in intuitive control and sensory feedback. For decades, this has been the standard solution for limb loss, enabling movement but not restoring the full sense of self. BCIs promise to dramatically change this narrative by developing prosthetics that are controlled in the same way as natural limbs: through the power of thought.

This is not merely theoretical. Researchers at the University of Pittsburgh have developed a BCI that allows a paralyzed individual to control a robotic arm just by thinking about the movement[14,15].

The potential for BCI prosthetics goes far beyond replicating the movement of natural limbs. With the integration of sensory feedback, these advanced prosthetics could deliver tactile information back to the brain, enabling the wearer to feel pressure, temperature, and even texture. This two-way communication, mirroring the natural dialogue between our brains and our bodies, could provide an unprecedented level of control and realism for prosthetic users[16,17].

Envision the operating room of the future, a sanctum of

sterility and precision. In stark contrast to the bustling surgical theaters of today, this room is silent and uninhabited. There are no surgeons or nurses, no hum of conversation, or rustle of gowned figures moving about. The only occupant is a surgical robot, its armature gleaming under the lights, a beacon of the medical miracles to come.

The surgeon? They could be in a separate room or even thousands of miles away. They're equipped with *augmented reality* (AR) goggles or a holographic interface, granting them a high-resolution 3D view of the patient's internal structures. The sterility of the operating room would remain uncompromised, and the potential for human error significantly reduced.

And the cornerstone of this futuristic vision? A BCI that translates the surgeon's thoughts and intentions into precise movements of the surgical robot. As the surgeon navigates through the patient's body, their thoughts are instantaneously transformed into robot actions, eliminating the need for physical controls and reducing the risk of hand tremors or fatigue compromising the surgery's success. This mind-machine melding transcends the limits of human steadiness, offering a level of surgical precision that is currently beyond our grasp[18].

But the promise of BCI-controlled robotic surgery goes

beyond improved precision and sterility. It also ushers in the age of truly remote surgery. Today, remote surgeries or telesurgeries, while feasible, are hampered by factors such as time delay and the need for a human operator at the patient's end. BCIs, coupled with advanced robotics and real-time holographic imaging, could overcome these barriers, making it possible for a surgeon in New York to operate on a patient in Nairobi, with a level of precision and safety that would surpass even the best surgeons today.

Cybernetic Vehicles

Drones, both in the consumer space and in various industries such as logistics, surveillance, and filmmaking, have rapidly become an integral part of our technological landscape. Today, most of these devices are controlled through manual inputs such as joysticks or touchscreens. But imagine piloting a drone not with your hands, but with your thoughts. BCI technology is opening the doors to this tantalizing possibility.

In experimental settings, researchers have already demonstrated the feasibility of this concept. At the University of Florida, for instance, a competition was held where participants raced drones solely through mental commands[19,20]. By wearing EEG headsets, which record the electrical activity of the brain, the pilots were able to direct the drones along a ten-yard course.

In a future where BCIs have matured and been fully integrated into our transportation systems, our interaction with drones and vehicles will fundamentally change. A drone operator could, for example, seamlessly switch from observing a wildfire to delivering a package, all with a simple change of thought. Search and rescue missions could be more precise and faster, with pilots intuitively navigating challenging terrains based on their perception and intent.

The use of BCIs in the military is almost a certain guarantee. The present-day fighter pilot is encased within a cockpit, surrounded by an array of switches, buttons, and dials, all requiring constant attention in addition to the actual combat strategies. Physical fatigue and information overload are serious concerns in such a high-pressure environment. Now, picture a future where a pilot, through a BCI, directly interfaces with the aircraft's system. Complex maneuvers, weapons deployment, and systems management can all be executed with thought alone, significantly reducing the cognitive load and physical demands[21,22].

This shift to thought-controlled air power could

revolutionize aircraft design. The traditional cockpit with its multitude of controls could give way to a minimalist, streamlined design, further enhancing the aircraft's efficiency and performance.

Taking it a step further, BCIs could completely transform warfare by making the conventional chain-of-command obsolete. Picture the command center of the future. Nestled within a fortified bunker or airborne in a high-tech aircraft, it is a far cry from the flurry of maps, radios, and personnel seen in present-day war rooms. At the heart of this center, a commander observes a live, three-dimensional holographic rendering of the battlefield. It is a window into the theater of conflict, presenting real-time information with an unmatched level of detail and accuracy.

In this revolutionized command center, a commander, through a BCI, can bypass the traditional channels of orders and relay instructions directly to the units on the field. However, we're not just talking about human soldiers. The real innovation is the direct control of weapon systems[23,24]. A battalion of tanks, a swarm of drones, and even autonomous submarines prowling the ocean depths could all be controlled directly by a commander outfitted with a BCI.

Each of these assets could be manipulated at the

speed of thought. A subtle shift of focus, a momentary spark of strategic insight, and the battlefield morphs in response. Imagine drones shifting formation, tanks adjusting their firing solutions, or naval units altering their course, all within fractions of a second. The agility and responsiveness of this thought-controlled force would be unprecedented, giving commanders a level of strategic fluidity that is simply unattainable today.

This is not just about speeding up the pace of operations; it is about unlocking a new paradigm of warfare. The concept of "commander's intent," a cornerstone of military strategy, could be actualized in real time, reducing misunderstanding and delay. The barrier between strategic planning and operational execution would blur, and tactical decisions could adapt fluidly to the ever-changing dynamics of the battlefield.

With BCIs enabling remote control of vehicles and weapons systems, the need for soldiers on the front lines could be reduced, preserving lives without compromising operational effectiveness.

Artificial Telepathy

BCIs, as we know, tap into the brain's electrical activity and translate these patterns into commands for devices. Currently, these are primarily used to control prosthetic limbs or allow paralyzed individuals to communicate. However, a logical extension of this technology might enable the transfer of these thought patterns directly to another person's BCI, facilitating *telepathic* communication[25,26].

Consider the following scenario: Person A thinks about a specific idea, their BCI converts this thought into a digital signal. This signal is then transmitted over a network to person B's BCI which decodes the signal and recreates the neural activity from person A. Voila, the thought has been transferred from person A to person B and telepathy is achieved! This isn't mere theory, scientists are saying this technology is just around the corner[27,28].

So, how would such a leap in communication impact the future? The implications are truly monumental. Firstly, it could revolutionize how we interact with one another. No longer would language barriers impede understanding, for thoughts and concepts could be shared directly, bypassing the necessity of translation or interpretation. The potential for miscommunication or misunderstanding would decrease drastically, creating a world more unified in understanding.

Next, imagine the transformative effect on education.

Learning could be as easy as downloading a document, with concepts directly transmitted into the minds of students, bypassing all language barriers. Complex theories, abstract concepts, or intricate procedures could be understood intuitively, fostering a deeper understanding and advancing education and learning beyond anything we've known.

Telepathic BCIs could also have a profound impact on our emotional connectivity. Sharing thoughts directly could entail sharing emotions, sensations, or experiences, forging deeper empathetic links between individuals. Experiencing the world from another person's perspective could usher in an unprecedented era of understanding and empathy.

Moreover, such technology could be a boon for those unable to communicate traditionally due to disability or disease. It could provide a voice to those who've been voiceless, allowing them to express their thoughts and emotions directly.

However, alongside these fantastic possibilities, a telepathic future also raises critical questions about privacy and consent. The ability to access and share thoughts necessitates robust safeguarding measures to prevent unauthorized access and ensure ethical use. The development and regulation of telepathic BCIs would need to strike a delicate balance between unlocking their transformative potential and preserving our fundamental rights.

Mind Control

Traditional BCI systems allow the human brain to interact directly with external devices, from moving a robotic arm with thoughts alone to typing words on a screen using only brain activity. But what if this concept could be reversed? What if, instead of the brain controlling an external device, the device could influence the brain itself?

The concept of a machine that could manipulate our most intimate organ might sound like something from the far future, but rapid advances in neurotechnology have already made this concept a reality. There is an existing system called the *Deep Brain Stimulation (DBS)*, which uses a BCI-like system to treat patients suffering from Parkinson's disease[29,30]. Electrodes implanted in specific brain regions send electrical impulses that control abnormal brain activity, significantly reducing tremors and improving the patient's quality of life.

The key here is that when certain neural patterns are detected, electrical impulses are used to influence and change the brain activity. This same concept could operate on different levels. On a basic level, it could be employed to provide sensory feedback, closing the loop in traditional BCI applications. An example would be a prosthetic hand that not only moves according to the user's thoughts but can also relay sensory information back to the brain, allowing the user to "feel" the texture of a fabric or the temperature of a drink.

On a more sophisticated level, this concept might have the potential to modulate cognitive processes and emotional states. For example, by leveraging neurofeedback principles, these "two-way" BCIs could help individuals train their brains to enter specific mental states, potentially enhancing focus, creativity, or relaxation[31]. Therapeutically, such technologies could revolutionize mental health treatment, offering new avenues to manage conditions like anxiety, depression, and PTSD[32,33].

However, as we peer deeper into the realm of such possibilities, we arrive at a future where these technologies could have the ability to influence, or even control human behavior and thought processes. Here, the potential applications become both exhilarating and terrifying. Could we enhance learning and memory, effectively creating super-learners? Could we manipulate emotional responses, instilling happiness or dampening anger at will? Could we implant thoughts or skills directly into the brain, like the instant learning depicted in science fiction?

Such advances could herald a new era of human enhancement, bringing unprecedented possibilities for personal development, education, and mental health. However, it would also force us to grapple with profound ethical and societal questions. Who would have access to these technologies, and who would regulate their use? How would they impact our sense of identity, agency, and authenticity?

Chapter References

1. Brown University. (2021, August 12). Toward next-generation brain-computer interface systems. *ScienceDaily*. https://www.sciencedaily.com/releases/2021/08/210812135910.htm

2. Gonfalonieri, A. (2020, October 6). What brain-computer interfaces could mean for the future of work. *Harvard Business Review*. https://hbr.org/2020/10/what-brain-computer-interfaces-could-mean-for-the-future-of-work

3. Mridha, M. F., Das, S. C., Kabir, M. M., Lima, A. A., Islam, M. R., & Watanobe, Y. (2021). Brain-Computer Interface: Advancement and Challenges. *Sensors (Basel)*, 21(17), 5746. https://doi.org/10.3390/s21175746

4. Vaidyanathan, V. (2018, November 28). What is a brain computer interface? *Science ABC*. https://www.scienceabc.com/innovation/what-is-a-brain-computer-interface.html

5. Strickland, E. (2017, August 7). Startup Neurable unveils the world's first brain-controlled VR game. *IEEE Spectrum*. https://spectrum.ieee.org/brainy-startup-neurable-unveils-the-worlds-first-braincontrolled-vr-game

6. Laser Focus World. (2017, August 8). Startup Neurable Unveils the World's First Brain-Controlled VR Game. https://www.laserfocusworld.com/optics/article/16557134/startup-neurable-unveils-the-worlds-first-braincontrolled-vr-game

7. Musk, E., & Neuralink. (2019). An Integrated Brain-Machine Interface Platform With Thousands of Channels. *Journal of Medical Internet Research*, 21(10), e16194. https://doi.org/10.2196/16194

8. Lewis, T., & Stix, G. (2019, July 17). Elon Musk's secretive brain tech company debuts a sophisticated neural implant. *Scientific American*. https://www.scientificamerican.com/article/elon-musks-secretive-brain-tech-company-debuts-a-sophisticated-neural-implant1/

9. IEEE. (2018, April 26). Brain computer interface virtual reality with EEG signals. *Innovate*. https://innovate.ieee.org/innovation-spotlight/brain-computer-interface-virtual-reality-eeg/

10. Hall, S. B., & Baier-Lentz, M. (2022, February 7). 3 technologies that will shape the future of the metaverse – and the human experience. *World Economic Forum*. https://www.weforum.org/agenda/2022/02/future-of-the-metaverse-vr-ar-and-brain-computer/

11. Ban, N., Qu, C., Feng, D., Pan, J. (2023). A Hybrid Brain-Computer Interface for Smart Car Control. In: Ying, X. (eds) Human Brain and Artificial Intelligence. HBAI 2022. *Communications in Computer and Information Science*, vol 1692. Springer. https://doi.org/10.1007/978-981-19-8222-4_12

12. Zhuang, W., Shen, Y., Li, L., Gao, C., & Dai, D. (2020). A brain-computer interface system for smart home control based on single trial motor imagery EEG. *International Journal of Sensor Networks*, 34(4), 214-225. https://doi.org/10.1504/IJSNET.2020.111780

13. Pietzak, R. (2016, October 13). Paralyzed Man Feels Again using a Mind-Controlled Robotic Arm. *UPMC*. https://www.upmc.com/media/news/bci_scitransl-lms

14. Hofheinz, E. (2016, October 29). Brain-computer interface helps paralyzed man feel. *Orthopedics This Week*. https://ryortho.com/breaking/brain-computer-interface-helps-paralyzed-man-feel/

15. Chatterjee, A., Aggarwal, V., Ramos, A., Acharya, S., & Thakor, N. V. (2007). A brain-computer interface with vibrotactile biofeedback for haptic information. *Journal of NeuroEngineering and Rehabilitation*, 4, Article 40. https://doi.org/10.1186/1743-0003-4-40

16. Schwartz, A. B., Cui, X. T., Weber, D. J., & Moran, D. W. (2006). Brain-Controlled Interfaces: Movement Restoration with Neural Prosthetics. *Neuron*, 52(1), 205-220. https://doi.org/10.1016/j.neuron.2006.09.019

17. Olivieri, E., Barresi, G., & Mattos, L. S. (2015). BCI-based user training in surgical robotics. *Annual International Conference of the IEEE Engineering in Medicine and Biology Society*, 2015, 4918–4921. https://doi.org/10.1109/EMBC.2015.7319495

18. Furness, D. (2016, April 27). The University of Florida just held the world's first mind-controlled drone race. *Digital Trends*. https://www.digitaltrends.com/cool-tech/mind-controlled-drone-race-university-of-florida/

19. Catwell. (2016, May 10). University of Florida holds the world's first brain-controlled drone race. *Element14 Community*. https://community.element14.com/technologies/robotics/b/blog/posts/university-of-florida-holds-the-world-s-first-brain-controlled-drone-race

20. Vahle, M. W. (2020, July). Opportunities and implications of brain-computer interface technology (Wright Flyer Paper No. 75). *Air University Press*. https://www.airuniversity.af.edu/Portals/10/AUPress/Papers/WF_0075_VAHLE_OPPORTUNITIES_AND_IMPLICATIONS_OF_BRAIN_COMPUTER_INTERFACE_TECHNOLOGY.PDF

21. Binnendijk, A., Marler, T., & Bartels, E. M. (2020). Brain-Computer Interfaces: U.S. Military Applications and Implications, An Initial Assessment. *RAND Corporation*. https://www.rand.org/pubs/research_reports/RR2996.html

22. Best, J. (2020, July 28). Mind-controlled drones and robots: How thought-reading tech will change the face of warfare. *ZDNet*. https://www.zdnet.com/article/mind-reading-particles-for-the-military-the-bcis-that-enable-soliders-to-fly-planes-with-their-thoughts-alone/

23. GlobalData. (2022, November 28). Mind and matter: the application of brain-computer interfaces. *Army Technology*. https://www.army-technology.com/comment/mind-and-matter-the-application-of-brain-computer-interfaces/

24. Grau, C., Ginhoux, R., Riera, A., Nguyen, T. L., Chauvat, H., Berg, M., Amengual, J. L., Pascual-Leone, A., & Ruffini, G. (2014). Conscious Brain-to-Brain Communication in Humans Using Non-Invasive Technologies. *PLOS ONE*, 9(8), e105225.

25. Iozzio, C. (2014, October 2). Scientists prove that telepathic communication is within reach. *Smithsonian Magazine*. https://www.smithsonianmag.com/innovation/scientists-prove-that-telepathic-communication-is-within-reach-180952868/

26. Bates, K. (2015, March 8). Brain-to-brain interfaces: the science of telepathy. *The Conversation*. https://theconversation.com/brain-to-brain-interfaces-the-science-of-telepathy-37926

27. GLOOM. (2014, August). Brain-To-Brain Communication Is Now Possible: Virtual Telepathy. *Mental Health Daily*. https://mentalhealthdaily.com/2014/09/10/brain-to-brain-communication-is-now-possible-virtual-telepathy/

28. Johns Hopkins Medicine. (n.d.). Deep Brain Stimulation. https://www.hopkinsmedicine.org/health/treatment-tests-and-therapies/deep-brain-stimulation

29. Cleveland Clinic. (n.d.). Deep Brain Stimulation (DBS): What It Is, Purpose & Procedure. https://my.clevelandclinic.org/health/treatments/21088-deep-brain-stimulation

30. Bitbrain team. (2020, May 21). Modern BCI-based Neurofeedback or EEG Biofeedback for Cognitive Enhancement. *Bitbrain*. https://www.bitbrain.com/blog/neurofeedback

31. Zagorski, N. (2023). FDA Clears Neurofeedback Intervention for PTSD. *Psychiatric News*. https://doi.org/10.1176/appi.pn.2023.08.8.60

32. Duke, G., Yotter, C. N., Sharifian, B., Duke, G., & Petersen, S. (2023, September 8). The effectiveness of microcurrent neurofeedback on depression, anxiety, post-traumatic stress disorder, and quality of life. *Journal of the American Association of Nurse Practitioners*. Advance online publication. https://doi.org/10.1097/JXX.0000000000000945

Robotics

From the rudimentary Automata of the ancient Greeks to the metallic Golem of Jewish folklore, and from the whimsical creations of Leonardo Da Vinci to the eloquent machines of Isaac Asimov's universe, our stories have always had a place for these fascinating constructs. They are mirrors to our own existence, offering us a unique perspective to ponder upon the questions of life, consciousness, and the ever-blurring line between the natural and the artificial.

Cinema, too, has been an integral part of this journey. Iconic creations like R2-D2 from *Star Wars*, the ominous T-800 from *Terminator*, and the philosophical replicants of *Blade Runner*, have all imprinted upon us the endless possibilities and moral conundrums that come with robotic intelligence. These fantastical depictions have ignited our imaginations, pushing us to make them a reality.

In the physical world, robots have moved from the realm of fantasy to factories, homes, hospitals, and even outer space. They assemble our vehicles, assist in delicate surgeries, defuse explosives, and explore distant planetary bodies. As we strive towards a future that has for so long lived in our stories, the advancements in technology continue to open up new frontiers for robotics.

Take, for instance, the remarkable progress we've made in fields like photonics and electromagnetic engineering. The use of light in computing could herald a new age of robotic intelligence with processing speeds beyond our current comprehension. Robots could perceive, analyze, and react to their surroundings in a fraction of the time it takes us[1,2,3].

Similarly, with breakthroughs in nuclear technology, such as SMRs, we could potentially power robots for extended durations, allowing them to undertake long-term missions in space or the deep sea without the need for refueling[4].

Advancements in BCIs promise a future where controlling these machines could be as seamless as thinking. We might communicate with robots telepathically, instruct them with mere thoughts, or experience the world through their sensors[5]. Similarly, BCIs would allow our robotic comrades to tell us information that our senses wouldn't be able to perceive.

Industrial Robots

When people think of robots, the image that often comes to mind is a humanoid creation from a movie. But while such robots remain largely within the realm of fiction, another type of robot has become an integral part of our everyday lives. We may not always see them, but industrial robots are the invisible driving force behind the products we use daily. From your morning coffee maker to the car you drive, industrial robots have likely had a hand in creating them.

Industrial robots have been used in manufacturing since the 1960s when the Unimate robot was introduced in a General Motors factory[6,7]. However, their role has expanded enormously over the decades, thanks to advancements in technology. Today, they perform a myriad of tasks from assembling products, handling materials, welding, painting, to quality inspection and beyond.

A great example of industrial robots are those in the

Gigafactory that was built by Tesla. Here, advanced robots named after X-Men characters work alongside human employees to produce the electric batteries used in their cars. Robots like Wolverine and Iceman perform high precision tasks at extraordinary speeds, thereby increasing efficiency and production capacity[8,9].

KUKA, a German robotics company, provides another compelling example. Its KR QUANTEC robot series can be used in a wide range of applications from foundry installations to cleanroom applications[10,11]. Their superior precision and speed make them particularly suitable for high-tech industries.

Industrial robots' future applications appear limitless. As they become smarter and more autonomous, they could handle even more complex tasks, potentially taking over entire production lines. We could also see more widespread use of robots in industries where they are currently underutilized, such as food and beverage production or clothing manufacturing.

The combination of robotics with other technologies opens up even more possibilities. For instance, smart factories, where industrial robots communicate and coordinate with each other to optimize production, are already becoming a reality[12,13]. Imagine a factory where every robot, conveyor belt, and piece of machinery is connected, continuously communicating, and working in unison. A manufacturing problem in one part of the factory could be instantaneously detected and compensated for elsewhere, minimizing downtime and maximizing efficiency. Companies like Siemens are already making strides in this space with their concept of the "digital factory"[14,15].

When big data is integrated with industrial robots, the potential is astounding. Robots can analyze this data to optimize their performance, predict and prevent breakdowns, and continuously improve the manufacturing process. Fanuc, a leading industrial robot manufacturer, is using AI and big data to create "learning robots" that can self-improve their operations over time[16,17].

Instead of a human operator designing a product and setting up the 3D printer, imagine an industrial robot doing it all. This would include autonomously designing, printing, and even improving the product based on continuous feedback. The *Dreamcatcher* project by Autodesk offers a glimpse into this future, combining AI, generative design, and robotics to create an autonomous manufacturing system[18,19].

Wheeled Robots

One of the most widely used robots currently is the wheeled robot. They come in a variety of shapes and sizes to take on various roles. One of the most renowned is the Mars rover, such as Perseverance, whose six rugged wheels enable it to traverse the treacherous Martian terrain. It showcases an amalgamation of autonomy, scientific instrumentation, and adaptability, with its wheels designed to navigate rocky surfaces, climb steep hills, and endure the Martian environment[20,21]. Its capabilities extend from capturing stunning visuals of the red planet to collecting invaluable soil samples, contributing immensely to our understanding of our celestial neighbor.

In the domain of everyday life, wheeled robots like the Roomba have become synonymous with convenience and modern living. Roomba, with its clever combination of sensors and algorithms, is designed to navigate through homes, avoiding obstacles and efficiently cleaning floors[22,23]. Its ability to adapt to different floor types and automatically dock for charging showcases the integration of autonomy and utility in wheeled robotic design, making it a beloved addition to many households.

Exploring the educational landscape, we find robots like the Sphero, a spherical robot designed to inspire the next generation of inventors. With its ability to roll in any direction, change colors, and be programmed via a smartphone, Sphero offers a playful yet educational platform[24,25]. It provides a hands-on experience in coding and robotics, nurturing creativity and problem-solving skills among learners.

In agriculture, wheeled robots such as the AgBot II are making substantial contributions. This autonomous robot, equipped with sensors and cameras, can navigate through fields, identify weeds, and administer the appropriate amount of herbicide, reducing the environmental impact and increasing efficiency in crop management[26,27].

In the realm of logistics and warehousing, wheeled robots like those developed by Amazon are optimizing operations. These robots navigate through warehouses, carrying shelves of products to human operators, thereby reducing the time taken to fulfill customer orders and enhancing overall efficiency[28,29]. There are also thousands of six-wheeled robots created by Starship Technologies that are operating around the globe to deliver food, groceries, and supplies[30,31].

Wheeled robots are also making strides in the healthcare sector, with robots like TUG autonomously delivering medications, meals, and supplies within hospitals, thereby streamlining operations and allowing healthcare professionals to focus on patient care[32,33].

Even security and law enforcement is starting to use

these type of robots. Recently, the New York Police Department introduced a wheeled robot to help patrol the subway. This robot is the K5 and was created by the California-based company Knightscope. Weighing in at almost 400 pounds and standing around 5-foot-3, this autonomous robot is equipped with four cameras and is designed for surveillance[34,35].

Quadruped Robots

Although wheeled robots are serving many useful roles, they will be outshined by quadruped robots. The robots *Spot* by Boston Dynamics and ANYmal by ANYbotics are showcasing how advanced these robots are becoming. These robotic counterparts to our four-legged friends are rewriting the rules of mobility and autonomy, showcasing their prowess across numerous applications[36,37].

At their core, quadruped robots are a triumph of engineering. Their designs borrow heavily from the biomechanics of the animals they wish to emulate[38]. The elegance of their bounding or careful trot is a testament to the sophisticated algorithms and engineering design that underpin their movements.

Boston Dynamics, a forerunner in robotics, has been in

the spotlight with Spot, its commercial quadruped robot. It's able to navigate complex terrains, climb stairs, and maintain balance even when kicked. Its modular design allows for various attachments, like an arm that can open doors or a 360-degree camera system for surveying[39,40].

Meanwhile, across the Atlantic, Swiss company ANYbotics has made strides with its quadruped robot, ANYmal. This robot can autonomously perform industrial inspection tasks, even in hazardous environments, reducing the risk for human workers. It uses a combination of visual and thermal cameras, microphones, and gas-detection sensors to carry out its inspections[41].

The versatility of these types of robots is already being utilized and showcased for military applications. Because of their design and profile, quadruped robots are ideal to carry heavy loads. For instance, the US Marines tested a robotic mule called LS3 that was developed by Boston Dynamics[42,43]. This mechanical mule is designed to carry up to 400 pounds of gear. If each infantry squad was assigned one of these robotic mules, they could mount some of their non-essential gear on the mule to carry. This would make the soldiers lighter, faster, and more agile. This type of robot could also save lives by transporting the wounded. One day there could even be large, horse-sized versions of these robots that could serve as a new modern form of cavalry.

Another contender in this arena is Vision 60. This robot-dog created by Philadelphia-based Ghost Robotics. In 2020, these robots were spotted being used a US Air Force military exercise for patrol and security duties[44]. More recently, an iteration of this robot was seen at a convention with a sniper rifle integrated on its back[45]. Known as the Special Purpose Unmanned Rifle (SPUR), this robot is capable of engaging targets at three-quarters of a mile away.

But what does the future hold for these mechanical quadrupeds? The possibilities seem endless. Because of their construction and design, they can go almost anywhere on land. Whether it is dense forests, rocky terrains, or urban landscapes with rubble and stairs, these environments pose considerable challenges. This is where quadruped robots will shine. Their agility and stability, combined with their ability to handle diverse terrains, make them exceptionally suited for such situations.

Looking ahead, one could imagine quadruped robots undertaking bomb disposal or search and rescue missions. Equipped with appropriate tools and sensors, these robots could safely neutralize explosive devices or locate and retrieve injured people during a disaster.

Quadruped robots are even finding a role in space

exploration. NASA's Jet Propulsion Lab has been developing a quadruped robot, MarsDog, designed to navigate the challenging terrains of Mars[46]. Unlike wheeled rovers, MarsDog could potentially access hard-to-reach areas, providing a new level of exploration for future missions.

Swarm Drones

In the stillness of the Ukrainian fields, the whir of propellers began to echo, resonating across the broad expanses and frigid nights, casting an eerie prelude to a future that no one could have imagined. The conflict with Russia was being reshaped, not by hulking tanks or jet fighters, but by devices no larger than a suitcase[47,48,49]. Drones, the inexpensive harbingers of this technological revolution, began to hover above the battlefield, rewriting the rules of engagement with every sortie.

These drones, the pride of garages and hobbyist workshops, were proving to be lethal opponents against armored vehicles and weapon systems that were hundreds if not thousands of times more expensive. They signify a profound paradigm shift, where greater mass and firepower doesn't automatically equate to supremacy on the battlefield.

In the midst of the tumult and the chaos, these agile drones are often cobbled together using off-the-shelf parts and appear harmless in their simplicity. A drone worth a few hundred dollars was becoming the Achilles' heel of vehicles and weaponry that cost many times more. The economic metrics of warfare were being irrevocably altered. This was a classic example of disruption on the battlefield, and a vivid illustration of the adage "less is more."

In this evolving narrative of warfare, speed, agility, and innovation were wresting control from size, firepower, and brute force. A new breed of warriors was emerging, ones who wielded code and joysticks rather than rifles and grenades. This shows that the future battlefield will not necessarily be dominated by those with the largest arsenals, but by those who can leverage technology the most creatively and effectively.

From a wider lens, the rise of drones was underscoring a larger trend towards automation and unmanned systems in warfare. The cold logic of machines was beginning to make headway into an arena traditionally defined by human valor and strategic cunning. The dispassionate precision of algorithms and sensors was introducing a level of efficiency and ruthlessness that could not be matched by even the most disciplined and experienced human soldier.

Yet, with every flight that these drones undertake, they raise profound ethical questions. As drones become increasingly autonomous, the lines between human control and machine autonomy are starting to blur[50,51]. This raises a myriad of philosophical dilemmas about accountability, legality, and the very nature of warfare.

Still, as these drones swoop down on their unsuspecting targets, the course of battles and the complexion of the war are being changed in ways that are both tangible and irreversible. The humble drone, cheap and unsophisticated, was reshaping the nature of warfare, making us rethink the value of investment in military technology. Among the war-torn landscapes of Ukraine, a new age was being born, where the humble drone reigned supreme and where less, indeed, proved to be more.

However, these drones are still mostly remote controlled. Their true power will be realized as they become smarter and more autonomous. One impressive example of this emerged from the high-tech labs of Zhejiang University in China. The dedicated team of scientists there successfully developed an autonomous swarm of drones designed to navigate intricate landscapes, even as complex as dense bamboo forests, entirely unaided by human intervention[52,53].

The demonstration involved a squadron of ten palm-sized drones, skillfully maneuvering through a thick forest with the sheer prowess of their infrared sensors and advanced algorithms. With no need for human guidance or a previously mapped area for path calculation, these drones, incredibly, plotted their own dynamic, real-time routes, adapting to the unpredictable twists and turns of the dense forest[52,54].

Consider the enormous potential applications this breakthrough introduces. These relatively inexpensive but increasingly smarter drones will become extremely popular because they will save money for their owners, companies, and governments. Half of security is surveillance, and any place that uses security staff will save money using these types of drones, from malls and churches to prisons and military bases. Why pay a human to walk a route around a perimeter, when a palm-sized drone can do it a lot faster at maximum operational efficiency? The drone would not only be more efficient, but it would be able to perform its route nonstop. Equipped with infrared sensors, it would instantly be able to detect intruders or scan personnel to verify identification.

The scope for employing these diminutive drones in military strategy stretches far beyond the horizon, their potential teeming with a myriad of applications. They can operate as clandestine scouts, their tiny forms avoiding detection as they penetrate enemy lines, setting the stage for full-blown operations. Alternatively, they might serve as crafty diversions in the pulsing heart of military stand-offs, strategic feints that could change the tide of battle in an instant. The conflict in Ukraine has already shown their ability in having a direct role on the battlefield[55]. Strapping explosives to these drones and sending them in swarms to attack enemy armor has proven an extremely cost-effective way of engaging the enemy[55].

Imagine these machines in perfect harmony, a symphony of hundreds of drones in the sky, choreographed to orchestrate critical supply drops. They carry medical supplies, ammunition, and even the wounded, all while being unfazed by the chaos below. Assigned to infantry squads, these drones morph into guardian angels, their sensors scanning the terrain ahead, peeking into potentially hostile buildings, and monitoring the squad's surroundings for unseen threats.

They could meticulously scan fields for mines, unmask IEDs, and reveal traps, turning potential disasters into manageable threats. With each successful detection, a wealth of information is harvested and fed up the chain-of-command.

Humanoid Robots

As we voyage into the future, our world will undoubtedly host a legion of different humanoid robots. No longer confined to production lines or experimental labs, they will walk among us, partake in our societies, and redefine the boundaries of what we deem possible. These are not mere mechanized mimics of the human form. They represent an embodiment of our collective dreams, made real by leaps in scientific understanding and technological innovation.

Depending on the role the robot is designed for, construction and components will vary greatly. There will be "base" humanoid robot models made for general purpose. Taking into account the different advanced materials becoming available, we can guess what basic robot construction will consist of. There's a good chance humanoid robot endoskeletons will be made of graphene[56]. This is because graphene is many times stronger than steel while being a lot lighter at the same time. Shape-memory alloys could be used to build joints and mechanical systems within the robots, offering them the flexibility and range of motion close to that of a human. For their "skin", metallic glasses are good candidates because these materials are known for their extraordinary strength and resistance to wear and tear. Auxetic materials, which expand instead of contracting under stress, could be used in areas that require the robot to absorb shocks, for instance, in the soles of their feet or palms of their hands. Geckskin, a biomimetic material designed to mimic the adhesive capabilities of gecko feet, could be integrated into their fingers and feet to allow them to climb walls or hold onto objects with remarkable ease.

These robots could be powered by small modular reactors, making them capable of self-sustaining for extended periods of time. Their senses could be tremendously advanced, surpassing human limitations. Piezoelectric materials could give robots a very precise sense of touch, allowing them to detect pressure changes or vibrations[57,58]. Acoustic metamaterials could be used to create ultra-sensitive audio sensors, enabling robots to hear across a vast range of frequencies[59]. They could use photonic crystals and graphene-based sensors to detect light and heat, giving them advanced visual and thermal sensing capabilities[60].

Most "base" humanoid robots will simply be helpers. They will be friendly, intuitive, and designed to seamlessly integrate into our daily lives. These robots understand our needs and preferences, thanks to the symbiotic connection enabled by BCIs[5]. From house chores to personalized tutoring and elderly care, these companion robots greatly enhance the quality of life in our homes.

Although the basic humanoid robot will be impressive

enough, there will be more advanced robot models with specialized construction and equipment fit for their role. Consider medical surgery robots, their hands, equipped with optical tweezers, will be capable of performing microscopic surgeries, manipulating cells and even individual DNA strands[61]. Their vision, augmented by negative refraction optics, can detect abnormalities invisible to the human eye, making them a crucial ally in our fight against diseases[62].

Envision emergency responder robots, the heroes of the future. Outfitted with unique thermal insulating aerogel panels, they march into blazing fires, tirelessly battling the flames while human firefighters command from a safe distance[63]. Their advanced optics cut through the densest smoke, ensuring no one is left behind[64,65].

Finally, picture humanoid robots as future entertainers, captivating audiences with their intricate dance routines, their movements an impossible combination of precision and grace, a testament to the advanced geometric modeling that brought them to life[66,67].

Future humanoid robots might even be made to look and feel like us. Leading this quest for more realistic robots is Professor Shoji Takeuchi and his dedicated team at the University of Tokyo[68,69,70]. Their experimental process, intricate as it is fascinating, involves immersing a plastic robotic finger in a cocktail of collagen and human skin cells known as fibroblasts[68,69,70]. After a three-day bath, these organic components adhere to the finger, forming a layer uncannily similar to the dermis, which is the second major layer of human skin.

However, the replication of our complex skin architecture doesn't stop there. The next step involves gently introducing another type of skin cells, *keratinocytes*, onto the finger. This meticulously created layer represents the epidermis, the outermost layer of our skin, thereby providing the finishing touch to this bioengineered marvel. What emerged from this process is a synthetic skin 1.5 mm thick that astonishingly mirrors the properties of human skin[68,69,70]. As the robotic finger articulates, the artificial skin displays the natural stretch, contraction, and even the subtle wrinkling characteristic of a human finger.

Chapter References

1. Shastri, B. J., Tait, A. N., Ferreira de Lima, T., et al. (2021). Photonics for artificial intelligence and neuromorphic computing. *Nature Photonics*, 15, 102–114. https://doi.org/10.1038/s41566-020-00754-y

2. University of Oxford. (2022, June 16). Researchers develop the world's first ultra-fast photonic computing processor using polarisation. https://www.ox.ac.uk/news/2022-06-16-researchers-develop-worlds-first-ultra-fast-photonic-computing-processor-using

3. Schenker, Paul & Elfes, Alberto & Hall, Jeffrey & Huntsberger, Terrance & Jones, Jack & Wilcox, Brian & Zimmerman, Wayne. (2003). *Photonics Technologies for Robotics, Automation, and Manufacturing* (pp. 43-59).

4. World Nuclear News. (2021, January 13). US order promotes SMRs for space exploration and defence. https://www.world-nuclear-news.org/Articles/US-order-promotes-SMRs-for-space-exploration-and-d

5. Bryan, M., et al. (2011). An adaptive brain-computer interface for humanoid robot control. *2011 11th IEEE-RAS International Conference on Humanoid Robots* (pp. 199-204). Bled, Slovenia. https://doi.org/10.1109/Humanoids.2011.6100901

6. Association for Advancing Automation. (n.d.). Unimate. *Automate.org*. https://www.automate.org/a3-content/joseph-engelberger-unimate

7. Peterson, D. (2023, September 6). Origin Story: Meet Unimate, the First Industrial Robot. *Control.com*. https://control.com/technical-articles/origin-story-meet-unimate-the-first-industrial-robot/

8. Casgains Academy. (2021, March 4). Inside Tesla's crazy AI manufacturing revolution. *StreetFins*. https://streetfins.com/inside-teslas-crazy-ai-manufacturing-revolution/

9. Mascellino, A. (2020, March 04). KUKA Showcases New KR QUANTEC Foundry Robots. *Control Automation*. https://control.com/news/kuka-showcases-new-kr-quantec-foundry-robots/

10. KUKA. (2019, January 17). KUKA launches new generation of successful KR QUANTEC robot series. https://www.kuka.com/en-us/company/press/news/2018/12/quantec-new-generation

11. Automation & Control. (n.d.). KUKA KR QUANTEC Series. https://automation-control.com.au/brands/kuka/kuka-kr-quantec-series/

12. Burkacky, O., Kolesova, Z., & Lingemann, S. (2020, October 2). Smarter factories: How 5G can jump-start Industry 4.0. *McKinsey & Company*. https://www.mckinsey.com/capabilities/mckinsey-digital/our-insights/digital-blog/smarter-factories-how-5g-can-jump-start-industry-40

13. Bansal, N. (2019, June). This is how a smart factory actually works. *World Economic Forum*. https://www.weforum.org/agenda/2019/06/connectivity-is-driving-a-revolution-in-manufacturing/

14. Ohr, R.-C. (2022, July). Merging Real and Digital Worlds: Siemens' First Digital Native Factory. *Siemens Blog*. https://blog.siemens.com/2022/07/merging-real-and-digital-worlds-siemens-first-digital-native-factory/

15. Siemens Advanta. (n.d.). Lean Digital Factory Leverages the Potentials of Digitalization and Automation. https://www.siemens-advanta.com/cases/digital-factory

16. Tobe, F. (2016, June 17). Industrial robot companies investing in the cloud and Big Data. *Control Engineering*. https://www.controleng.com/articles/industrial-robot-companies-investing-in-the-cloud-and-big-data/

17. FANUC Corporation. (n.d.). Learning Robot Series. https://fanuc.co.jp/en/product/robot/function/gakushu.html

18. Sculpteo. (n.d.). Dreamcatcher: a research platform for generative design. https://www.sculpteo.com/en/glossary/autodesks-dreamcatcher/

19. Autodesk Research. (n.d.). Project Dreamcatcher: Generative Design Solutions in CAD. https://www.research.autodesk.com/projects/project-dreamcatcher

20. NASA's Jet Propulsion Laboratory. (n.d.). Rover Wheels. https://mars.nasa.gov/mars2020/spacecraft/rover/wheels/

21. NASA's Jet Propulsion Laboratory. (n.d.). Rover Body. https://mars.nasa.gov/mars2020/spacecraft/rover/body/

22. Lal, R., & Johnson, S. (2017, November). iRobot: Moving Beyond the Roomba. *Harvard Business School*. https://www.hbs.edu/faculty/Pages/item.aspx?num=53360

23. Congdon, B. (2023, October 12). 10 Amazing Roomba Robot Vacuum For 2023. *Robots.net*. https://robots.net/tech/10-amazing-roomba-robot-vacuum-for-2023/

24. Aurora. (2019, July 22). What is Sphero and How Does it Work? *iD Tech*. https://www.idtech.com/blog/what-is-sphero-how-does-it-work

25. Sphero. (n.d.). indi Educational Robot Student Kit. https://sphero.com/collections/for-school/products/indi-student-kit

26. Queensland University of Technology. (n.d.). AgBot II Robotic Site-specific Crop and Weed Management Tool. https://research.qut.edu.au/qcr/projects/agbot-ii-robotic-site-specific-crop-and-weed-management-tool/

27. Calderone, L. (2020, June 11). Agbots in Farming. *AgriTechTomorrow*. https://www.agritechtomorrow.com/article/2020/06/agbots-in-farming/12203

28. Thaler, S. (2023, October 18). Amazon revamps warehouses with robots to reduce delivery times. *New York Post*. https://nypost.com/2023/10/18/amazon-revamps-warehouses-with-robots-to-reduce-delivery-times/

29. Waredock. (n.d.). What is Amazon Robotic Fulfillment Center? https://www.waredock.com/magazine/what-is-amazon-robotic-fulfillment-center/

30. Starship Technologies. (n.d.). Autonomous robot delivery - The future of delivery - today! *Starship Technologies*. https://starship.co/

31. Shankland, S. (2015, November 2). Startup bets its wheeled robots, not airborne drones, will deliver your groceries. *CNET*. https://www.cnet.com/tech/tech-industry/startup-bets-its-wheeled-robots-not-airborne-drones-will-deliver-your-groceries/

32. Simon, M. (2017, November 10). Tug, the busy little robot nurse, will see you now. *Wired*. https://www.wired.com/story/tug-the-busy-little-robot-nurse-will-see-you-now/

33. Mercy. (n.d.). TUG Autonomous Mobile Robots. https://www.mercy.net/about/mercy-technology-services/tug-robot/

34. Wessling, B. (2023, September 29). NYPD deploys Knightscope security robot in Manhattan subway. *Mobile Robot Guide*. https://mobilerobotguide.com/2023/09/29/nypd-deploys-knightscope-security-robot-in-manhattan-subway/

35. Siff, A. (2023, September 22). Mayor Adams debuts 420-pound NYPD robot assigned to patrol NYC subway stations. *NBC New York*. https://www.nbcnewyork.com/news/local/eric-adams-debuts-420-pound-robot-assigned-to-patrol-nyc-subway-station/4704333/

36. Ackerman, E. (2015, February 10). Spot Is Boston Dynamics' Nimble New Quadruped Robot. *IEEE Spectrum*. https://spectrum.ieee.org/spot-is-boston-dynamics-nimble-new-quadruped-robot

37. Dormehl, L. (n.d.). Move Over, Spot. Anymal Is a Four-Legged Robot With Sorts of Tricks. *Digital Trends*. https://www.digitaltrends.com/cool-tech/anybotics-anymal-dog-robot-capabilities-and-uses/

38. Fukuhara, A., Gunji, M., & Masuda, Y. (2022). Comparative anatomy of quadruped robots and animals: A review. *Advanced Robotics*, 36(13), 612-630. https://doi.org/10.1080/01691864.2022.2086018

39. Moses, J., & Ford, G. (2021). See Spot save lives: Fear, humanitarianism, and war in the development of robot quadrupeds. *Digi War 2*, 64–76. https://doi.org/10.1057/s42984-021-00037-y

40. Leonida, S. (2021, February 19). Boston Dynamics Expands Autonomous Capabilities of SPOT Robot. *Control Automation*. https://control.com/news/boston-dynamics-expands-autonomous-capabilities-of-spot-robot/

41. The Robot Report Staff. (2019, August 20). ANYmal C Legged Robot Is Optimized for Industrial Inspection. *The Robot Report*. https://www.therobotreport.com/anymal-c-legged-robot-optimized-industrial-inspection/

42. Greenemeier, L. (n.d.). Robot Pack Mule to Carry Loads for G.I.s on the Move. *Scientific American*. https://www.scientificamerican.com/article/boston-dynamics-ls3/

43. Guizzo, E. (2010, February 1). Boston Dynamics Wins Darpa Contract To Develop LS3 Robot Mule (It's a Bigger BigDog). *IEEE Spectrum*. https://spectrum.ieee.org/boston-dynamics-ls3-robot-mule

44. Mizokami, K. (2020, September 11). The Air Force Is Testing Robo-Guard Dogs to Protect Its Planes. *Popular Mechanics*. https://www.popularmechanics.com/military/weapons/a33983077/robot-guard-dogs-us-air-force/

45. Mizokami, K. (2021, October 15). Welp, Now We Have Robo-Dogs With Sniper Rifles. *Popular Mechanics*. https://www.popularmechanics.com/military/weapons/a37939706/us-army-robot-dog-ghost-robotics-vision-60/

46. Malewar, A. (2020, December 19). NASA is working on Mars Dog, a four-legged robot for Mars exploration. *Inceptive Mind*. https://www.inceptivemind.com/nasa-plans-mars-dog-four-legged-robot-mars-exploration/16798/

47. Fuchs, H. (2022, May 4). Drones Are Changing Modern Warfare. *DW*. https://www.dw.com/en/ukraine-how-drones-are-changing-the-way-of-war/a-61681013

48. Kahn, L. (2022, March 2). How Ukraine Is Using Drones Against Russia. *Council on Foreign Relations*. https://www.cfr.org/in-brief/how-ukraine-using-drones-against-russia

49. Shankland, S. (2022, April 19). Ukraine Is Fighting Russia With Drones and Rewriting the Rules of War. *CNET*. https://www.cnet.com/news/ukraine-is-fighting-russia-with-drones-and-rewriting-the-rules-of-war/

50. Konert, A., Balcerzak, T. (2021). Military autonomous drones (UAVs) - from fantasy to reality. Legal and ethical implications. *Transportation Research Procedia*, 59, 292-299. https://doi.org/10.1016/j.trpro.2021.11.121

51. O'Halloran, B. (2019, January 28). The Ethical Concerns Of Drone And Automated Warfare. *SIR Journal*. http://www.sirjournal.org/op-ed/2019/1/28/the-ethical-concerns-of-drone-and-automated-warfare

52. Aubourg, L. (2022, May 4). Drone swarms can now fly autonomously through thick forest. *Tech Xplore*. https://techxplore.com/news/2022-05-drone-swarms-autonomously-thick-forest.html

53. Zarley, B. D. (2022, May 18). Watch a drone swarm navigate a bamboo forest. *Freethink*. https://www.freethink.com/hard-tech/drone-swarm-navigate-bamboo-forest

54. Chung, J. (2022). Researchers Program Drone Swarm to Navigate Autonomously Through a Forest Using Custom Algorithm. *TechEBlog*. https://www.techeblog.com/drone-swarm-navigate-autonomous-forest-algorithm/

55. Financial Review. (2022, October 18). Cheap and deadly. Why kamikaze drones are swarming Ukraine's skies. https://www.afr.com/policy/foreign-affairs/cheap-and-deadly-why-drones-are-swarming-ukraine-s-skies-20221018-p5bqpl

56. Arsh Basheer, A. (2023). Graphene materials for fabrication of robots. *Materials Chemistry and Physics*, 302, 127781. https://doi.org/10.1016/j.matchemphys.2023.127781

57. Kim, S., Shin, H., Song, K., & Cha, Y. (2019). Flexible piezoelectric sensor array for touch sensing of robot hand. *Proceedings of the 16th International Conference on Ubiquitous Robots (UR)* (pp. 21-25). Jeju, Korea (South). https://doi.org/10.1109/URAI.2019.8768644

58. Fretty, P. (2020, October 21). Do Robots Need a Sense of Touch? *New Equipment Digest*. https://www.newequipment.com/research-and-development/article/21145372/do-robots-need-a-sense-of-touch

59. Ma, K., et al. (2022). A wave-confining metasphere beamforming acoustic sensor for superior human-machine voice interaction. *Science Advances*, 8(eadc9230). https://doi.org/10.1126/sciadv.adc9230

60. Li, T., Liu, G., Kong, H., Yang, G., Wei, G., & Zhou, X. (2023). Recent advances in photonic crystal-based sensors. *Coordination Chemistry Reviews*, 475, 214909. https://doi.org/10.1016/j.ccr.2022.214909

61. Xie, M., Shakoor, A., & Wu, C. (2018). Manipulation of biological cells using a robot-aided optical tweezers system. *Micromachines*, 9(5), 245. https://doi.org/10.3390/mi9050245

62. Datta, S., Mukherjee, S., Shi, X., Haq, M., Deng, Y., Udpa, L., & Rothwell, E. (2021). Negative index metamaterial lens for subwavelength microwave detection. *Sensors*, 21(14), 4782. https://doi.org/10.3390/s21144782

63. Cabot Corporation. (n.d.). Aerogel. https://www.cabotcorp.com/solutions/products-plus/aerogel

64. Pizzuto, C. (2023, April 18). Disaster robots: Revolutionizing emergency response with autonomous robots. *AI for Good*. https://aiforgood.itu.int/disaster-robots-revolutionizing-emergency-response-with-autonomous-robots/

65. Khan, F., Xu, Z., Sun, J., Khan, F. M., Ahmed, A., & Zhao, Y. (2022). Recent advances in sensors for fire detection. *Sensors (Basel)*, 22(9), 3310. https://doi.org/10.3390/s22093310. https://www.ncbi.nlm.nih.gov/pmc/articles/PMC9100504/

66. Wang, H., Lu, J., & Yuan, Z.-S. (2014). Analysis and design of humanoid robot dance. *2014 7th International Conference on Intelligent Computation Technology and Automation* (pp. 88-91). Changsha, China. https://doi.org/10.1109/ICICTA.2014.29

67. Sousa, P., Oliveira, J. L., Reis, L. P., & Gouyon, F. (2011). Humanized Robot Dancing: Humanoid Motion Retargeting Based in a Metrical Representation of Human Dance Styles. In L. Antunes & H. S. Pinto (Eds.), *Progress in Artificial Intelligence*. EPIA 2011 (Vol. 7026, pp. 00-00). Springer. https://doi.org/10.1007/978-3-642-24769-9_29

68. Takeuchi, S. (2022). Scientists covered a robot finger in living human skin. *New Scientist*. https://www.newscientist.com/article/2323290-scientists-covered-a-robot-finger-in-living-human-skin/

69. Ravisetti, M. (2022, June 9). Scientists Craft 'Living Skin' for Robots, Made of Human Cells. *CNET*. https://www.cnet.com/science/biology/scientists-craft-living-skin-for-robots-made-of-human-cells/

70. Dionisio, C. (2022, June 21). These Scientists Created Robots Covered in Living Skin. *Discovery*. https://www.discovery.com/science/japanese-scientists-create-a-new-self-healing-skin-for-robots

Quantum Technologies

At the heart of quantum technology lies quantum mechanics, a branch of physics that describes how the tiniest particles in the universe behave. Unlike classical physics, which describes our everyday world, quantum physics is filled with phenomena that appear strange to us. This is where the magic and allure of quantum technology truly lie.

If you've heard about Schrödinger's cat, then you've already had a taste of one of the most bizarre yet fascinating concepts in quantum mechanics: *quantum superposition*. It is a principle that defies our conventional understanding of reality, hinting at a universe far stranger than we can imagine.

At its core, quantum superposition refers to the ability of quantum particles to exist in multiple states at once. An electron, for instance, can be in more than one place simultaneously. This isn't a matter of simply not knowing where the particle is or what state it is in, the mind-bending reality is that the particle truly occupies all those states at once[1,2].

Schrödinger's cat, a thought experiment proposed by physicist Erwin Schrödinger, is often used to illustrate this. Imagine a cat inside a closed box, along with a radioactive atom that, within the hour, may decay (and consequently kill the cat) or may not. According to quantum mechanics, until we open the box, the cat is both alive and dead at the same time[3,4]. Only when we open the box to observe does the cat "collapse" into one state or the other: alive or dead. Strange, isn't it?

One of the most well-known examples of quantum superposition in action is the double-slit experiment. When particles of light (photons) or matter are fired at a barrier with two slits, they don't pass through one slit or the other, as you'd expect in the everyday world. Instead, each particle interferes with itself, passing through both slits simultaneously and creating an interference pattern on a screen behind the barrier. This clearly demonstrates the particle's ability to be in two places at the same time, a manifestation of quantum superposition[5,6].

Quantum superposition tears down our traditional notions of reality and rebuilds them in a more complex, fascinating, and counterintuitive way. It is a concept that can be difficult to comprehend, let alone accept. But it is this very principle that promises to revolutionize our world, from computing and communication to encryption and beyond. As we move forward into a future molded by quantum mechanics, we continue to push the boundaries of what is possible, constantly challenging and expanding our understanding of the universe.

At the heart of quantum physics there's a phenomenon so strange that even Albert Einstein called it "spooky action at a distance." This is *quantum entanglement*, a phenomenon where two particles are linked together regardless of the distance separating them. Imagine a pair of particles that are created together, such as two photons emitted from the same atom. According to quantum theory, these particles are "entangled," meaning their properties are intrinsically connected no matter how far apart they may be[7,8,9]. Change the state of one particle, and the other will instantaneously reflect that change. It is as if they exist in a shared state, mirroring each other's behavior.

This shared existence persists regardless of distance— whether the particles are millimeters or galaxies apart. It is a concept that defies our everyday understanding of reality, for it suggests a form of instantaneous communication faster than the speed of light, which according to Einstein's Theory of Relativity, is not possible.

Now, you might ask, "How does this work?" Well, nobody knows exactly why. This is one of the great mysteries of quantum mechanics. The entangled particles don't send any signal through space; they simply know the state of their partner instantaneously. This behavior seems to defy the laws of classical physics, making quantum entanglement one of the key distinctions between the quantum and classical worlds.

As for real-life examples, scientists have been experimenting with quantum entanglement for years. In a 2015 experiment, scientists at QuTech in Delft, Netherlands made a significant breakthrough by being the first to generate long-lived quantum entanglement over a distance of 1.3 kilometers, providing full experimental proof of quantum entanglement for the first time. This experiment, which involved entangling distant single electrons on diamond chips using photons as mediators, laid the groundwork for their ongoing efforts to develop a quantum internet[10].

So, what does this mean for us? Why is quantum entanglement important? While the theory might seem abstract and far removed from our daily lives, it is actually at the heart of many emerging technologies. Quantum entanglement is the fundamental principle behind quantum computers, which promise to revolutionize computing by solving problems beyond the reach of even the most powerful classical computers[11,12].

Quantum entanglement is a surreal concept that challenges our classical understanding of the world. Yet, it holds the promise of igniting a new technological revolution that may redefine our future.

Apart from superposition and entanglement, there is a third logic-defying phenomena in quantum mechanics called *quantum tunneling*. Imagine a ball that you want to roll over a hill. Traditionally, you would need to give the ball enough energy to reach the top of the hill and descend on the other side. In the realm of quantum mechanics, the ball can simply pass through the hill, appearing on the other side without ever climbing to the top. That's quantum tunneling in a nutshell.

Quantum tunneling is a fascinating phenomenon that allows particles to pass through barriers that should, according to the laws of classical physics, be insurmountable. The particles don't go over, around, or under these barriers. Instead, they "tunnel" directly through them, even when they technically shouldn't have enough energy to do so. In essence, it is like walking through walls[13,14,15].

How does this work? The answer lies in the dual nature of particles in quantum mechanics. Particles such as electrons not only have characteristics of matter but also of waves[13,14,15]. When these "wave-particles" encounter a barrier, the wave associated with them can sometimes continue through the barrier and come out on the other side. And where the wave goes, the particle can follow, effectively "tunneling" through the barrier.

A real-world example of quantum tunneling can be seen in the process of radioactive decay[14]. Certain atomic nuclei can transform into different elements through a process that involves the emission of alpha particles, which are essentially helium nuclei. These alpha particles are initially trapped within the atomic nucleus, a barrier they shouldn't be able to overcome. But due to quantum tunneling, they manage to escape, leading to the decay of the original atom.

Quantum tunneling isn't just a curiosity, this phenomenon is already an integral part to several modern technologies. Tunnel diodes, for instance, use quantum tunneling to allow electrons to move quickly through a thin barrier, leading to very fast electronic switches[16]. It is this ability to transition from off to on states extremely rapidly that makes tunnel diodes particularly useful in certain radio-frequency applications.

Quantum tunneling exemplifies how quantum mechanics challenges our everyday experiences and intuitions. It is a principle that seems to flout the conventional rules, giving us a glimpse of a world where particles can be many places at once, and apparently insurmountable barriers are simply another path to be explored. As we continue to unravel these quantum curiosities, who knows what other walls we might learn to tunnel through in our journey to the future?

These amazing phenomena that quantum mechanics reveals opens up a future with technologies that not only seems amazing and impossible to us, but could also make us rethink what reality is and what is really possible.

Quantum Encryption

In the vast, complex world of data security, one technology promises to offer an unprecedented level of protection: Quantum encryption. Also known as *quantum key distribution* (QKD), it leverages the quirky and unpredictable behavior of quantum particles to create encryption keys that are supposedly unbreakable[17,18,19]. Let's peel back the layers of this fascinating field, investigate its current state, and envision its potential implications for the future.

Quantum encryption utilizes the principles of quantum mechanics, particularly those of superposition and entanglement. The key concept here is that any measurement of a quantum system disturbs the system. This means that, if an eavesdropper tries to intercept a quantum-encrypted message, they would inevitably alter the state of the particles and reveal their presence.

In recent years, the development of quantum encryption has made promising strides. For instance, China launched the world's first quantum satellite, Micius, in 2016, which successfully demonstrated intercontinental quantum key distribution between China and Austria[20,21]. In 2020, Toshiba Europe announced a breakthrough in QKD technology, creating a prototype that could transport quantum keys over 600 kilometers of fiber optic cables, setting a new record for the longest QKD link[22,23].

In the realm of the military and national security, the implications are monumental. Quantum encryption could secure communication lines, protecting sensitive data from potential adversaries. It could also offer an impenetrable shield for intelligence operations, ensuring that classified information remains confidential.

Furthermore, the advent of quantum computers poses a *Catch-22* situation. While they would empower quantum encryption, they could also potentially crack traditional encryption methods. Therefore, it is essential to prepare our cybersecurity infrastructure for this impending quantum shift.

Quantum Radar

Quantum radar, in theory, would exploit the bizarre properties of quantum entanglement to detect and track objects with unprecedented accuracy. In quantum entanglement, a pair of particles are linked in such a way that the state of one instantaneously influences the state of the other, no matter how far apart they are[7].

The current state of quantum radar development is nascent but promising. Several nations, including China and Canada, have reported significant advances. China, for instance, announced in 2016 that it had developed a single-photon quantum radar, which, they claim, can detect targets 100 kilometers away[24,25]. Meanwhile, the University of Waterloo's Institute for Quantum Computing has been granted funding to develop a proof-of-concept quantum radar system for Canada's Department of National Defense[26,27].

Nevertheless, it is important to note that quantum radar is still largely in the experimental phase. The technology demands complex, delicate systems to produce and maintain entangled particles, and verifying entanglement over long distances remains a significant challenge.

The potential applications of quantum radar are vast and could fundamentally transform military operations, aviation, and even weather forecasting. Its primary advantage is its potential to detect stealth aircraft[24]. Traditional radar systems detect objects by bouncing radio waves off them, but stealth aircraft are designed to absorb or deflect these waves, making them nearly invisible. Quantum radar, however, could potentially see through these stealth technologies by identifying disturbances in entangled particle pairs.

For military and defense agencies, this capability would be a game-changer, neutralizing the advantages of stealth technology and giving new meaning to "seeing the unseen." It could also improve the safety and efficacy of rescue missions, as quantum radar might detect small and distant objects in difficult environmental conditions, such as dense fog or rough seas[28,29].

Furthermore, quantum radar could enhance the ability to monitor weather patterns and predict storms[30,31]. Traditional radar can be confounded by obstacles or the ground, but quantum radar could offer a more precise, unobstructed view of atmospheric conditions.

Despite the challenges and uncertainty surrounding its development, the potential of quantum radar is immense. It could pierce through the cloak of invisibility, offering us an unprecedented view of our world and the objects that move within it. The road to realization may be steep, but the destination promises to be worth the climb. As quantum science continues to unravel, we're inching closer to illuminating the unknown with the power of quantum radar.

Quantum Modeling

Quantum molecular modeling, a blend of quantum physics, computational chemistry, and material science, is opening up new horizons in the design and understanding of complex molecular systems. While still a nascent field, it shows immense promise and potential for a wide range of future applications.

At its core, quantum molecular modeling leverages the principles of quantum mechanics to predict and explain the behavior of molecules[32,33]. Traditional computational methods have been limited by the sheer computational complexity of modeling systems of many interacting particles. However, with the advent of quantum computers, the prospect of accurately simulating such complex systems has become more feasible.

Several pioneering companies and research institutions are currently at the forefront of quantum molecular modeling development. For instance, IBM has used a quantum computer to simulate the molecular structure of beryllium hydride, marking the first time a molecule has been simulated on a quantum computer[34,35]. Google's quantum team has similarly made strides, demonstrating how a quantum computer can be used to model chemical reactions[36,37].

Despite these significant breakthroughs, quantum molecular modeling is still in its infancy. Quantum computers themselves are relatively new technology, with limited processing power compared to what is theoretically possible. Nevertheless, the progress in this field is accelerating, and as quantum computers evolve, so too will the capabilities of quantum molecular modeling.

In material science and engineering, this technology could drastically accelerate the process of discovering new materials with desirable properties, such as high-strength alloys, superconductors, or efficient solar cells. By accurately modeling the quantum behaviors of atoms in these materials, scientists could pinpoint the structural attributes that yield the best performance, helping to guide the creation of innovative materials[38].

Pharmaceutical development could also benefit immensely from quantum molecular modeling. The process of developing a new drug often involves a trial-and-error search for molecules that can interact with biological systems in specific ways. Quantum molecular modeling could potentially streamline this process by accurately predicting how candidate molecules would behave, saving time and resources in the drug discovery process[39].

Moreover, understanding complex molecular reactions is fundamental in areas like catalysis, photosynthesis, and battery technology. Quantum molecular modeling could revolutionize these fields by providing detailed insights into the underlying molecular processes, leading to more efficient industrial catalysts, bio-inspired energy systems, and longer-lasting batteries.

Quantum molecular modeling, while still in its early stages, carries the potential to usher in a new era of materials and molecular design. As quantum computing technology matures, we will be increasingly able to harness the power of quantum mechanics to engineer novel materials and gain profound insights into the universe at a molecular level. The possibilities are endless, and the future is bright for this burgeoning field.

Teleportation

If you're a fan of *Star Trek*, then you're undoubtedly familiar with the phrase, "Beam me up, Scotty!" This iconic line has become synonymous with the concept of teleportation: the idea of disappearing from one location and instantaneously reappearing in another. It is an idea that has tantalized sci-fi enthusiasts and perplexed scientists for generations. But how far are we from turning this cinematic fantasy into a scientific reality?

To the disappointment of many, we're still a long way from teleporting humans or objects across space in an instant. But that's not to say we haven't made progress in teleportation technology. In fact, some very real, albeit limited, forms of teleportation already exist in the field of quantum physics.

Over the last few decades, physicists have successfully teleported information between particles thanks to quantum entanglement. In a landmark experiment a few decades ago, scientists at the University of Innsbruck in Austria successfully transferred properties from one photon to another over a distance of one meter[40,41]. Fast forward to 2017, we see Chinese researchers breaking records by teleporting photons from a ground station to a satellite orbiting the Earth, covering a distance of up to 1,400 kilometers[42,43].

Despite these achievements, quantum teleportation is currently restricted to the realm of subatomic particles. So, while it is fascinating, you will not be beaming to work or a vacation spot anytime soon.

But let's indulge our imaginations for a moment and ponder a future where teleportation technology has fully blossomed. The applications could be extraordinary and wide-ranging.

In communication, teleportation could revolutionize data transfer, resulting in ultra-secure and instant information sharing. Using entangled particles to transmit data could usher in a new era of unhackable quantum networks.

In medicine, imagine if doctors could teleport drugs or microscopic medical bots to any part of the body, making surgeries non-invasive and much safer.

In logistics, instant teleportation could revolutionize transportation and distribution systems, negating the need for traditional shipping and dramatically reducing the time and energy spent on transporting goods.

For space exploration, teleportation could become the ultimate tool. Imagine teleporting supplies, equipment, or even astronauts to far-off planets or galaxies. This technology could unlock the secrets of the universe like never before.

Quantum Telescopes

Imagine a telescope that can surpass the limitations of its predecessors by observing phenomena never before seen, and able to delve even deeper into the cosmic mystery that is our universe. Welcome to the concept of *quantum telescopes*, a promising development in the world of astronomy, promising to bring a profound change in our understanding of the cosmos[44,45,46].

Presently, the pinnacle of telescopic technology is embodied in the James Webb Space Telescope (JWST), launched by NASA, which uses an array of 18 gold-coated, beryllium mirrors to collect and focus light[47,48]. This feat of engineering operates in the infrared spectrum, peering through cosmic dust to observe distant celestial bodies and events. However, the quantum telescope, once realized, could dwarf even the remarkable capabilities of the JWST.

The quantum telescope would take advantage of quantum entanglement, which allows particles to be linked in such a way that the state of one instantly affects the state of the other, no matter the distance between them[7]. This phenomenon, which Einstein famously referred to as "spooky action at a distance," forms the crux of quantum telescopes[8].

The hypothetical quantum telescope would employ a large network of detectors, possibly spread across the globe or even in space, to capture individual photons from astronomical sources. These photons, once entangled, would form a vast, interconnected network. With the right setup, these photons' quantum states could be measured in a way that lets them behave as though they originated from a telescope much larger than any physically possible. Essentially, this "telescope" would be as big as the distance between the detectors. This concept is known as *quantum interferometry* and has been considered theoretically feasible, although practically challenging[49,50,51].

Such a telescope would have extraordinary implications for astronomy. It could provide unprecedented resolution, potentially allowing us to directly observe exoplanets and perhaps even their atmospheric properties, giving us a greater chance of finding signs of life. It could yield detailed images of other galaxies and help us understand black holes and dark matter in ways that were previously impossible. The sheer magnitude of the effective aperture size of a quantum telescope could potentially surpass even our wildest expectations, bringing the universe closer than ever.

The road to a functional quantum telescope is fraught with technological and theoretical challenges. For one, entangling photons over large distances and maintaining their entangled state long enough to measure them is no small feat. Also, detecting single photons with high efficiency and precision, necessary for such a telescope, presents its challenges. But these hurdles are the driving force of innovation.

Chapter References

1. Ball, P. (2018). Quantum Physics May Be Even Spookier Than You Think. *Scientific American*. https://www.scientificamerican.com/article/quantum-physics-may-be-even-spookier-than-you-think/

2. Letzter, R. (2019). Giant Molecules Exist in Two Places at Once in Unprecedented Quantum Experiment. *Scientific American*. https://www.scientificamerican.com/article/giant-molecules-exist-in-two-places-at-once-in-unprecedented-quantum-experiment/

3. Johnson, L. (2019, December 5). Schrodinger's Cat (Simplified): What Is It & Why Is It Important? *Sciencing*. https://sciencing.com/schrodingers-cat-simplified-what-is-it-why-is-important-13722577.html

4. New Scientist. (n.d.). What is Schrodinger's cat? https://www.newscientist.com/definition/schrodingers-cat/

5. LibreTexts. (n.d.). 1.37: The Double-Slit Experiment. https://chem.libretexts.org/Bookshelves/Physical_and_Theoretical_Chemistry_Textbook_Maps/Quantum_Tutorials_(Rioux)/01%3A_Quantum_Fundamentals/1.37%3A_The_Double-Slit_Experiment

6. Calosi, C., & Wilson, J. (2021). Quantum indeterminacy and the double-slit experiment. *Philosophical Studies*, 178, 3291–3317. https://doi.org/10.1007/s11098-021-01602-7

7. Muller, A. (2022). What is quantum entanglement? A physicist explains the science of Einstein's 'spooky action at a distance'. *The Conversation*. https://theconversation.com/what-is-quantum-entanglement-a-physicist-explains-the-science-of-einsteins-spooky-action-at-a-distance-191927

8. Emspak, J. (Date not provided). What is quantum entanglement? *Space.com*. https://www.space.com/31933-quantum-entanglement-action-at-a-distance.html

9. Popkin, G. (2018, April 25). Einstein's 'spooky action at a distance' spotted in objects almost big enough to see. *Science*. https://www.science.org/content/article/einstein-s-spooky-action-distance-spotted-objects-almost-big-enough-see

10. TU Delft. (2018, June 13). Delft Scientists Make First 'On Demand' Entanglement Link. *The Kavli Foundation*. https://www.kavlifoundation.org/news/delft-scientists-make-first-on-demand-entanglement-link

11. Xia, S., & Zhao, J. (2023). Static Entanglement Analysis of Quantum Programs. *arXiv*. https://arxiv.org/abs/2304.05049

12. Genkina, D. (2023, October 19). Quantum Computers Run on Just the Right Amount of Connectivity. *Joint Quantum Institute*. https://jqi. umd.edu/news/quantum-computers-run-just-right-amount-connectivity

13. Venkatesh. (n.d.). What Is Quantum Tunneling? *Science ABC*. https://www.scienceabc.com/pure-sciences/what-is-quantum-tunneling. html

14. OpenStax. (n.d.). 7.6 The Quantum Tunneling of Particles through Potential Barriers. *University Physics Volume 3*. https://openstax.org/ books/university-physics-volume-3/pages/7-6-the-quantum-tunneling-of-particles-through-potential-barriers

15. Cooling, S. (2023, August 4). Quantum Tunneling. *Techopedia*. https://www.techopedia.com/definition/quantum-tunneling

16. Lincoln, J. (2021). Quantum tunneling experiments with tunnel diodes. *The Physics Teacher*, 59(1), 76–77. https://doi.org/ 10.1119/10.0003028

17. Caltech Science Exchange. (n.d.). Quantum Cryptography and Quantum Encryption Explained. https://scienceexchange.caltech.edu/ topics/quantum-science-explained/quantum-cryptography

18. National Security Agency. (n.d.). Quantum Key Distribution (QKD) and Quantum Cryptography (QC). https://www.nsa.gov/Cybersecurity/ Quantum-Key-Distribution-QKD-and-Quantum-Cryptography-QC/

19. Gillis, A. S. (2022, November). What is Quantum Key Distribution (QKD) and How Does it Work? *TechTarget*. https://www.techtarget.com/ searchsecurity/definition/quantum-key-distribution-QKD

20. China National Space Administration. (2018, January 23). China's "Micius" completes intercontinental quantum key distribution. https:// www.cnsa.gov.cn/english/n6465652/n6465653/c6799624/content.html

21. Kwon, K. (2020, June 25). China reaches new milestone in space-based quantum communications. *Scientific American*. https://www. scientificamerican.com/article/china-reaches-new-milestone-in-space-based-quantum-communications/

22. Toshiba Europe Ltd. (2021, June 8). Toshiba Announces Breakthrough in Long Distance Quantum Communication. https://www. toshiba.eu/pages/eu/Cambridge-Research-Laboratory/toshiba-announces-breakthrough-in-long-distance-quantum-communication

23. Swayne, M. (2021, June 14). Toshiba Europe Announces Long Distance Quantum Communication Over 600 Kilometers. *The Quantum Insider.* https://thequantuminsider.com/2021/06/14/toshiba-europe-announces-long-distance-quantum-communication-over-600-kilometers/

24. Chen, S. (2016, September 21). The end of stealth? New Chinese radar capable of detecting 'invisible' targets 100km away. *South China Morning Post.* https://www.scmp.com/news/china/article/2021235/end-stealth-new-chinese-radar-capable-detecting-invisible-targets-100km

25. Kania, E., & Armitage, S. (Year). Disruption Under the Radar: Chinese Advances in Quantum Sensing. *Jamestown Foundation.* https://jamestown.org/program/disruption-under-the-radar-chinese-advances-in-quantum-sensing/

26. Baugh, J. (2018, April 12). Quantum radar will expose stealth aircraft. *Institute for Quantum Computing.* https://uwaterloo.ca/institute-for-quantum-computing/news/quantum-radar-will-expose-stealth-aircraft

27. Mandelbaum, R. F. (2018, April 23). Canada's Defense Department Is Funding a Quantum Radar System. *Gizmodo.* https://gizmodo.com/canadas-defense-department-is-funding-a-quantum-radar-s-1825470931

28. Yirka, B. (2022, January 10). A new look at quantum radar suggests it might boost accuracy more than thought. *Phys.org.* https://phys.org/news/2022-01-quantum-radar-boost-accuracy-thought.html

29. Assouly, R., Dassonneville, R., Peronnin, T., et al. (2023). Quantum advantage in microwave quantum radar. *Nature Physics*, 19, 1418–1422. https://doi.org/10.1038/s41567-023-02113-4.

30. Enos, G. R., Reagor, M. J., Henderson, M. P., Young, C., Horton, K., Birch, M., & Rigetti, C. (2021). Synthetic weather radar using hybrid quantum-classical machine learning. *arXiv.* https://arxiv.org/abs/2111.15605

31. Swayne, M. (2021, December 7). Quantum Machine Learning May Improve Weather Forecasting. *The Quantum Insider.* https://thequantuminsider.com/2021/12/07/quantum-machine-learning-may-improve-weather-forecasting/

32. Aminpour, M., Montemagno, C., & Tuszynski, J. A. (2019). An overview of molecular modeling for drug discovery with specific illustrative examples of applications. *Molecules*, 24(9), 1693. https://doi.org/10.3390/molecules24091693

33. Ollitrault, P. J., Miessen, A., & Tavernelli, I. (2021). Molecular Quantum Dynamics: A Quantum Computing Perspective. *Accounts of Chemical Research*, 54(23), 4229-4238. https://doi.org/10.1021/acs.accounts.1c00514

34. Reilly, M. (2017, September 13). IBM Has Used Its Quantum Computer to Simulate a Molecule—Here's Why That's Big News. *MIT Technology Review*. https://www.technologyreview.com/2017/09/13/149180/ibm-has-used-its-quantum-computer-to-simulate-a-molecule-heres-why-thats-big-news/

35. McRae, M. (2017, September 14). IBM Just Broke The Record of Simulating Chemistry With a Quantum Computer. *ScienceAlert*. https://www.sciencealert.com/ibm-has-simulated-the-most-complex-molecule-yet-with-a-quantum-computer

36. Crane, L. (2020, August 27). Google performed the first quantum simulation of a chemical reaction. *New Scientist*. https://www.newscientist.com/article/2253089-google-performed-the-first-quantum-simulation-of-a-chemical-reaction/

37. Yirka, B. (2020, August 28). Google conducts largest chemical simulation on a quantum computer to date. *Phys.org*. https://phys.org/news/2020-08-google-largest-chemical-simulation-quantum.html

38. Morawietz, T., & Artrith, N. (2021). Machine learning-accelerated quantum mechanics-based atomistic simulations for industrial applications. *Journal of Computational Aided Molecular Design*, 35, 557–586. https://doi.org/10.1007/s10822-020-00346-6

39. Batra, K., Zorn, K. M., Foil, D. H., Minerali, E., Gawriljuk, V. O., Lane, T. R., & Ekins, S. (2021). Quantum Machine Learning Algorithms for Drug Discovery Applications. *Journal of Chemical Information and Modeling*, 61(6), 2641-2647. https://doi.org/10.1021/acs.jcim.1c00166

40. Science. (1997, December 10). Behold the Quantum Teleporter. https://www.science.org/content/article/behold-quantum-teleporter

41. Bouwmeester, D., Pan, JW., Mattle, K. et al. Experimental quantum teleportation. *Nature 390*, 575–579 (1997). https://doi.org/10.1038/37539

42. Emerging Technology from the arXiv. (2017, July 10). First Object Teleported from Earth to Orbit. *MIT Technology Review*. https://www.technologyreview.com/2017/07/10/150547/first-object-teleported-from-earth-to-orbit/

43. Ren, J. G., Xu, P., Yong, H. L., Zhang, L., Liao, S. K., Yin, J., Liu, W.

Y., Cai, W. Q., Yang, M., Li, L., Yang, K. X., Han, X., Yao, Y. Q., Li, J., Wu, H. Y., Wan, S., Liu, L., Liu, D. Q., Kuang, Y. W., He, Z. P., ... Pan, J. W. (2017). Ground-to-satellite quantum teleportation. *Nature*, 549(7670), 70–73. https://doi.org/10.1038/nature23675

44. Ananthaswamy, A. (2021, April 19). Quantum Astronomy Could Create Telescopes Hundreds of Kilometers Wide. *Scientific American*. https://www.scientificamerican.com/article/quantum-astronomy-could-create-telescopes-hundreds-of-kilometers-wide/

45. Williams, M. (2023, February 13). Are We Entering the Era of Quantum Telescopes? *Universe Today*. https://www.universetoday.com/159741/are-we-entering-the-era-of-quantum-telescopes/

46. Cartwright, J. (2014, April 29). Quantum telescope could make giant mirrors obsolete. *Physics World*. https://physicsworld.com/a/quantum-telescope-could-make-giant-mirrors-obsolete/

47. NASA. (2023). James Webb Space Telescope (JWST) - NSSDCA/COSPAR ID: 2021-130A. https://nssdc.gsfc.nasa.gov/nmc/spacecraft/display.action?id=2021-130A

48. NASA. (2016, April 29). James Webb Space Telescope's Golden Mirror. https://www.nasa.gov/image-article/james-webb-space-telescopes-golden-mirror/

49. Spagnolo, N., Aparo, L., Vitelli, C., et al. (2012). Quantum interferometry with three-dimensional geometry. *Scientific Reports*, 2, 862. https://doi.org/10.1038/srep00862

50. Castleberry, K. (2021, November 17). A Magic Recipe for a Quantum Interferometer. *JILA*. https://jila.colorado.edu/news-events/articles/magic-recipe-quantum-interferometer

51. De Martini, F., Denardo, G., & Zeilinger, A. (1994). *Quantum Interferometry* (pp. 1-322). https://doi.org/10.1142/9789814535311

Directed Energy Weapons

In countless imaginings of the future, there's a mesmerizing allure to the mastery and harnessing of potent energy. From the chambers of scientific laboratories to the expansive universes of cinema, the concept of energy weaponry has long captivated our collective imagination. The allure of these weapons lies in their combination of raw power and surgical precision, a promise of the future of warfare, one that stands at the intersection of science and fantasy.

The genesis of this fascination can be traced back to 1960, with the invention of the laser. Scientists marveled at the ability to produce a beam of light so focused that it could cut through metal or perform intricate eye surgeries[1,2]. Yet, even as lasers found practical applications, they were already sparking dreams of formidable weapons that seemed straight out of a science fiction novel.

It was Hollywood, with its flair for the fantastic, that first brought these dreams to life. Who can forget the iconic Death Star in *Star Wars*, its colossal laser capable of obliterating entire planets? Or the elegant lightsabers, their crackling energy blades becoming a symbol of the eternal struggle between good and evil? These cinematic portrayals depicted laser weapons as tools of immense, almost mythical, power.

Yet, energy weaponry was not confined to the realm of space opera. In the gritty, cyberpunk world of *Blade Runner*, lasers became high-tech tools in the hands of futuristic law enforcement. In the James Bond series, they were wielded with lethal elegance by both villains and the iconic spy himself.

Simultaneously, science fiction literature also embraced the concept. In the pages of novels like *Dune*, laser weapons came in all shapes and sizes, from handheld blasters to gigantic starship-mounted cannons, underscoring the limitless potential of energy-based warfare.

Today, reality is starting to echo fiction as laser

weapons are slowly but surely stepping off the silver screen and onto the global stage. While we're still some way from handheld laser guns and planet-destroying super-weapons, military forces around the world are experimenting with laser systems capable of shooting down drones or neutralizing incoming missiles[3,4].

In the heart of military research labs, the hum of laser weaponry grows louder. Take, for example, the US Navy's *Laser Weapon System* (LaWS), a stark testament to the dawn of this new era[5,6]. Deployed on the USS Ponce, the LaWS has already demonstrated its potential, using concentrated energy to neutralize threats with pinpoint precision.

Other laser weapons already being integrated into current warships are the *High Energy Laser with Integrated Optical-dazzler and Surveillance* (HELIOS) weapon system from Lockheed Martin, and the *Optical Dazzling Interdictor, Navy* (ODIN) systems from Naval Surface Warfare Center in Dahlgren, VA[7,8,9,10]. These systems not only able to fire a concentrated energy beam, but have low-power modes that have the ability of destroying electronics and disorientating sensors. Such weapon outputs would be able to take down future threats such as swarms of drones.

Furthermore, laser weaponry is not merely confined to

the dominion of naval warfare. Ground-based laser systems, like the *High Energy Laser Mobile Demonstrator* (HEL MD) developed by the US Army, can incinerate drones and mortars, providing a futuristic defense mechanism[11,12].

Even the air is not devoid of this revolution. In the aeronautical realm, companies like Lockheed Martin are testing laser weapons that can be mounted on aircraft[13,14]. It is not hard to imagine a near future where dogfights in the sky are not determined by traditional bullets and missiles, but by the precision and relentless power of lasers.

These weapons systems will truly shine in space, the ultimate strategic high ground. Mounted on satellites, they will be able to interact with any point on the globe. This presents an intimidating new presence of military power, with a weapons that is always present, always operational, and pinpoint accurate. The concept of mounting laser weapons on satellites is a topic of ongoing research and strategic discussions among military powers. The Pentagon has shown interest in testing a space-based weapon in 2023, with officials requesting a $304 million fund for researching space-based lasers among other technologies[15].

Picture a destroyer slicing through the waves, not burdened by tons of explosive ordnance, but empowered by an arsenal of light. Instead of launching prohibitively expensive projectiles, a pulsating laser cannon thrums to life. Each shot costs mere cents, a revolution not just in capability but also in cost-effectiveness.

The complex ballet of predicting a target's movement, factoring in wind speed and the earth's curvature, is replaced by a laser's unwavering accuracy. Traveling at the speed of light, laser weaponry offers near-instantaneous impact. The laser, guided by advanced targeting systems, strikes with pinpoint precision, reducing collateral damage and ensuring the highest probability of neutralizing the intended threat.

The limitations of fire rates and ammunition supply, a longstanding shackle on the effectiveness of warfare, vanish under the relentless beam of a laser. Picture a weapon that unleashes an uninterrupted torrent of destruction, its stream of energy only limited by the power supplied to it. The naval vessel, thus equipped, becomes an unstoppable force, its laser weaponry providing an unending supply of firepower so long as the power flows.

This potential of unlimited firepower from laser weapons would be a major game-changer for air forces as well. The traditional notion of roaring jets needing to refuel and restock on ammunition could become as outdated as the concept of a cavalry charge. Tomorrow's aerial champions might be drones and advanced aircraft that, once aloft, never need to touch the ground again. They would soar, tireless and relentless, backed by the power of the sun. Solar panels, evolving far beyond our current understanding, would drink in sunlight, allowing these guardians to remain ever-vigilant.

In the hands of skilled remote pilots, safe in secure locations far from the theater of conflict, these airborne titans would dominate the skies. Such a shift would not merely represent an incremental advancement, but a tectonic upheaval in the art of warfare. The sunlit day might soon be shadowed by the silent vigil of these futuristic sentinels.

As we continue down the laser-illuminated path of future warfare, it is impossible to overlook the profound implications of such systems.

Microwave Weaponry

Similar in concept but different in application, microwave weaponry will also become a staple of military arsenals. These aren't mere replacements to the laser weapons of the same era, but rather, they serve a unique and indispensable role. While laser weaponry carves precise incisions into the chaos of battle, microwave weaponry sweeps across the theater, disrupting and disabling with wide-reaching effect.

The weaponization of microwaves has been a reality for some time now. One significant product of this unsettling transformation is the *Active Denial System* (ADS), an ostensibly harmless device that carries the disquieting undertones of a potent weapon[16,17]. This technology, designed for area denial, perimeter security, and crowd control, emits a 95 GHz wave, a frequency that manifests in a physical wavelength of a scant 3.2 mm, to enact its silent, invisible dominance.

The ADS doesn't wound or maim—no, its artistry lies in subtler torment. With a potency of 100 kilowatts, it releases a burning heat that climbs to an unbearable degree almost instantly. Its victims find retreat the only option, driven back without a scratch on their skin, without a single drop of blood shed, a spectacle of forced submission.

Under the rose-tinted glasses that this is a humane tool of de-escalation and non-lethal incapacitation, lies the uncomfortable reality that a tool that can cause unbearable discomfort from a distance with the flip of a switch, is a tool that is ripe for misuse. If these systems were installed the way cameras are today, it paints a rather dystopian outlook on things.

Although effective as conventional weaponry, microwave weaponry truly shines against electrical systems, which will be the heart and blood of future warfare. Even the most fortified bunker, immune to the might of conventional explosives, will be rendered impotent and mute as its intricate network of communication and electronic systems succumbs to the silent onslaught.

This is not mere fiction but a testament to our rapid technological advancement. Epirus, an industry leader in this field, has recently been awarded a contract by the US Army to deliver prototypes of a new microwave weapon, dubbed Leonidas[18,19]. Unlike its laser counterparts, Leonidas is a master of adaptation and versatility. It can singularly target a drone or erect a microwave barricade against an onslaught of enemy swarms. It could even weave a protective shield over friendly skies, allowing our drones safe passage while neutralizing hostile ones sharing the same airspace.

Meanwhile, the US Air Force has taken impressive strides with its *Counter-Electronics High Power Microwave Advanced Missile Project* (CHAMP)[20,21]. Developed by Boeing's Phantom Works and successfully tested in 2012, these missiles carry the promise of a new era. CHAMP rides the skies not with a payload of explosives, but with a storm of microwaves, ready to strike down any form of electronics the enemy dares to deploy.

A subtler but no less impressive ability that futuristic microwave technology will allow, is through the phenomena known as the *microwave auditory effect*. Sometimes referred to as the *Frey effect*, this discovery was made by American neuroscientist Allan H. Frey in 1961[22,23].

While working on radar equipment, he inadvertently discovered that a pulsed or modulated microwave signal could be heard by certain people as a buzzing, clicking, hissing, or popping sound, even in the absence of any other detectable sound. Intrigued, Frey started to research this phenomenon, eventually concluding that the sounds were not due to any form of known biological anomaly or illness, but instead were an example of a new form of sound perception. This creates the perception of sound by affecting the central nervous system directly instead of the natural auditory pathway of vibrating air entering the ear canals[22].

The ability to induce sound perception remotely and without the target's knowledge offers a troubling avenue for exploitation. The possibility for harassment or psychological manipulation is self-evident, with malicious actors potentially using the technology to confuse, distract, or even intimidate individuals. Individuals who are unaware of the existence of such technology could truly believe that they are hearing God or a spiritual entity and carry out any task given to them.

Acoustics and Sonic Weaponry

The battlefield, traditionally associated with the clamor of gunfire and explosive blasts, might be due for a new kind of auditory experience. Sound, a fundamental and ubiquitous aspect of our environment, is being viewed through a fresh lens as technology advances—specifically as a potential weapon. Sonic weaponry, utilizing the power and properties of sound waves, promises to rewrite combat rules, presenting possibilities as intriguing as they are disquieting.

Most of us have experienced the discomfort caused by loud noises, but sonic weaponry takes this concept to an entirely new level. A prime example of this is known as the *Long Range Acoustic Device (LRAD)*[24]. Used by police and military forces for communication and crowd control, these devices emit powerful, directed sound waves.

One of the primary uses is to communicate messages

or sirens over long distances, piercing through ambient noise and allowing warnings or instructions to be issued effectively even in chaotic circumstances. There are US Navy ships outfitted with LRADs, and it allows them to communicate with vessels 3,000m (9,800 ft) away when radio communication fails or is unresponsive[25,26].

At higher power levels, this type of device can cause severe discomfort, disorientation, and even physical pain to those in their path. The human ear can typically stand a sound pressure level of 120 dB before feeling pain. LRADs are capable of producing 135 dB or more of acoustic energy[24].

At the high end of the sound spectrum are ultrasonic waves, with frequencies above the upper limit of human hearing. Despite their invisibility to our senses, ultrasonic waves can be concentrated and directed with precision. One potential military application of ultrasonics is through the use of sonic lasers, or *sasers*. Operating on similar principles as lasers but using sound waves, such devices could theoretically produce ultrasonic beams with the power to cause physical damage or incapacitation from a distance[33,34].

Another fascinating prospect is the possibility of using advanced sonic weaponry and acoustic technologies for new forms of indirect and psychological warfare.

Scientists are exploring the potential of using acoustic devices to create "sonic nets"[27,28]. These are zones of silenced audio, effectively blocking out communication channels or masking the sound of movements, adding a new layer of stealth in warfare.

Beyond the range of human hearing lies the domain of infrasound, sound waves with frequencies below 20 Hz. Despite being inaudible, these low-frequency vibrations can have significant physiological and psychological effects on humans[29,30]. Studies have linked exposure to infrasound to feelings of unease, fear, and even hallucinations[31,32]. Weaponizing this effect could result in a form of psychological warfare that undermines enemy morale and disrupts their cognitive functions without causing physical harm.

Chapter References

1. Engineering and Technology History Wiki. (2022, June 14). IEEE Milestone: First Working Laser, 1960. https://ethw.org/Milestones:First_Working_Laser,_1960

2. Gbur, G. J. (2020, April 28). A Brief History of Lasers: 60th anniversary of the laser. *Cambridge Blog*. http://www.cambridgeblog.org/2020/04/a-brief-history-of-lasers-60th-anniversary-of-the-laser/

3. Mizokami, K. (n.d.). The Army's Laser Weapon Is Finally Here: DE M-SHORAD, Explained. *Popular Mechanics*. https://www.popularmechanics.com/military/weapons/a45500360/army-first-laser-unit/

4. Morgan, R. (2022, April 15). Pics: US Navy laser shoots down cruise missile target for first time. *American Military News*. https://americanmilitarynews.com/2022/04/pics-us-navy-laser-shoots-down-cruise-missile-target-for-first-time/

5. LaGrone, S. (2014, December 10). U.S. Navy Allowed to Use Persian Gulf Laser for Defense. *USNI News*. https://news.usni.org/2014/12/10/u-s-navy-allowed-use-persian-gulf-laser-defense

6. Peach, M. (2014, December 10). US Navy ship-mounted 30kW laser weapon tested in Persian Gulf. *Optics.org*. https://optics.org/news/5/12/18

7. Lockheed Martin. (2021, January 9). More Than a Laser, HELIOS is an Integrated Weapon System. https://www.lockheedmartin.com/en-us/news/features/2021/more-than-a-laser-helios-is-an-integrated-weapon-system.html

8. Naval Technology. (n.d.). Lockheed Martin delivers first HELIOS weapon system to US Navy. https://www.naval-technology.com/news/lockheed-martin-helios-us-navy/

9. Tingley, B. (2021, July 12). Here's Our Best Look Yet At The Navy's New Laser Dazzler System. *The Drive*. https://www.thedrive.com/the-war-zone/41525/heres-our-best-look-yet-at-the-navys-new-laser-dazzler-system

10. Vavasseur, X. (2020, March 1). U.S. Navy Fits Destroyer with ODIN Laser Weapon to Counter Drones. *Naval News*. https://www.navalnews.com/naval-news/2020/03/u-s-navy-fits-destroyer-with-odin-laser-weapon-to-counter-drones/

11. U.S. Army. (2015, September 9). The Army High-Energy Laser Mobile Demonstrator. https://www.army.mil/standto/archive/2015/09/09/

12. Boeing. (Date not provided). Boeing, US Army demonstrate high energy laser in maritime environments. *Army Technology.* https://www.army-technology.com/news/newsboeing-us-army-demonstrate-high-energy-laser-in-maritime-environments-4363299/

13. Bisht, I. S. (2022, July 12). Lockheed delivers first jet-mounted laser weapon to USAF. *The Defense Post.* https://www.thedefensepost.com/2022/07/12/lockheed-jet-mounted-laser-weapon/

14. Airforce-Technology.com. (n.d.). Agents of SHiELD – the US Air Force's new aircraft-mounted laser weapon. *Airforce Technology.* https://www.airforce-technology.com/features/agents-shield-us-air-forces-new-aircraft-mounted-laser-weapon/

15. Tucker, P. (2019, March 14). Pentagon Wants to Test A Space-Based Weapon in 2023. *Defense One.* https://www.defenseone.com/technology/2019/03/pentagon-wants-test-space-based-weapon-2023/155581/

16. Joint Intermediate Force Capabilities Office. (n.d.). Active Denial System FAQs. https://jnlwp.defense.gov/About/Frequently-Asked-Questions/Active-Denial-System-FAQs/

17. Paleja, A. (2021, October 4). US Military's 'Active Denial System' Is a 95 GHz Heat Ray. *Interesting Engineering.* https://interestingengineering.com/innovation/us-militarys-active-denial-system-is-a-95-ghz-heat-ray

18. Epirus, Inc. (2022). Leonidas High-Power Microwave (HPM) System, USA. *Army Technology.* https://www.army-technology.com/projects/leonidas-high-power-microwave-hpm-system-usa/

19. Saballa, J. (2023, January 24). US Army Buys Directed Energy Weapon System to Counter Drone Swarms. *The Defense Post.* https://www.thedefensepost.com/2023/01/24/epirus-counter-drone-microwave/

20. Air Force Technology. (2012, October 22). USAF's CHAMP missile completes first weapons test flight. https://www.airforce-technology.com/news/newsusaf-champ-missile/

21. Toor, A. (2012, October 24). Boeing's CHAMP missile uses radio waves to remotely disable PCs. *The Verge.* https://www.theverge.com/2012/10/24/3546690/boeing-us-air-force-champ-missile-test-launch

22. Foster, K. R., Garrett, D. C., & Ziskin, M. C. (2021). Can the Microwave Auditory Effect Be "Weaponized"? *Frontiers in Public Health*, 9. https://doi.org/10.3389/fpubh.2021.788613

23. Hahn AI. (n.d.). Microwave Auditory Effect: The Science Behind Sound Perception. https://hahn.ai/blog/blog41.html

24. Acentech. (2020, August 10). Long Range Acoustic Devices (LRAD) and Public Safety. *Acentech*. https://www.acentech.com/resources/long-range-acoustic-devices-lrad-and-public-safety/

25. Defenshield. (n.d.). LRAD 500X™ - Long Range Acoustic Devices. https://defenshield.com/product/lrad-500x/

26. Naval Technology. (2013, June 16). US Navy orders long-range acoustic devices. https://www.naval-technology.com/news/newsus-navy-orders-long-range-acoustic-devices/

27. Swaddle, J. P., Moseley, D. L., Hinders, M. H., & Smith, E. P. (2016). A Sonic Net Excludes Birds from an Airfield: Implications for Reducing Bird Strike and Crop Losses. *William & Mary*. https://jpswad.people.wm.edu/Swaddle_et_al-2016-Ecological_Applications.pdf

28. Loughran, J. (2016, May 6). Sonic nets installed in airfields shown to prevent bird collisions. *Engineering & Technology (E&T)*. https://eandt.theiet.org/content/articles/2016/05/sonic-nets-installed-in-airfields-shown-to-prevent-bird-collisions/

29. Mühlhans, J. H. (2017). Low frequency and infrasound: A critical review of the myths, misbeliefs and their relevance to music perception research. *Musicae Scientiae*, 21(3), 267-286. https://doi.org/10.1177/1029864917690931

30. Traynor, R. (2015, March 4). Sonic Warfare: Noise as a Weapon. *Hearing International*. https://hearinghealthmatters.org/hearing-international/2015/sonic-warfare-noise-as-a-weapon/

31. Jauchem, J. R., & Cook, M. C. (2007). High-Intensity Acoustics for Military Nonlethal Applications: A Lack of Useful Systems. *Military Medicine*, 172(2), 182–189. https://doi.org/10.7205/MILMED.172.2.182

32. English, L. (2016, October 9). The Sound of Fear: The history of noise as a weapon. *FACT Magazine*. https://www.factmag.com/2016/10/09/sound-fear-room40-boss-lawrence-english-history-noise-weapon/

33. Fox, S. (2009, June 19). Saser: The Sonic Laser. *Popular Science*. https://www.popsci.com/scitech/article/2009-06/saser-sonic-laser/

34. Live Science Staff. (2022, October 14). Sasers: Sound-based Lasers Invented. *Live Science*. https://www.livescience.com/3705-sasers-sound-based-lasers-invented.html

Scalar Technologies

The term *scalar field* might sound arcane, but it is a common concept in physics[1,2]. Temperature distribution in a room, for example, can be described as a scalar field. At every point in the room, there is a temperature value, a scalar, that changes in space. Scalar fields contrast with vector fields, which have both a magnitude and a direction at every point, like the velocity of the wind in the atmosphere.

In physics, there is a concept known as a *scalar potential*[3]. You can visualize the scalar potential as a landscape of hills and valleys, where the height of the land at any point represents the scalar potential at that point. When an object sits on a tall hill, it has more potential to speed down quickly, therefore it has more "potential energy" because of the height of the hill. Similarly, in physics a scalar potential tells us about the "potential energy" at different points in space.

Because of quantum mechanics, even empty space, devoid of any visible objects or forces, still has scalar potential energy[4]. This is what is sometimes referred to as *zero-point energy* or *vacuum energy*. Developing technologies involving the manipulation and utilization of this scalar potential energy would lead to amazing capabilities beyond our current expectations.

Why would these technologies be so groundbreaking? In order to understand these possibilities, it's important to understand what is called the scalar *Aharonov-Bohm effect*. The Aharonov-Bohm effect is a fascinating phenomenon in quantum mechanics. Proposed by Yakir Aharonov and David Bohm in 1959, this effect challenges our conventional understanding of physics, emphasizing the role of electromagnetic potentials in quantum systems[5]. Classical physics asserted that charged particles were influenced solely by electric and magnetic fields, not potentials. However, Aharonov and Bohm theorized that these potentials had a direct impact on the phase of a particle's wave function, a fundamental aspect of its quantum behavior. The confirmation of the Aharonov-Bohm effect had profound implications for our understanding of quantum mechanics and the role of potentials[6,7]. It highlighted that potentials are not just mathematical tools, but have physical reality and can influence particles even in regions where the associated fields are zero[8,9]. In simpler terms, the Aharonov-Bohm effect says that the scalar potential can change the way a particle moves, even when it is not touching or interacting with the particle directly[6,7].

So what would technologies that harness scalar potential energies entail? For one, it would mean being able to harness energy from a power source that is available literally everywhere and never runs out[10]. It could result in achieving the dream of infinite energy for everyone. It could also mean wireless power transmission, new types of superweapons, and new forms of propulsion magnitudes beyond in capability to anything we have[10,12]. Although this type of technology seems like fantasy, it has been theorized for over 100 years. *Scalar energy* was first proposed by James Clerk Maxwell in the mid 1800's and was later refined by a Yugoslavian immigrant called Nikola Tesla[11,17].

Wireless Energy Transfer & Instantaneous Communication

"The present is theirs; the future, for which I really worked is mine."

   -Nikola Tesla

One of the most brilliant inventors and visionaries of his time, Nikola Tesla was a man who envisioned a world powered by limitless energy, instant communication across distances, and remarkable technological advancements[15]. His inventive mind left an indelible mark on our society, his contributions paving the way to our present modern civilization[13,14]. If you are reading this book and don't know who Nikola Tesla is, just know that without him we wouldn't have the following: radio, television, AC electricity, fluorescent lighting, neon lighting, radar, microwaves, and X-rays[13,14].

In 1899, Nikola Tesla received $100,000 from John Jacob Astor to develop a new lighting system, but instead used the funds to establish a high voltage and high frequency lab on a remote hillside in Colorado Springs[19]. Though he operated the lab for less than a year, it was here that he had his major breakthroughs that hardened his theories about long-distance wireless energy transmission using his *magnifying transmitter*[18]. The magnifying transmitter, an advanced form of a *Tesla coil*, generated scalar potential waves with a longitudinal electrical field and resonated with the natural frequencies of the Earth, creating standing waves of electrical energy that could be harnessed elsewhere[27,28]. He produced artificial lightning at the lab, with millions of volts, arcing over more than 100 feet of open space[20]. He also energized the Earth, and lit light bulbs up to 26 miles away from his lab, proving that the ground, as well as the air, could be used as a conductor[21,22]. With a 200 ft pole topped by a large copper sphere rising above his laboratory he generated potentials that discharged lightning bolts up to 135 feet long. People walking along the streets would see sparks jumping between their feet and the ground[22]. Horses at the livery stable would receive shocks through their metal shoes and bolt from the stalls[22].

Eventually his high draws of energy destroyed the local power station, six miles away, putting an end to his experiments there[22]. He returned to New York, and the Colorado Springs lab remained, but was eventually torn down in 1904, and its contents sold[23].

On February 19, 1900, Nikola Tesla filed patent *No. 649,921* for his *Apparatus for Transmission of Electrical Energy*[24]. Over a year after, Tesla began construction of his most ambitious project. Nestled within the scenic landscape of Shoreham, Long Island, an imposing wooden structure stood that reached approximately 187 feet in height, crowned with a 68-foot copper dome[25]. Beneath the ground, a network of iron pipes plunged 120 feet below the surface, forming an essential part of the tower's operations. This was the *Wardenclyffe Tower*, Tesla's grand vision of free electricity to the world, a concept far ahead of its time[15,16]. An intriguing blend of technological innovation and unbridled ambition, the story of the Wardenclyffe Tower offers a captivating glimpse into Tesla's extraordinary dream of a world where wires and powerlines are a thing of the past.

Tesla's vision didn't stop at wireless power transmission. He also believed that the Wardenclyffe Tower could act as a global communication hub[16]. Tesla believed the Earth itself could be used as a conductor. By utilizing the Earth's natural resonant frequency, a form of vibration that Tesla theorized the Earth naturally produced, he intended to send communication signals to any corner of the globe instantaneously[26]. It was a vision of a globally connected world in an age when even landline telephones were a luxury.

Unfortunately, the tower was never completed. Nikola Tesla lost funding for the project, and was forced to abandon it[29]. However, his work continues to inspire and influence society today.

There is an existing patent for a device that generates and/or utilizes scalar-longitudinal waves[40]. This device, described in patent *no. 9,306,527* outlines the applications with such a device. These include passive imaging of a living organism based on gradient-driven current across cellular membranes, enhancing a decay rate of a radioactive material, enhancing a fusion rate reaction to produce heat and/or electrical power, communication through water and ground, and reception of solar-generated scalar-longitudinal waves to produce electrical power[40].

Resonant inductive coupling is another modern technology implemented using Tesla's foundational work on wireless energy transmission[30]. Resonant inductive coupling uses tuned magnetic coils to wirelessly transfer power. The principle is simple, yet powerful: two coils, each tuned to the same natural frequency, can exchange energy efficiently through the medium of a magnetic field. This method echoes Nikola Tesla's century-old dream of wireless power transmission.

In a future, where wireless energy transmission is mastered, all of our technologies will benefit. Ditching all the wires and power cables will make technology not only a lot more reliable and durable, but a lot more aesthetic and safer as well. Many building fires for example, are started when rats chew through electrical wiring and cause short circuits. Also, power cables that run through trees can get worn down over time, eventually causing short circuits.

Undoubtedly almost every vision of the future comes with people driving around in flying cars. Wireless energy transmission could bring a future where vehicles aren't self-powered anymore. No more need for complicated combustion engines or needing to re-fuel. By leveraging beams of energy from ground stations, our future flying vehicles can recharge on the fly, ensuring a much safer vehicle that will require a lot less maintenance. This same principle could also power logistical vehicles that would bring a new level of efficiency and speed in the transport of goods.

Although the wireless charging pads we use for our phones might seem amazing enough, in the future, you might never even need to charge your phone altogether. It might not even have a battery; instead it would just pull energy wirelessly as needed. These devices would also be thin as paper while still being flexible and durable because they would no longer require a bulky battery or complicated cabling.

Not limited to small devices or vehicles, wireless power transmission will be able to power distant settlements and cities. Even the most remote island will be able to have as much energy as it needs, all without going through the fiscal and logistical challenge of running undersea power cables to the island. They would be free from the need of consistent shipments of fuel, which is the sole lifeline for many remote outposts and settlements.

Scalar Weapons

On January 7, 1943, at the height of WWII, Nikola Tesla was found dead in his New York hotel at the age of 86[31]. His nephew, Sava Kosanović, went to the room the next day, and claimed that certain key possessions of Tesla had been taken—namely, "technical papers" and a black notebook containing notes on some kind of government work[31,32]. The bureau was concerned that he might turn over such coveted information to the "enemy", so the following day the Office of Alien Property Custodian confiscated all of Tesla's items, which amounted to "two truckloads"[31]. What causes additional controversy is the fact that Tesla was a US citizen and it is incomprehensible why the Department of Justice's Alien Asset Custody Office could even be authorized to take over Tesla's assets and have jurisdiction at that time. Coincidentally, just before his death, Tesla announced he has perfected his "teleforce" invention. Tesla teased his "teleforce" weapon for decades, saying it could shoot down airplanes from 250 miles away[33]. The press at the time thought this wasn't a captivating enough name and re-named it to the "death ray"[33,34].

To this day Tesla's papers on his "death ray" remain classified. However, some declassified papers have been released showcasing scalar wave technology being weaponized. One of these claimed that the soviets had scalar wave weapons by utilizing *scalar wave interferometry*[35].

The term "interferometry" is borrowed from the field of optics, where it traditionally refers to the process of overlapping two or more light waves to measure their phase differences and produce an interference pattern[36]. This principle allows precise measurements in a range of scientific and technical applications, from astronomy to quantum mechanics. When applied to scalar energy, the theory suggests that two scalar longitudinal waves can overlap and interfere with each other[35,37]. Because of the Aharonov-Bohm effect, it is proposed that scalar wave interferometry can manipulate electromagnetic fields at a distance instantaneously[35].

How is this possible? It's built off of Tesla's idea for wireless and lossless energy transfer at a distance instantly[35]. These "waves" of scalar energy don't "travel" in the classical sense of going from point A to point B, this is because scalar waves are pure longitudinal waves of compression and rarefaction of the vacuum itself[35]. This "locked-in stress energy" of the vacuum is available literally everywhere[35]. By using the quantum phenomena shown in the Aharonov-Bohm effect, it's analogous to "putting energy here" and "extracting it out there"[35].

These effects of such technologies range from minor influences on people's consciousness to major destruction that rivals and even surpasses the power of atomic weapons[35].

These system would be able to produce enormous amounts of energy at a desired location, which would result in an explosion not unlike an explosion from an atomic bomb. In contrast, instead of teleporting large amounts of energy to an area, these systems could theoretically also extract energy from an area, with the result being a "cold bomb" that would freeze an area instantaneously[35].

Likewise, these scalar interferometer systems could be used with microwaves. This would create an EMP at the target location that would fry any electronics in the area.

Although horrifyingly destructive, these scalar wave weapons could be extremely effective for defense as well.

Theoretically these scalar wave systems could be used to form an impenetrable force field[35]. This could be the ultimate missile defense system. Even hypersonic nuclear missiles, feared because their speed makes them almost impossible to intercept, would be rendered useless.

In a more insidious form, these systems could be used in what is referred to as *psychoenergetics*. The human brain works using electricity and different wave frequencies. Brain waves are classified into several distinct categories based on their frequencies. Each category corresponds to a different state of consciousness, from deep sleep to heightened alertness. These brain waves include delta, theta, alpha, beta, and gamma waves.

Scientific experiments decades ago verified that the mind is scalar in nature, and that these scalar systems could theoretically be used to manipulate and influence these waves, causing a direct effect on human consciousness and behavior[41]. These effects could be malevolent or benevolent. On one hand, these could cause calm feelings or even euphoria. On the other hand, they could be used to cause negative emotions. With increased levels of power, this form of scalar weaponry could cause unconsciousness and/or death to beings within a target area without leaving behind any physical signs[42].

Future conflicts with the existence of such weapon systems will be much less theatrical and much more calculated and unsettling in their efficiency. Gone will the days where the default option was to rely on explosive ordnance which is costly, unpredictable, and often yielding chaotic results.

Scalar systems offer precision previously undreamed of. Need to incapacitate a hostile force's electronics without causing a single human casualty? it is possible. Conversely, should the objective be to neutralize combatants without so much as scratching the infrastructure? Scalar systems can achieve that too.

The age-old dilemma, where an attack on weaponry might unintentionally harm civilians, or targeting combatants could inadvertently destroy vital infrastructure, would seem archaic. Scalar systems promise a future of warfare defined not by its indiscriminate destruction, but by its chilling precision.

The applications don't stop there, it's postulated that scalar wave interferometry could be utilized to interfere with the Earth's magnetic fields, generating disturbances capable of affecting weather patterns[12]. For instance, by creating an area of high energy density in the atmosphere, this could theoretically heat the air, causing it to expand and create a low-pressure system. This low-pressure system would attract air from surrounding high-pressure areas, stirring winds and potentially fostering storm systems and tornados.

The theory would propose that by creating zones of intense heat (low pressure) and cold (high pressure) in the atmosphere, the necessary instability could be induced. The heat would cause the air to rise rapidly, while the cold air would sink, setting up a powerful convection current. If these pressure differentials could be arranged in a particular pattern, perhaps it could induce the required wind shear, causing the air to rotate and potentially triggering a tornado.

This also includes the ability to induce an earthquake by building up energy in a specific location beneath the Earth's surface[35]. This could be akin to adding energy to a system that's already in a delicate equilibrium. Eventually, this addition of energy might disturb the equilibrium enough to cause the Earth's crust to slip along a fault line, triggering an earthquake.

Anti-gravity and Field Propulsion

In the ever-evolving landscape of human innovation, the emergence of scalar wave systems would cast a shadow of awe and trepidation. These formidable tools have the duality of a double-edged sword. On one side, they harbor the potential for profound malevolence, capable of reshaping the theater of warfare in ways we can scarcely imagine.

Yet, it is the other edge of this blade that truly captivates the spirit of human endeavor. Scalar technology systems, when harnessed for benevolent purposes, might very well be the key that unlocks our terrestrial bounds. Rather than being confined to the Earth, this groundbreaking technology holds the promise of expanding our horizons, liberating humanity to reach further, dream bigger, and find new homes among the stars.

Scientists have already discovered that the Aharonov-Bohm effect also applies to gravity[6]. It has also been noted that scalar interferometer systems can be used to create an inertial field, or in other words, anti-gravity[35].

This idea again goes back to the pioneering work of Nikola Tesla. Before his death at a conference on May 12, 1938, Tesla discussed a "space drive"[43,44]. He also talked about his theory of gravity, a form of unified field theory.

Simply put, this theory proposes that gravity, electricity, and magnetism are all tied together[45,46]. It's an elegant theory that postulates that these forces are different forms from a single underlying foundational field. Much like how water, ice, and vapor are different forms of water, electricity, magnetism, and gravity are different states from one underlying field, which he referred to as the aether or ether.

If we consider the possibility that gravity is a distinct field, parallel in essence to the forces of electricity and magnetism, the implications are colossal. It invites us to reimagine gravity as something that can be created and manipulated, just like electric and magnetic fields.

Understanding of this theory could be used to generate gravitational fields. Think of it as lighting a beacon in the depths of the cosmos, creating an artificial gravity well that could pull a spaceship towards a distant star or galaxy.

Imagine a spacecraft outfitted with an apparatus capable of influencing this superpotential field with laser-like precision. It would initiate the sequence by aiming these waves in the desired direction of travel. Forming a gravitational field at a certain point in space, the spacecraft would start to "fall" into this newly created gravity well.

In this scenario, space travel is less about propulsion

and more about attraction. There would be no need for powerful rocket engines to fight against the Earth's gravity or to propel the ship across the vast emptiness of space. Instead, the ship would follow the pull of the artificially created gravitational field. As the spacecraft falls into the field, it could continuously adjust the location of the gravitational point, maintaining a perpetual free fall towards its destination, drawn ever onward by the pull of the artificial gravity well.

Chapter References

1. Siegel, E. (2021, March 19). Ask Ethan: What Is A Scalar Field? *Forbes*. https://www.forbes.com/sites/startswithabang/2021/03/19/ask-ethan-what-is-a-scalar-field/

2. Akin, J. E. (2005). Scalar fields. In J. E. Akin (Ed.), *Finite Element Analysis with Error Estimators* (pp. 281-383). Butterworth-Heinemann. https://doi.org/10.1016/B978-075066722-7/50042-4.

3. Arfken, G. B., Griffing, D. F., Kelly, D. C., & Priest, J. (1984). Electric potential. In G. B. Arfken, D. F. Griffing, D. C. Kelly, & J. Priest (Eds.), *International Edition University Physics* (pp. 514-534). Academic Press. https://doi.org/10.1016/B978-0-12-059858-8.50033-9

4. Scientific American. (1997, August 18). FOLLOW-UP: What is the 'zero-point energy' (or 'vacuum energy') in quantum physics? Is it really possible that we could harness this energy? https://www.scientificamerican.com/article/follow-up-what-is-the-zer/

5. Imry, Y., & Webb, R. A. (1989). Quantum Interference and the Aharonov-Bohm Effect. *Scientific American, 260*(4), 56–65. http://www.jstor.org/stable/24987212

6. Conover, E. (2022, January 13). An eerie quantum effect of magnetic fields also applies to gravity. *Science News*. https://www.sciencenews.org/article/quantum-particles-gravity-spacetime-aharonov-bohm-effect

7. Lindley, D. (2011, July 22). Landmarks: Ghostly Influence of Distant Magnetic Field. *Physics*. https://physics.aps.org/story/v28/st4

8. Allman, B. E., Cimmino, A., Klein, A. G., Opat, G. I., Kaiser, H., & Werner, S. A. (1992). Scalar Aharonov-Bohm experiment with neutrons. *Physical Review Letters*, 68(16), 2409-2412. https://link.aps.org/doi/10.1103/PhysRevLett.68.2409

9. Allman, B. E., Cimmino, A., Klein, A. G., Opat, G. I., Kaiser, H., & Werner, S. A. (1993). Observation of the scalar Aharonov-Bohm effect by neutron interferometry. *Physical Review A*, 48(3), 1799-1807. https://link.aps.org/doi/10.1103/PhysRevA.48.1799

10. Reed, D. (2019). Unravelling the potentials puzzle and corresponding case for the scalar longitudinal electrodynamic wave. *Journal of Physics: Conference Series*, 1251(1), 012043. https://dx.doi.org/10.1088/1742-6596/1251/1/012043

11. Eyges, Leonard (1972). *The Classical Electromagnetic Field*. New York: Dover. ISBN 9780486639475

12. Bearden, T. E. (2005). Scalar electromagnetic weapons and their terrorist use: Strategic aspects of the asymmetric war on the US. *World Affairs: The Journal of International Issues*, 9(4), 58–85. https://www.jstor.org/stable/48531830

13. Learnodo Newtonic. (n.d.). Nikola Tesla's 10 major contributions and accomplishments. https://learnodo-newtonic.com/nikola-tesla-contributions

14. Tesla Science Center at Wardenclyffe. (n.d.). Nikola Tesla inventions. https://teslasciencecenter.org/nikola-tesla-inventions/

15. Tesla Science Center at Wardenclyffe. (n.d.). Tesla's wireless power. https://teslasciencecenter.org/teslas-wireless-power/

16. Tesla Science Center at Wardenclyffe. (n.d.). The Tower. https://teslasciencecenter.org/history/tower/

17. Adachi, K. (2003, April). Radiant energy - Unraveling Nikola Tesla's greatest secret. *ExtraOrdinary Technology*, 23-26. https://teslauniverse.com/nikola-tesla/articles/radiant-energy-unraveling-nikola-teslas-greatest-secret

18. Bakshi, S. (2022, March 9). Magnifying transmitter - An electrical Tesla coil. *Voltage Lab*. https://www.voltagelab.com/magnifying-transmitter/

19. Center for Land Use Interpretation. (n.d.). Tesla's Colorado Springs Lab Site, Colorado. https://clui.org/ludb/site/teslas-colorado-springs-lab-site

20. Perreault, B. A. (2020, May 12). Nikola Tesla Free Energy: Unraveling Greatest Secret. *NuEnergy*. https://www.nuenergy.org/nikola-tesla-radiant-energy-system/

21. Denver Gazette. (n.d.). LOOKING BACK: How Tesla's experiments plunged one Colorado city into darkness. https://denvergazette.com/outtherecolorado/features/looking-back-how-teslas-experiments-plunged-one-colorado-city-into-darkness/article_10a9c9ec-987a-5eb2-a176-beab06fd91d4.html

22. Patowary, K. (2020, August 4). Nikola Tesla's experimental laboratory in Colorado Springs. *Amusing Planet*. https://www.amusingplanet.com/2020/08/nikola-teslas-experimental-laboratory.html

23. Tesla Universe. (n.d.). June, 1904 - Colorado Springs Lab Torn Down - Nikola Tesla Colorado Springs Timeline. https://teslauniverse.com/nikola-tesla/timeline/colorado-springs/19040600-colorado-springs-lab-torn-down

24. Bieberich, J. (n.d.). The complete Nikola Tesla U.S. patent collection - Grant date listing. *Massachusetts Institute of Technology.* http://web.mit.edu/most/Public/Tesla1/grant_tesla.html

25. Atlas Obscura. (n.d.). Tesla's Wardenclyffe Laboratory – Shoreham, New York. https://www.atlasobscura.com/places/tesla-s-wardenclyffe-laboratory

26. Open Tesla Research. (n.d.). Earth Resonance. https://teslaresearch.jimdofree.com/wardenclyffe-lab-1901-1906/connection-to-earth/earth-resonance/

27. Csanyi, E. (2011, May 11). Magnifying transmitter – Nikola Tesla. *Electrical Engineering Portal.* https://electrical-engineering-portal.com/magnifying-transmitter-nikola-tesla

28. Nedic, Slobodan. (2016). Longitudinal Waves in Electromagnetism: Towards Consistent Framework for Tesla's Energy and Information Transmission, along w/ Energy Harvesting. https://www.researchgate.net/publication/339747101_Longitudinal_Waves_in_Electromagnetism_Towards_Consistent_Framework_for_Tesla's_Energy_and_Information_Transmission_along_w_Energy_Harvesting

29. Tesla Science Center at Wardenclyffe. (n.d.). The Journey. https://teslasciencecenter.org/history/journey/

30. Das Barman, S., Reza, A. W., Kumar, N., Karim, M. E., & Munir, A. B. (2015). Wireless powering by magnetic resonant coupling: Recent trends in wireless power transfer system and its applications. *Renewable and Sustainable Energy Reviews*, 51, 1525-1552. https://doi.org/10.1016/j.rser.2015.07.031

31. Coulon, J. (n.d.). Did the U.S. Government Steal Nikola Tesla's Research Papers? *Popular Mechanics.* https://www.popularmechanics.com/science/energy/a44197280/did-the-us-government-steal-nikola-teslas-research/

32. Pruitt, S. (2018, May 3). The FBI has finally declassified its files on Nikola Tesla, but questions remain. *History.* https://www.history.com/news/nikola-tesla-files-declassified-fbi

33. Kean, S. (2020, October 6). The Undying Appeal of Nikola Tesla's "Death Ray". *Science History Institute.* https://www.sciencehistory.org/

stories/magazine/the-undying-appeal-of-nikola-teslas-death-ray

34. All That's Interesting. (2021, October 16). The Baffling Mystery Of The Nikola Tesla's Death Ray. *All That's Interesting*. https://allthatsinteresting.com/tesla-death-ray

35. Bearden, T. E. (1984). STAR WARS NOW! The Bohm-Aharonov Effect, Scalar Interferometry, and Soviet Weaponization. https://www.cia.gov/readingroom/docs/CIA-RDP96-00788R001900680014-4.pdf

36. Zygo Corporation. (n.d.). Interferometry: Measuring with Light. *Photonics Media*. https://www.photonics.com/Articles/Interferometry_Measuring_with_Light/a25128

37. Reed, D., & Hively, L. M. (2020). Implications of gauge-free extended electrodynamics. *Symmetry*, 12(12), 2110. https://doi.org/10.3390/sym12122110

38. Hegerfeldt, G.C., & Neumann, J.T. (2008). The Aharonov–Bohm effect: the role of tunneling and associated forces. *Journal of Physics A: Mathematical and Theoretical*, 41, 155305. https://www.semanticscholar.org/paper/The-Aharonov%E2%80%93Bohm-effect%3A-the-role-of-tunneling-and-Hegerfeldt-Neumann/4884b4c06ce4fb0a0f05051b9f2e8e4c16545353

39. Lai, W., Xing, Y., & Ma, Z. (2013). Dephasing of electrons in the Aharonov–Bohm interferometer with a single-molecular vibrational junction. *Journal of Physics: Condensed Matter*, 25(20), 205304. https://dx.doi.org/10.1088/0953-8984/25/20/205304

40. Hively, L. M. (2016). Systems, apparatuses, and methods for generating and/or utilizing scalar-longitudinal waves (United States Patent No. 9,306,527). https://patents.google.com/patent/US9306527B1/en

41. Byrd, E. (2021, July 1). Scalar Technologies - Eldon Byrd. *United States Psychotronics Association*. https://www.psychotronics.org/scalar-technologies-by-eldon-byrd-a-masterclass-on-scalar-waves/

42. Verismo, C. (2016, July 19). 12 Things You Should Know About Scalar Weapons. *Stillness in the Storm*. https://stillnessinthestorm.com/2016/07/12-Things-You-Should-Know-About-Scalar-Weapons/

43. Csanyi, E. (2013, February 6). Did Tesla Discover the Secrets of Antigravity? *Electrical Engineering Portal*. https://electrical-engineering-portal.com/did-tesla-discover-the-secrets-of-antigravity

44. Piacenza, G. (2015, November 29). Scalar waves: What might

they be? Are they in our technological future? *ExoNews*. https://exonews. org/scalar-waves-what-might-they-be/

45. Rovayo, A. (2020, November 11). Nikola Tesla: Dynamic theory of gravity. An Idea (by Ingenious Piece). *Medium*. https://medium.com/an-idea/nikola-tesla-dynamic-theory-of-gravity-9db68097db64

46. Nedic, Slobodan. (2015). Thermo-Gravitational Oscillator and Tesla's Energy Source Ether. https://www.researchgate.net/publication/280304207_Thermo-Gravitational_Oscillator_and_Tesla's_Energy_Source_Ether

Nanotechnology

The genesis of nanotechnology dates back to a prophetic lecture delivered in 1959 by renowned physicist Richard Feynman. In *There's Plenty of Room at the Bottom*, Feynman's address pondered the potential of manipulating and controlling things on a small scale[1,2]. He speculated that it would be possible to write the entire *Encyclopedia Britannica* on the head of a pin and proposed machines small enough to "swallow the doctor," foreshadowing the rise of medical nanobots.

But Feynman's visionary talk remained more science fiction than science fact until the development of the *scanning tunneling microscope (STM)* in 1981 by Gerd Binnig and Heinrich Rohrer[3,4]. The STM, which allowed scientists to see atoms for the first time, was a watershed moment for nanotechnology. It opened the door to the world of the infinitesimally small and provided researchers with a tool to not just observe but also manipulate individual atoms.

Since then, nanotechnology has evolved from a nascent scientific discipline into a field that influences many areas of our lives. Today, it has become an interdisciplinary field involving physics, chemistry, biology, materials science, and engineering.

In the healthcare sector, *nanoparticles* are being utilized for targeted drug delivery[5], which could revolutionize cancer treatment by delivering potent drugs directly to the tumor while sparing healthy cells. Nano-sized biosensors are being developed for early disease detection, and research is being conducted to use nanotechnology for tissue regeneration and to halt aging processes[6].

Meanwhile, in energy, nanotechnology has significantly enhanced the efficiency of solar cells, potentially making renewable energy more feasible on a large scale[7,8]. It also shows promise in enhancing battery capacity and lifespan[9].

Despite these advancements, nanotechnology is still very much a frontier field. The possibilities are vast, but so are the challenges. Creating structures and machines at such a small scale is a monumental task. There are also concerns about the environmental and health impact of nanoparticles. Although there is still much innovation that needs to be made to reach Feynman's visions of nano-robots manipulating matter atom by atom, we have made progress with the introduction of *molecular machines*, which earned Jean-Pierre Sauvage, Sir Fraser Stoddart, and Bernard L. Feringa a Nobel Prize in 2016[10,11,12].

Improving nanotechnology will culminate in awe-inspiring and terrifying abilities that have not been seen since the detonating of the first atomic bombs. These advancements, as they converge, will be so revolutionary and all-powerful that they will be indistinguishable from magic. Everything from computing and construction, to medicine and warfare will be redefined.

Nanoelectronics

In our present day, our electronic and computer components seem to be small enough already. The *M2* chip by Apple for example, contains 20 billion transistors, all in a processor that's around the size of a thumbnail[13]. If our electronics keep improving and getting smaller at the same pace, where does it lead? It leads to the domain of nanoelectronics. Emerging at the intersection of nanotechnology and electronics, nanoelectronics is the domain of electrical engineering that works with components and structures at the nanoscale, that's one-billionth of a meter. It is a field that promises to redefine the fabric of our electronic devices and has profound implications for the future of computing, communication, energy harvesting, and sensing technologies.

To understand the current state of nanoelectronics, we must first tip our hat to the traditional, silicon-based semiconductor industry. For decades, engineers have been religiously following *Moore's Law*. This was a prediction made by Gordon Moore in 1965 that the number of transistors on a chip will double approximately every two years[14,15]. This principle has guided us through the era of microelectronics, shrinking our transistors and electronic components to a level previously unimaginable. Yet, as we reach the limits of silicon and the physical barriers of the quantum realm, we look to nanoelectronics to continue our pursuit of miniaturization and increased performance.

Scientists are now striving to use single molecules as electronic components, creating the ultimate miniature circuits[16,17,18]. Imagine the power of a modern supercomputer that can fit in the palm of your hand. It may sound like science fiction, but research in this field is steadily progressing, with scientists having already created single molecule transistors and diodes. IBM has already demonstrated the possibility of storing data on a single atom[19,20,21]. In a 2017 experiment, IBM scientists stored one bit of data on a single holmium atom. When considering the number of atoms on a typical hard drive today, atomic-scale storage would represent an astronomical increase in potential data density. Future smartphones and personal computers might hold petabytes of data, effectively providing users with what seems like infinite storage. Recently, scientists at Delft University in the Netherlands developed an atomic-scale "hard drive" that can store the entire U.S. Library of Congress on a 0.1mm wide cube, demonstrating the massive storage capacity that atomic-scale memory can offer[22].

Nanoengines

Another exciting result in the future of nanotechnology will be the development of *nanoengines*, which could revolutionize energy production and ultimately unlock an almost infinite power source. Nanoengines, as their name suggests, are infinitesimal machines designed to convert energy into motion at a molecular or atomic scale[23,24,25]. The principle is not far removed from a traditional internal combustion engine, which transforms chemical energy into mechanical power. But when scaled down to nanometers, or billionths of a meter, these tiny engines operate under the unique rules of quantum physics, opening up a host of unprecedented possibilities.

Nanoengines, with their negligible size and weight, generate energy remarkably efficiently, opening the way to potentially boundless energy applications. A key concept underpinning the power of nanoengines is Brownian motion. This is the random movement of particles in a fluid due to their collisions with other particles. Some researchers have developed nanoengines that convert this omnipresent thermal motion into directed movement, effectively utilizing heat waste as a power source[24,26]. This concept is revolutionary, as it breaks the traditional confines of energy production and points towards an incredibly efficient, and nearly limitless, energy source.

Furthermore, nanoengines can be engineered to respond to various stimuli, like light, heat, or chemical reactions[26]. This adaptability opens up a myriad of application possibilities.

The power of nanoengines lies not only in their energy production capabilities, but also in their potential to exploit the constant, untapped energy sources surrounding us. Imagine a world where your smartphone never needs charging because it is powered by the heat in your pocket or the light from the room, or where electric cars draw their power from the very asphalt they drive on. These nanoengines could also be used as the power source for nanobots, an important step towards unlocking the full and impressive potential of nanorobotics[27,28,29].

Nanorobotics

Advances in nanotechnology such as nanoengines and nano-computing will lead to *nanobots* or *nanorobots*, these are nano-sized robots capable of modifying matter atom by atom[30,31,32]. The implications and possibilities are limited only by our imagination. The possibilities with such technology will start to look more like magic than science.

With the dexterity of these nanobots, objects and structures could materialize before our very eyes, seemingly conjured from the ether. Picture a world where a damaged structure self-repairs, where a broken device mends itself, or where medicine is delivered to the precise cell it needs to target, all thanks to these atomic architects.

A colossal construction site brimming with bulky cranes, excavators, and a hive of busy construction workers would become a relic of the past. The construction workers are no longer dressed in their trademark hard hats, and the force of the grinding machinery is replaced with an eerie, tranquil silence. The center of this silence, and the new architects of our world, are an army of nanobots invisible to the naked eye.

Nanobots, microscopic robots that could be as small as a few atoms in size, will be the new geniuses of engineering, seamlessly constructing our homes, bridges, and skyscrapers. They will be able to work from the atomic level upwards to create structures with an unparalleled level of precision and strength. No longer would construction be about moving and assembling huge chunks of material; it would be an intricate dance of atomic assembly, performed by these nanoscale maestros.

Already, nanotechnology has given us a peek into this potential future. We have successfully developed molecules that can perform basic tasks, and molecular 3D printers that can print on an atomic scale[33,34]. Researchers at the University of Manchester in England have already developed the first prototypes for robots made entirely of atoms, that can be programmed to move and build with molecules[35]. This robot is made up of just 150 carbon, hydrogen, oxygen and nitrogen atoms. This tiny robot uses a single atom to "grab" molecules. Depending on the electric properties of the robot, it can "grip" or release molecules.

All this could culminate in nanobots capable of precise atomic-level construction. In the future, these nanobots could be programmed to work collectively, swarming over a construction site like a team of miniaturized construction workers. They would take raw materials, break them down to their atomic constituents, and methodically assemble them into the desired structure. This is "bottom-up" construction at its best, which means a level of precision and efficiency that is unprecedented.

Buildings and structures created by nanobots would not only be incredibly robust but also highly adaptable. Because the nanobots can move and rearrange atoms, they can modify a structure after it has been built, making alterations or repairs without the need for demolition or reconstruction. Walls could shift, buildings could grow, adapt, and evolve in real-time in response to changes in their environment or their inhabitants' needs. The future would not be one of static, fixed infrastructure but a dynamic, ever-changing landscape.

Picture a skyscraper, pulsing and evolving in real-time. No longer are buildings static monuments to the era they were built in; they are living, breathing entities. Imagine the 30th floor of an office building that, come Tuesday, it needs a 31st. And by Wednesday morning, with nary a crane in sight or the clash of construction to be heard, it stands tall with an added tier.

These aren't just builders, they are maestros of metamorphosis. Rooms could expand to host a grand gala in the evening and contract into intimate spaces by morning. Fancy a window with a view of the west skyline today and the north by tomorrow? The nanobots could reconfigure the space every day if needed, to be a certain way in the morning, and a different way by evening.

Moreover, the aesthetic possibilities are endless. Today, the shapes and designs of our buildings are often limited by what can be achieved with cranes, concrete, and steel. With nanobots, these limitations would vanish, and architects would be able to create designs that were once too complex for practical use. Buildings could take on any form, any texture, and any color, at the whims of the designers. Our cities would transform from concrete jungles into stunning landscapes of architectural artistry.

The future of construction with nanobots offers a vision of a world built not by the hands of laborers but by the consistent and tireless work of atomic architects. It will be a world of unlimited creativity, efficient use of resources, and unimaginable precision. As fantastical as it may sound now, remember that every giant leap for humanity once started with an idea that seemed too grand, too incredible. With time, effort, and ingenuity, we have always found a way to bring these ideas to life.

Not limited to building, these machines will prove themselves the ultimate movers as well, being able to relocate furniture, paintings, and electronics effortlessly. Imagine a host preparing for a dinner party, and realizing that the grand piano in the living room would be better suited in the ballroom for the evening's entertainment. With the precision beyond any artist, the nanobots transport the instrument while leaving behind any dust or buildup, and reposition it to the desired room in a calculated location to perfectly complement the room's acoustics.

These amazing little machines will not just impact our world, they will impact us directly. They will be so innovative to the way we deal with healthcare that it might make sickness and death a symptom of the past. Imagine a future surgeon as he deploys an army of nanobots into the patient's body. These microscopic entities are designed with a precision that transcends human capability. They navigate the labyrinth of the human body, traveling through veins, arteries, and cellular structures to complete their task. Guided by the surgeon's neural interface, these nanobots perform a delicate operation, making minuscule repairs, removing harmful cells, or delivering targeted treatments. There's no physical intrusion, no risk of infection. just a seamless procedure that once would've been called a miracle.

Nanobots might become so good at repairing our tissue and healing us that medicine will no longer be needed. Imagine having a personal swarm of nanobots living in your bloodstream, a sort of microscopic maintenance crew. These nanobots would perform routine checks and balances on your bodily functions, repairing DNA strands damaged by exposure to radiation or toxins, spotting and neutralizing potential cancerous cells before they become a problem, or even cleaning arteries to prevent cardiovascular diseases. At the first sign of any tissue damage, they swarm to the site like bees to a flower. Whether it is a bullet graze or internal bleeding, they commence repair operations at a staggering speed. They promote clotting, stanch the flow of blood, and initiate tissue repair, reducing healing times from days to mere minutes. They could also then override specific nerve pathways, instantly stopping any unnecessary pain and suffering.

Furthermore, these nanobots could optimize our health by fine-tuning our biochemistry based on real-time monitoring. Feeling stressed? Your nanobot army could release the necessary hormones to help you relax. Need a burst of energy? The nanobots could stimulate the release of adrenaline. They could be the perfect personal health assistants, constantly rejuvenating our bodies and potentially expanding our lifespans, possibly even indefinitely.

Such a technology would no doubt be utilized in the military to push the average soldier's abilities to something akin to a superhero. The U.S Army has even partnered with the Massachusetts Institute of Technology (MIT) to establish the Institute for Soldier Nanotechnologies[36]. Like an army of microscopic medics, these nanobots would constantly monitor the vitals of the soldier. Information like heart rate, oxygen levels, and stress hormones will all be detected, analyzed, and communicated instantaneously. This stream of data, both intimate and comprehensive, paints a living and dynamic portrait of the soldier's health. Commanders, thus, make decisions based on an unparalleled awareness of their troops' condition, a luxury once unthinkable.

These nanobots would be able to form a network and communicate with each other. This ability would be leveraged to give soldiers on the battlefield the ability to communicate using thought alone. The nanobots would interpret the brain's electrical signals and broadcast to the bots of another soldier, or perhaps of an entire squad. The nanobots receiving the message would then re-create the electrical patterns in their host's brain, essentially functioning as a Brain-Computer Interface (BCI). This feed of invaluable data will prove itself the ultimate decentralized communication network. Billions of coordinated nanorobots could form a secure, dynamic network that's resistant to jamming or interception. By continuously shifting transmission frequencies and communication paths, they could keep communication open even in the most adverse conditions.

Even stranded alone and injured, a soldier with nanobots coursing through his veins would not be out of the fight for long. His minuscule allies would analyze and consume available matter in the environment to construct medical supplies, or even advanced prosthetics, right there on the field. The waiting game for resupply would be outdated. In hostile environments, they could gather and purify water, extract nutrients from otherwise inedible material, or filter out harmful gases or radiation.

Beyond the body, in a scenario where a soldier is under attack or on the defensive, his personal nanorobot army would help transform the environment to give them the advantage. Wreckage from a destroyed vehicle or even the natural environment could be quickly and efficiently transformed into useful tools or structures. Bunkers could rise from rubble, barriers from boulders, or a bridge from a fallen tree. At a simple command, the nanobots could disassemble surrounding matter and reconstruct it into advanced weaponry. This can be an impenetrable shield, a high-powered laser, or even an exosuit like the one used in *Iron Man*. Deployed as a protective swarm around strategic assets or important personnel, they could intercept and neutralize incoming threats. From dismantling explosive devices to obstructing the path of bullets, their coordinated response could provide an unprecedented shield against attacks.The battlefield could change in an instant, dynamically reacting to the ever-shifting tides of war. The real key to this concept is the swarm's adaptability. They could adjust their action based on the nature of the situation, whether it is a single sniper bullet or a deadly gas, their ability to change roles will be instant and effective.

These roles will also include repairing and maintenance. Whether it is damage to a vehicle's armor, a malfunctioning piece of equipment, or wear and tear on a weapon system, nanobots could swiftly diagnose and repair the issue at the microscopic level. This would drastically reduce downtime and strain on logistics, ensuring that military assets remain operational when they're needed most.

Beyond a support role on the battlefield, nanobots will prove themselves irreplaceable at data gathering and reconnaissance. These invisible spies would be able to infiltrate any installation easily, providing detailed insight into their structure, personnel, and operational capabilities. They would have the ability to monitor conversations, access digital systems, and even subtly manipulate the environment. A thin layer of nanobots spread over an area would be able to relay information about their locations back to the headquarters, which would then be quickly translated into holographic mappings of the area. The data gathered by these nanobots, with their ability to map every square inch of an area down to each blade of grass, would not only be comprehensive but also astoundingly precise. This would provide an unprecedented level of situational awareness, thus granting strategists and commanders a granular understanding of the battlefield layout and enemy positioning, further enhanced by real-time updates.

After data-gathering is complete, these minuscule machines would be able to take on an offensive role as well. Their potential to be used for sabotage could redefine the concept of a "surgical strike." They could embed themselves into complex machinery, weapon systems, or vital infrastructure, and wreak havoc from the inside out. Imagine an enemy's radar system suddenly malfunctioning, their weapons jamming, or their power grid collapsing, all without a single missile launched or a bullet fired.

This ability to cause damage from the inside out will of course mean that they will have the ability to perform sinister tasks such as assassination. These invisible assassins would simply have to enter the bloodstream and link together to form a blockage to a major artery. Once the target is eliminated, the bots would de-link and continue to their next task, vanishing without leaving any trace of foul play with the victim appearing to die naturally from a heart attack or stroke. They could lie dormant in a target for an indefinite period, activated remotely when the time is right.

On an even more insidious note, they will also be able to perform roles in psychological warfare. They could influence mood, induce fatigue, or even trigger hallucinations, causing disarray and sowing seeds of doubt and confusion within their ranks. This form of covert manipulation could destabilize an enemy force without engaging in direct combat, preserving resources and minimizing casualties.

Among the numerous speculative scenarios about the future of nanotechnology, one stands out for its stark dystopian tone: the *grey goo* scenario[37]. Coined by the renowned engineer and futurist Eric Drexler in his seminal book *Engines of Creation*, the term "grey goo" has since entered the lexicon of speculative science and technology, representing a cautionary tale about the potential perils of uncontrolled self-replicating machines.

The scenario plays out like this: imagine a swarm of nanobots, each one no larger than a speck of dust, engineered with the capability to replicate themselves using the atoms and molecules found in their environment. At first glance, this self-replication seems advantageous, allowing rapid multiplication and the ability to repair any damage by simply creating replacements.

However, consider what would happen if these microscopic machines were to malfunction or fall into the wrong hands, and begin replicating uncontrollably. Like a mechanical cancer, they could potentially consume all available matter, organic and inorganic alike, to produce more of themselves. This relentless, unchecked proliferation would result in a runaway reaction where the entire planet could be reduced to "grey goo," a homogenous mass of self-replicating nanobots.

This dystopian vision, while currently in the realm of science fiction, underscores the need for stringent controls and fail-safe mechanisms in the design of future nanobots, particularly those capable of self-replication. It highlights the ethical imperative to proceed with caution in our exploration and application of nanotechnology, ensuring that the potential benefits do not come at the expense of existential risk.

These marvelous machines will have the potential for benevolent roles that will match and perhaps even surpass their malevolent use. They could be a permanent solution for minimizing the negative effects humanity has on the environment. From clearing rubble after a natural disaster to decontaminating polluted sites, these tiny agents could mitigate the environmental impact of human activity, helping restore ecosystems and ensuring the safety of local populations.

Nanobiotechnology

The term *nanobiotechnology* might appear a bit intimidating at first glance, but don't be fooled. It is a term that describes an awe-inspiring fusion of the minuscule with the biological. It involves applying the principles of nanotechnology, the science of manipulating matter on an atomic and molecular scale, to the biological realm. It is a field that offers potential to revolutionize medicine, agriculture, and even our understanding of life itself.

The art of nanobiotechnology lies in utilizing the natural behavior of biological materials and systems at the nanoscale to develop innovative solutions to some of humanity's biggest challenges. It is about working at scales where the divide between the living and non-living blurs, and nature's incredible machinery of life can be harnessed, modified, and optimized.

One of the most striking examples of

nanobiotechnology at work in our world today can be found in the realm of medicine. Here, nanoparticles are being designed and developed as carriers for drugs or even as therapeutics themselves[38,39]. By carefully crafting these particles, scientists can target disease at the cellular and even molecular level. This is no small feat; think of it as using a microscopic GPS to send healing agents directly to diseased cells, minimizing side effects and maximizing therapeutic effects. Nanoparticle-based therapies are already in clinical use in cancer treatment and hold immense promise for tackling other diseases[38,39].

Probably the most impressive form of nanobiotechnology would be the creation and altering of life itself. Imagine a world where life isn't solely born, it is designed. This isn't the stuff of science fiction, but a potential reality being explored by scientists[40,41]. As the manipulation of biological matter at an atomic and molecular scale becomes more refined, so too does the ability to construct life at its most fundamental level.

In the near future, this field will give the ability to modify and change the DNA of unborn offspring[42,43]. Parents, on the cusp of welcoming a new life into the world, will have the tools to sculpt a future for their child that was once the stuff of myth and legend.

This will go beyond being able to change eye color and

physique. This technology delves deeper, touching the very essence of human potential. What if the haunting specter of hereditary diseases could be banished to the annals of history? What if, through precise genetic tweaks, we could bolster resilience, amplify intellect, and nurture personalities brimming with empathy and passion? Through the manipulation of our genetic code, we might be able to unlock other "superhuman" capabilities. Enhanced senses, superior cognitive function, increased strength, endurance, or agility, or even the ability to heal faster than normal.

Envision a world where the marvels of our technological age such as BCIs are integrated into our biological architecture. As astounding as BCIs are, their functionality could be woven into our genetic fabric by using advanced nanobiotechnology to evolve our biological capabilities. By incorporating and tweaking the mechanics of BCIs, we could develop genetic modifications that allow us to directly transmit and receive information to and from one another's brains. This would be natural telepathy coded directly into our DNA, which means it would then be passed on to offspring.

Further into the future, nanobiotechnology could evolve to a point where we can not only modify existing life forms but design new ones from scratch[42,43]. Picture microorganisms, built not to reproduce or feed, but solely to consume plastic waste in our oceans. They could be designed to have lifespans that terminate once their task is done, ensuring no unforeseen ecological consequences.

In a world grappling with climate change, we could engineer bacteria that consume excess carbon dioxide and methane, effectively functioning as supercharged trees, but without the need for vast tracts of land[44].

Within our bodies, nano-engineered cells could operate far more efficiently than our own cells. They could be tasked with seeking and destroying cancer cells, managing insulin levels, or even repairing damaged tissue at a rate we've never seen before.

In the realm of agriculture, lifeforms could be designed for specific tasks. This could be nitrogen-fixing plants that rejuvenate the soil, or organisms that guard crops against pests without the need for chemical intervention[45].

Imagine microorganisms tailored to capture sunlight and directly convert it into electricity or organisms that can synthesize biofuels more efficiently than any existing plant.

For space exploration, we could create lifeforms that don't require sustenance in traditional senses. They could mine asteroids, terraform planets, or even act as biological sensors, searching for signs of life, all while enduring the vast spans of cosmic time and the harsh conditions of space.

Blurring the lines between the digital and organic, these new lifeforms could serve as living computers. Storing information not in silicon, but in bio-molecular structures, leading to computing processes that nature itself might envy.

On the softer side, organisms designed by humans could be made to respond to our own biology. imagine flora that changes colors with the seasons, not due to natural processes but in response to atmospheric music or the emotions of people around. Public spaces could become symphonies of color and sound, with nano-designed life responding to human interaction.

Chapter References

1. Toumey, C. (2009). Plenty of room, plenty of history. *Nature Nanotechnology*, 4, 783–784. https://doi.org/10.1038/nnano.2009.357

2. Feynman, R. P. (1960). There's Plenty of Room at the Bottom. *Engineering and Science*, 23(5), 22-36. https://resolver.caltech.edu/CaltechES:23.5.1960Bottom

3. Bellis, M. (2018, February 28). Scanning Tunneling Microscope. *ThoughtCo.* https://www.thoughtco.com/scanning-tunneling-microscope-4075527

4. Anirban, A. (2022). 40 years of scanning tunneling microscopy. *Nature Reviews Physics*, 4, 291. https://doi.org/10.1038/s42254-022-00462-2

5. Di Stefano, A. (2023). Nanotechnology in targeted drug delivery. *International Journal of Molecular Sciences*, 24(9), 8194. https://doi.org/10.3390/ijms24098194

6. Montelione, N., Loreni, F., Nenna, A., Catanese, V., Scurto, L., Ferrisi, C., Jawabra, M., Gabellini, T., Codispoti, F. A., Spinelli, F., Chello, M., & Stilo, F. (2023). Tissue Engineering and Targeted Drug Delivery in Cardiovascular Disease: The Role of Polymer Nanocarrier for Statin Therapy. *Biomedicines*, 11(3), 798. https://doi.org/10.3390/biomedicines11030798

7. Wang, L., Teles, M. P. R., Arabkoohsar, A., Yu, H., Ismail, K. A. R., Mahian, O., & Wongwises, S. (2022). A holistic and state-of-the-art review of nanotechnology in solar cells. *Sustainable Energy Technologies and Assessments*, 54, 102864. https://doi.org/10.1016/j.seta.2022.102864

8. Sood, A. (2016, November 15). Using nanotechnology to improve the efficiency of solar cells. *AltEnergyMag*. https://www.altenergymag.com/article/2016/11/using-nanotechnology-to-improve-the-efficiency-of-solar-cells/25041

9. Pokrajac, L., Abbas, A., Chrzanowski, W., Dias, G. M., Eggleton, B. J. , Maguire, S., Maine, E., Malloy, T., Nathwani, J., Nazar, L., Sips, A., Sone, J., van den Berg, A., Weiss, P. S., & Mitra, S. (2021). Nanotechnology for a Sustainable Future: Addressing Global Challenges with the International Network4Sustainable Nanotechnology. *ACS Nano*, 15(12), 18608-18623. https://doi.org/10.1021/acsnano.1c10919

10. The Royal Swedish Academy of Sciences. (2016, October 5). The Nobel Prize in Chemistry 2016. *NobelPrize.org*. https://www.nobelprize.

org/prizes/chemistry/2016/press-release/

11. Gallego, J. (2016, October 7). Nanomachines Score The 2016 Nobel Prize in Chemistry. *Futurism*. https://futurism.com/nanomachines-score-the-2016-nobel-prize-in-chemistry

12. Advanced Science News. (2016, October 5). Molecular machines honored in 2016 Nobel Prize in Chemistry. https://www.advancedsciencenews.com/molecular-machines-honored-in-2016-nobel-prize-in-chemistry/

13. Apple. (2022, June 6). Apple unveils M2, taking the breakthrough performance and capabilities of M1 even further. *Apple*. https://www.apple.com/newsroom/2022/06/apple-unveils-m2-with-breakthrough-performance-and-capabilities/

14. Kelleher, A. (2022, February 16). Moore's Law – Now and in the Future. *Intel*. https://www.intel.com/content/www/us/en/newsroom/opinion/moore-law-now-and-in-the-future.html

15. Computer History Museum. (n.d.). 1965: "Moore's Law" Predicts the Future of Integrated Circuits. https://www.computerhistory.org/siliconengine/moores-law-predicts-the-future-of-integrated-circuits/

16. Perrin, M. L., Burzurí, E., & van der Zant, H. S. J. (2015). Single-molecule transistors. *Chemical Society Reviews*, 44(4), 902-919. The Royal Society of Chemistry. https://doi.org/10.1039/C4CS00231H

17. Capozzi, B., Xia, J., Adak, O., et al. (2015). Single-molecule diodes with high rectification ratios through environmental control. *Nature Nanotechnology*, 10, 522–527. https://doi.org/10.1038/nnano.2015.97

18. Ouyang, Y., Wang, F., Zhang, M., Qin, Y., Tan, Y.-Z., Ji, W., & Song, F. (2023). Atom electronics in single-molecule transistors: single-atom access and manipulation. *Advances in Physics: X*, 8(1). https://doi.org/10.1080/23746149.2023.2165148

19. IBM. (2017, March 8). IBM Researchers Store Data on World's Smallest Magnet -- a Single Atom. https://uk.newsroom.ibm.com/2017-03-08-IBM-Researchers-Store-Data-on-Worlds-Smallest-Magnet-a-Single-Atom

20. Gibney, E. (2017). Magnetic hard drives go atomic. *Nature*. https://doi.org/10.1038/nature.2017.21599

21. Kumar, M. (2017, March 13). Scientists store one bit of data on a single atom — Future of data storage. *The Hacker News*. https://thehackernews.com/2017/03/atom-data-storage.html

22. Mearian, L. (2016). Atomic-scale memory can store 500 times more than today's best hard drive. *Computerworld*. https://www.computerworld.com/article/3096810/atomic-scale-memory-can-store-500-times-more-than-todays-best-hard-drive.html

23. Sun, F., & Singh, M. R. (2021). Modeling of piezoelectric power nano-generators using Brownian particles. *Journal of Intelligent Material Systems and Structures*, 32(7), 724-732. https://doi.org/10.1177/1045389X20965704

24. Johnson, D. (2018, April 5). "Rocking" Brownian Motor Pushes Nanoparticles Around. *IEEE Spectrum*. https://spectrum.ieee.org/nanomotors-swimming-without-fluid-flow-revolutionizes-nanofluidics

25. Knoll, A., & Schwemmer, C. (2018, March 30). IBM scientists demo rocking Brownian motors for nanoparticles. *Phys.org*. https://phys.org/news/2018-03-ibm-scientists-demo-brownian-motors.html

26. Alejo, T., Uson, L., & Arruebo, M. (2019). Reversible stimuli-responsive nanomaterials with on-off switching ability for biomedical applications. *Journal of Controlled Release*, 314, 162-176. https://doi.org/10.1016/j.jconrel.2019.10.036

27. Valev, V. (2016, May 24). Powering nanotechnology with the world's smallest engine. *The Conversation*. https://theconversation.com/powering-nanotechnology-with-the-worlds-smallest-engine-58969

28. Wavhale, R. D., Dhobale, K. D., Rahane, C. S., et al. (2021). Water-powered self-propelled magnetic nanobot for rapid and highly efficient capture of circulating tumor cells. *Communications Chemistry*, 4, 159. https://doi.org/10.1038/s42004-021-00598-9

29. Xu, D., Hu, J., Pan, X., Sánchez, S., Yan, X., & Ma, X. (2021). Enzyme-Powered Liquid Metal Nanobots Endowed with Multiple Biomedical Functions. *ACS Nano*, 15(7), 11543–11554. https://doi.org/10.1021/acsnano.1c01573

30. Mehta, M., & Subramani, K. (2012). Nanodiagnostics in Microbiology and Dentistry. In K. Subramani & W. Ahmed (Eds.), *Emerging Nanotechnologies in Dentistry* (pp. 365-390). William Andrew Publishing. https://doi.org/10.1016/B978-1-4557-7862-1.00021-3

31. Mattoo, S. (2022, November 18). Why Are Nanobots Considered a Medtech Success? *G2*. https://www.g2.com/articles/nanobots

32. Requicha, A. A. G. (2003). Nanorobots, NEMS, and nanoassembly. *Proceedings of the IEEE*, 91(11), 1922-1933. https://doi.org/10.1109/JPROC.2003.818333

33. Krassenstein, B. (2015, March 13). Breakthrough Molecular 3D Printer Can Print Billions of Possible Compounds. *3DPrint.com*. https://3dprint.com/50777/molecular-3d-printer/

34. Carl von Ossietzky Universität Oldenburg. (2021, December 21). 3D printing approaches atomic dimensions. *Phys.org*. https://phys.org/news/2021-12-3d-approaches-atomic-dimensions.html

35. University of Manchester. (2017, September 20). Scientists create world's first 'molecular robot' capable of building molecules. https://www.manchester.ac.uk/discover/news/scientists-create-worlds-first-molecular-robot-capable-of-building-molecules/

36. Institute for Soldier Nanotechnologies at MIT. (n.d.). Shaping the future of Warfighter capabilities. https://isn.mit.edu/

37. Francis, S. (2016, August 1). grey goo. *Encyclopedia Britannica*. https://www.britannica.com/technology/grey-goo

38. Gavas, S., Quazi, S., & Karpiński, T. M. (2021). Nanoparticles for Cancer Therapy: Current Progress and Challenges. *Nanoscale Research Letters*, 16(1), 173. https://doi.org/10.1186/s11671-021-03628-6

39. Dang, Y., & Guan, J. (2020). Nanoparticle-based drug delivery systems for cancer therapy. *Smart Materials in Medicine*, 1, 10-19. https://doi.org/10.1016/j.smaim.2020.04.001

40. Sivakami, A., Sarankumar, R., & Vinodha, S. (2021). Introduction to Nanobiotechnology: Novel and Smart Applications. In K. Pal (Ed.), *Bio-manufactured Nanomaterials*. Springer. https://doi.org/10.1007/978-3-030-67223-2_1

41. Kaur, K., & Thombre, R. (2021). Chapter 1 - Nanobiotechnology: methods, applications, and future prospects. In S. Ghosh & T. J. Webster (Eds.), *Nanobiotechnology* (pp. 1-20). Elsevier. ISBN 9780128228784. https://doi.org/10.1016/B978-0-12-822878-4.00001-8

42. Lagomarsino, V. (2019). Arrival of Gene-Edited Babies: What lies ahead? *Harvard University*. https://sitn.hms.harvard.edu/flash/2019/arrival-gene-edited-babies-lies-ahead/

43. Kupferschmidt, K. (2012, June 6). Sequencing the Unborn. *Science*. https://www.science.org/content/article/sequencing-unborn

44. Shahcheraghi, N., Golchin, H., Sadri, Z., et al. (2022, February 9). Nano-biotechnology, an applicable approach for sustainable future. *3 Biotech*, 12, 65. https://doi.org/10.1007/s13205-021-03108-9

45. Tripathi, A., & Prakash, S. (2022). Nanobiotechnology: Emerging trends, prospects, and challenges. In S. Ghosh, S. Thongmee, & A. Kumar (Eds.), *Agricultural Nanobiotechnology* (pp. 1-21). Woodhead Publishing Series in Food Science, Technology and Nutrition. Woodhead Publishing. ISBN 9780323919081. https://doi.org/10.1016/B978-0-323-91908-1.00006-7

AI

Long before the flash and hum of servers, before the hushed conversations of Silicon Valley visionaries, and even before the rise of the electronic computer itself, the concept of AI had already taken root deep within the human imagination. Our collective consciousness, teeming with ideas that straddle the boundary between the real and the unreal, had long been infatuated with the possibility of creating non-biological intelligence.

The rise of AI begins not with binary code or sophisticated algorithms, but with myths, legends, and dreams. Our ancestors imbued life into inanimate objects, whispering stories around campfires about enchanted beings and automatons that moved and thought like humans. This anthropomorphic urge, an integral part of our human condition, sparked the concept of entities that could mirror our own intelligence.

While it might be hard to envision ancient civilizations contemplating the complex idea of AI as we understand it today, they indeed harbored inklings of similar concepts. The essence of AI, machines or constructs possessing human-like intelligence, finds its roots in the anthropomorphic myths and automatons of ancient cultures. Ancient Greek mythology offered glimpses into this early conception of AI through Talos, a giant bronze automaton[1,2]. Crafted by Hephaestus, the god of blacksmiths and invention, Talos was tasked with patrolling the shores of Crete, hurling boulders at approaching enemy ships. In this tale, we can perceive a nascent understanding of man-made beings designed to carry out tasks, a foundational idea of modern AI. Similarly, Hephaestus was also said to have created artificial servants made of gold, which could anticipate his needs and assist him in his work. This image of self-operating, helpful machines bears a striking resemblance to our contemporary visions of AI. Ancient India's epic, the *Mahabharata*, also hinted at autonomous machines and AI[3,4]. The text describes machines that could behave like humans, called yantras, an allusion that echoes our contemporary fascination with humanoid robots. Ancient China contributed its own tales of artificial life with stories of mechanical engineers like Yan Shi who presented King Mu of Zhou with a life-sized automaton[5,6]. This mechanical figure could sing, dance, and even engage in simple conversations, much like the AI-powered personal assistants we have today. These stories and mythologies underscore a deep, historical fascination with the idea of creating non-biological intelligence, a theme that has persisted and evolved over millennia. Though ancient cultures lacked our understanding of technology and computation, they pondered, in their unique ways, the concept of artificial life and intelligence. In doing so, they laid the earliest imaginative groundwork for what we now know as AI.

As centuries unfolded, the desire for artificial companions found new expressions in literature, philosophy, and art. From Mary Shelley's creature in *Frankenstein* to Karel Čapek's industrious robots in *R.U.R*, from philosophical musings on the nature of mind and consciousness to depictions of mechanized men in the vivid panels of comic books, these embodiments of artificial intelligence provoked questions about the essence of life, the scope of human ingenuity, and the ethical complexities of creating sentient beings.

The Scientific Revolution and the Industrial Age brought significant advancements in understanding the physical world, setting the stage for the later development of artificial intelligence. As thinkers and inventors began to decode the laws of nature and harness the power of machines, the idea of creating artificial life and intelligence gained more concrete and scientific underpinnings. Figures like René Descartes introduced a mechanistic view of the world, likening the human body to a complex machine. This revolutionary perspective laid the groundwork for the idea that human intelligence, too, might be replicated mechanically[7,8]. The advent of automata, self-operating machines, during this period also embodied the nascent concept of AI. One notable example was Jacques de Vaucanson's Digesting Duck, an automated duck made of more than 400 moving parts in each wing[9,10]. While it couldn't 'digest' as its name suggested, it mimicked the action convincingly, showing that machines could simulate life-like, intelligent behavior. The idea of machine-aided calculation also emerged during this period. The designs for a mechanical calculator by Wilhelm Schickard and later Blaise Pascal and Gottfried Wilhelm Leibniz signified early attempts to offload intellectual labor to machines[11,12]. This concept was a crucial precursor to the development of computer-based AI.

The Industrial Age advanced these ideas further as machinery became central to production and daily life. The development of Charles Babbage's Difference Engine and

Analytical Engine, machines designed to automatically perform calculations, marked a pivotal step toward modern computers. Though never fully built in Babbage's time, Ada Lovelace recognized that the Analytical Engine could go beyond calculations, stating it might compose scientific pieces of music of any degree of complexity or extent[13,14]. This remarkable insight hinted at the concept of machines performing tasks requiring creativity, a central facet of modern AI. Another critical development was Samuel Butler's suggestion in his 1863 essay *Darwin Among the Machines*, where he proposed that machines could reproduce, evolve, and surpass humans in intelligence and dominance[15,16]. This was a provocative concept that foreshadowed current debates about AI surpassing human intelligence.

From the mechanistic philosophy of Descartes to the calculating engines of Babbage and Lovelace, the Scientific Revolution and the Industrial Age transformed the idea of AI from myth and fantasy into a scientific and technological possibility. These ideas and inventions played an instrumental role in shaping the trajectory of AI, turning ancient dreams of intelligent machines into a pursuit within the realm of reality.

By the 1930s and 40s, groundbreaking work in mathematics and logic laid a solid theoretical foundation for AI. In 1936, Alan Turing's seminal paper on computable numbers introduced the concept of a "universal machine" that could simulate any other machine given the appropriate input[17,18]. This universal machine would later be realized as the digital computer, the engine driving AI.

Post World War II, the first practical steps towards AI and robotics were taken. The invention of the transistor in 1947 and the integrated circuit in 1958 enabled computers to become smaller, cheaper, and more powerful, setting the stage for the rise of personal computing and later the internet[19,20]. In 1950, Turing proposed the *Turing Test* to determine if a machine could exhibit intelligent behavior indistinguishable from a human, a concept still central to AI[21,22]. The same year, Isaac Asimov published *I, Robot*, containing the "Three Laws of Robotics," which continue to inspire ethical discussions around AI and robotics[23,24]. The term "artificial intelligence" was coined by John McCarthy for the Dartmouth Workshop in 1956, marking the official birth of the field[25,26]. Early AI research led to the development of algorithms like the *Logic Theorist* and *General Problem Solver*, programs designed to mimic human problem-solving skills[27,28].

The late 20th century saw the introduction of Machine Learning, with algorithms learning from and making decisions based on data[29,30]. Pioneering work by researchers such as Frank Rosenblatt's *Perceptron* in 1958 and later the *backpropagation algorithm* in the 1980s enabled machines to learn from their mistakes and adjust their strategies, a cornerstone of modern AI[31,32].

A watershed moment for AI was in 1997 when IBM's Deep Blue defeated world chess champion Garry Kasparov[33,34]. Later, in 2011, IBM's Watson won Jeopardy!, demonstrating the ability of AI to understand and respond to natural language queries[35,36]. Around the same time, breakthroughs were made in AI's capability to recognize and generate human speech[37,38]. Apple's introduction of Siri in 2011, Amazon's Alexa in 2014, and Google's Assistant in 2016 have made AI-powered personal assistants a ubiquitous part of everyday life[39,40,41].

Finally, advancements in Deep Learning in the 21st century have propelled AI to unprecedented capabilities[42,43]. Breakthroughs in image recognition, natural language processing, and AlphaGo's 2016 victory over the world *Go* champion have demonstrated that AI can now perform tasks once thought exclusively human[44,45].

At the current moment we are at a pivotal moment in human history, where AI will soon be interwoven into every aspect of society[46,47,48]. Everything from transportation and medical care, to art and cyberspace will be revolutionized by AI. To truly illustrate how much of an impact AI will make, imagine if everyone on Earth had access to a personal genius that never gets tired, knows everything, and can perform any mental task in a fraction of the time it would take you. As if that wasn't enough, humanity might soon reach a singularity, where AI becomes smarter than any and every human in existence[49,50,51].

Autonomous Vehicles

One of the most obvious uses for AI will be to control vehicles which will undoubtedly lead to a revolution in transportation and logistics[52,53]. These vehicles will prove to be so efficient and so much safer than our current human-driven ones that in the future it might not even be an option to manually drive a vehicle anymore. Human error due to fatigue, distraction, or inexperience, is a leading cause of vehicular accidents. AI vehicles, perpetually vigilant and driven by algorithms that analyze vast amounts of data in real-time, will drastically reduce, if not eliminate, these accidents[54,55]. No more drunk driving incidents, no more crashes from dozing off truck drivers after a long haul, and no more accidents from misjudged lane changes.

AI vehicles can coordinate with each other, ensuring optimal speeds, minimal unnecessary braking, and synchronicity that's poetic in its precision[56,57,58]. The result?

Expedited commutes, reduced fuel consumption, and a significant decrease in vehicular emissions. Future commutes could be completely free of stop signs and traffic lights, there will be no need since future AI vehicles will be able to coordinate with each other seamlessly[59]. Imagine a future four way intersection in the road or the sky where vehicles crossing never slow down because they effortlessly calculate the speed and trajectory needed to pass perfectly through the space between each vehicle.

Autonomous trucks and supply vehicles will operate around the clock, unhindered by human limitations, ensuring superior logistics[52,53]. Ports and warehouses will deploy AI-driven vehicles and drones, streamlining the process of loading, unloading, and inventory management[60,61]. This will lead to faster shipping times, reduced costs, and a potential boom in global trade.

Additionally, with AI vehicles at the helm the need for parking spaces in city centers will diminish[62,63]. They will drop passengers off and park themselves in designated areas outside the city or continuously ferry other passengers. This frees up vast tracts of land, paving the way for more green spaces, recreational areas, or innovative urban infrastructure.

To truly convey the superiority that these autonomous vehicles will bring, it will help to take a look at how complicated and time consuming it is for humans to become proficient in piloting complex vehicles like fighter jets. The conventional process of developing a human fighter pilot in the United States to reach combat efficiency is arduous and expensive[64,65,66]. The process begins with earning at least a bachelor's degree, as this is a prerequisite for officer training. Prospective pilots then attend Officer Training School, or they may receive their commission through the Reserve Officers' Training Corps (ROTC) or the US Air Force Academy. Next comes *Initial Flight Training*, which lasts about a month. Here, candidates learn basic flight principles. Those who pass this phase move on to *Primary Flight Training*, which lasts about six months. Trainees learn basic flight skills primarily through simulator training. Following Primary Flight Training, students move on to Advanced Flight Training, lasting another six months. Here they begin training on the specific aircraft they will be piloting. They'll learn advanced combat maneuvers, low-level flight, and aircraft carrier operations if they're in the Navy. After completing Advanced Flight Training, pilots receive their "wings," but the training doesn't stop there. They then move onto further specialized training with the specific aircraft they'll be flying, and this training could last anywhere from a few months to a year. Finally, a person that went through this process can finally call themselves a fighter pilot that will be active for an average of around

15-20 years. Although this pilot might be the best to ever exist, they are still human.

In contrast, a fighter piloted entirely by AI would be superior in every way. Take, for instance, the years of extensive training a fighter pilot undergoes, comprising rigorous academic study, simulated training, and countless hours of live flight experience. This process is both time-consuming and resource-intensive, involving millions of dollars in expenditure, not just on training facilities and instructors, but also on aircraft fuel for training flights. However, AI presents an entirely different paradigm. Rather than years of learning, an AI pilot's "training" could be uploaded in a matter of seconds through a software update, an immense saving in time, resources, and effort. Recent developments have shown that AI pilots can outperform human pilots in simulated dogfights, showcasing their potential in combat scenarios[67,68,69].

An AI pilot would always operate at peak efficiency, unhindered by human needs such as sleep, food, or water. This relentless operational capacity affords significant strategic advantages. For example, an AI fighter pilot could undertake long-haul surveillance missions without needing to rotate pilots or engage in extended combat scenarios without performance degradation over time. Decisions, devoid of emotional biases or delays due to physical fatigue, would be swift, accurate, and calculated to the minutest detail.

In the domain of combat maneuvers, AI would truly shine. Human pilots are restricted by the physical limits of the human body. When a maneuver too intense is performed, the pilot risks blacking out due to extreme g-forces. In contrast, AI pilots have no such physical constraints. They could perform complex, high-g maneuvers that would be impossible for a human pilot, thereby revolutionizing air combat tactics and strategies[70,71,72]. Not long ago the AlphaDogfight Trials demonstrated that AI algorithms could handle several minutes of continuous high-G maneuvers, whereas real combat scenarios involving such maneuvers would likely induce loss of consciousness or G-LOC for human pilots due to the biological stresses of such maneuvers[70,71,72]. In these trials, AI demonstrated not only the ability to handle high-G forces but also showcased tactics that human pilots wouldn't think of or wouldn't attempt, like aggressive head-on gun attacks, which are considered high-risk and prohibited in training[70,71,72].

Moreover, there are huge implications with the capability of AI to analyze vast amounts of data. It can simultaneously interpret radar signatures, infrared emissions, and electronic communications to not only evade enemy defenses but even predict enemy movements and positions[73]. Advanced machine learning algorithms could help the AI adapt and improve after each mission, increasing its effectiveness over time[74].

When an autonomous plane takes off it may never need to land. With existing mid-flight refueling procedures, these aircraft could theoretically stay aloft indefinitely, only landing to re-arm. But even this could change in the near future, as technologies for mid-air re-arming develop[75,76]. In essence, the introduction of AI in fighter aviation presents an unprecedented shift, redefining the very boundaries of combat aviation. By eliminating the limitations posed by the human element, AI could elevate fighter aviation to heights previously thought unreachable. While the ethical and policy considerations of this shift remain to be fully understood, the technological potential is undeniable.

Of course, AI would not be used just for aviation. Recently a collaboration between Estonian robotics and autonomous systems developer Milrem Robotics have revealed the Type-X, an AI-piloted tank[77,78]. An AI-powered tank would have all the same advantages. However, the most ominous form of these autonomous vehicles would be an AI-piloted nuclear submarine[79,80].

Plunge beneath the ocean's shimmering surface and into the world of nuclear submarines, awe-inspiring leviathans that lurk in the abyss. These underwater colossi are powered by nuclear technology that endows them with an almost mythical endurance. They can traverse the world's oceans for up to two decades without needing to refuel[81,82]. Already, they are daunting adversaries, manned by elite crews who live and breathe the silent, submerged world for months on end. Consider the Ohio Class Submarine, a veritable titan beneath the waves. It comes equipped with 24 Trident II D-5 ballistic missiles, each of which can carry between 8-12 *Multiple Independently Targetable Re-entry Vehicles* (MIRV)[83,84]. Each MIRV is armed with a payload of either 100 or 475 kilotons[85]. Crunch the numbers, and you are looking at a total theoretical payload of 136,800 kilotons. To provide some perspective on the scale of this formidable firepower, consider Little Boy, the bomb that decimated Hiroshima in 1945. It yielded a comparatively paltry 15 kilotons[86]. So, an Ohio-class submarine, with its arsenal of Tridents, carries the equivalent of over 9,000 Hiroshima bombs. This realization alone is enough to send a shiver down your spine.

Imagine the world-destroying potential of such machinery under the control of artificial intelligence. With AI at the helm, these behemoths could become the tireless sentinels of our oceans, operational for decades without interruption. Unshackled from the constraints of human frailty, an AI-guided submarine could be fundamentally redesigned. No longer would it need to consider human comforts like bunk rooms and galleys, or be limited by the physical and psychological needs of a human crew. Instead, every nook and cranny could be devoted to advanced technology, improved structural integrity, and increased weaponry, propelling these deep-sea titans to even greater heights of maritime supremacy. This is not mere fantasy, as the United States and China are already developing such weapon systems[79,80].

AI and Entertainment

AI is already changing the technological landscape and disrupting industries. A plethora of AI systems are crafting texts, conjuring images, and choreographing videos with a finesse that challenges, and at times even eclipses, the very best of human creativity. As these capabilities evolve, we stand on the brink of a transformative era – one where the canvas of creation is bound only by the limitlessness of our imaginations.

Art, for centuries, has been exclusively a human endeavor where heart meets hand, and soul touches canvas. It was once believed to be a domain impervious to technological intrusion. Yet, in a twist worthy of the most riveting tales, art has emerged as AI's playground. Platforms like *Midjourney* exemplify this seismic shift[87,88]. Desiring a rendition of the Mona Lisa as if painted by Picasso? It can materialize on your screen in mere moments. Dreaming of concept art for a dystopian metropolis in your upcoming sci-fi saga? A brief descriptive paragraph is your paintbrush. Need a vivid scene of jubilant faces for an advertisement? The granularity of customization, down to expressions, attire, and even ambiance, is all possible.

People and corporations are already creating AI personalities to serve as social media influencers[89,90,91]. These AI personalities are tailored with specific appearances and characteristics. They come up with relevant things to post and promote according to the brand they were created for. These personalities are so popular and realistic already that people that interact with them on social media platforms think they are real people.

The ripples of this AI-driven renaissance don't stop at static images. Video games, the entertainment behemoths of our age, are poised for a metamorphosis[92,93,94]. Picture this: a gaming universe where non-player characters engage you with uniquely tailored dialogues, where the landscapes of missions and worlds are in perennial flux, offering an unprecedented freshness. Imagine mechanics so fluid that a fantasy quest today morphs into a space odyssey tomorrow, rendering every gaming session distinct.

Similarly, the cinematic world stands on the cusp of a revolution[95,96,97]. Today's blockbusters, which necessitate astronomical budgets and an army of talent, might one day be crafted in the quiet sanctum of a creator's room, orchestrated end-to-end by AI. A single visionary could sculpt worlds, weave narratives, and breathe life into characters, all within a span that previously took years and legions of filmmakers.

AI with a combination of emerging holographic technologies might also bring new forms of entertainment and interaction[98,99,100]. In a dimly lit, futuristic chamber, a glimmer of light began to coalesce, giving form to a scene that blurred the line between fantasy and reality. This was no ordinary display; this was the vanguard of next-gen entertainment, a mesmerizing fusion of AI prowess and cutting-edge holographic technology.

Imagine attending a soiree where you could mingle with the charismatic charms of James Dean or the effervescent spirit of Marilyn Monroe. These iconic celebrities, once confined to the pages of history, could now hold court, their personalities, quirks, and tales captured with breathtaking precision. Through the genius of artificial intelligence, every nuance, every inflection in their voice, every tilt of their head was recreated with meticulous attention to detail, making them virtually indistinguishable from their living counterparts[101,102,103].

But the magic doesn't stop at recreating the celebrities of yesteryears. You could converse with a Native American chief, or a philosopher from ancient Greece. Each aspect of his persona, from the patterns on his garments to the accent that colored his speech, would be rendered with uncanny accuracy, breathing life into legends and myths.

Stepping into the corporate realm, businesses would no longer rely on mere logos or static mascots. Instead, they would be represented by dynamic AI-driven holographic entities[104,105]. Picture a towering, shimmering figure representing a leading tech conglomerate, well-versed in the intricacies of its operations. This virtual spokesperson would not just parrot rehearsed lines. No, they would engage, debate, negotiate, and provide answers in real-time, their knowledge encompassing every facet of the company's vision and strategy.

In this breathtaking junction of art and algorithms, we're not just spectators but active participants, witnessing and shaping a world where AI doesn't replace human creativity but amplifies it. In this symphony of man and machine, every note resounds with the promise of boundless possibilities.

Intelligence, Surveillance, and Reconnaissance with AI

In the labyrinth of modern intelligence, surveillance, and reconnaissance (ISR), power coexists with vulnerability. At its core lies an overwhelming cascade of data that multiplies frenetically with each tick of the clock. While our current ISR capabilities are astonishing, they bump against a ceiling: the human element.

Imagine the vastness of the universe, with stars, galaxies, and cosmic events unfolding every millisecond. Now, transpose this image to the world of data, where every byte can be a beacon leading to crucial intelligence. Therein lies the crux of the problem; even with the best of human intentions and abilities, we are fundamentally unequipped to grapple with this deluge. Every piece of data, whether it's an image from a satellite or a coded message intercepted mid-air, requires human eyes to discern its value.

Tools like face-detection algorithms and fingerprint scanning systems have made significant strides. They act as our first line of defense, sifting through mountains of information, looking for the proverbial needle in the haystack. Yet, even these advanced systems are like diligent sentinels that, after identifying potential threats, turn to their human commanders for the final verdict. They may flag a face or a fingerprint, but it is up to us to confirm the match and interpret its implications.

This is where the transformative power of AI becomes invaluable. In this vast ocean of data, AI is the seasoned navigator we've been waiting for. Equipped with the capacity to process and analyze at speeds and accuracies that dwarf human capabilities, AI doesn't just identify patterns—it anticipates them. Today's facial recognition systems can identify known threats. However, future AI-driven systems will analyze minute facial expressions, gaits, and other subtle physiological signs to determine intent and emotions[106,107].

Consider satellite imagery analysis. Previously, human analysts had to painstakingly examine images pixel by pixel, looking for changes or signs of suspicious activity. Today, machine learning algorithms can be trained to identify and flag these activities autonomously. They can discern objects of interest, such as military vehicles or unusual construction activity, and even subtle changes in landscape that could indicate the presence of hidden structures or underground activities[108,109]. This automated analysis frees up human analysts to focus on more nuanced interpretation tasks.

With AI, surveillance and reconnaissance could take strange and unexpected forms. AI-driven robots modeled after animals or insects will be able to scout areas inconspicuously[110,111]. A robotic hawk might soar the skies while a mechanical beetle scuttles through enemy lines. Advanced AI tools will be able to detect anomalies through sound or ground vibrations – identifying, for example, the distant rumble of a concealed enemy tank or the whisper of a covert operative[112,113].

Furthermore, AI's capability to fuse data from multiple sources into a cohesive picture is a game-changer. For instance, an AI system could correlate social media chatter with signals intelligence and satellite imagery to offer a more comprehensive and accurate understanding of a situation. This capability, known as multi-intelligence fusion, provides a holistic picture that increases the speed and accuracy of decision-making[114].

AI and Robotics

The world of robotics, though dazzling in its advancements, is still in its infancy. Today's robots are mostly limited to a single role, mastering one craft but finding themselves out of depth beyond their specialized domain.

Consider the Roomba, the household name that has made floor-cleaning a hands-off task. Its diligent sweeps and nimble maneuvers around furniture are commendable. Yet, it is governed not by an intricate intelligence but by a series of sensors[115]. These sensors chart the terrain of your living room, ensuring the Roomba doesn't treat your prized potted plant like a patch of dirty carpet. It is methodical and efficient, but it is not "thinking."

Similarly, the modern camera-equipped drones soaring in our skies might seem like wonders. Their ability to tail users, capturing cinematic moments autonomously, is indeed a marvel. However, their genius lies in their programming and not in any inherent cognition. At their core, they're following a signal or frequency[116].

Now, imagine a future where the line between machine function and artificial intelligence blurs. AI promises not just to upgrade the robot's software but to transform its very essence. The potential? Robots that don't just "do" but "understand." Robots that can adapt, learn, and perhaps even surprise us. Instead of being tethered to one specific function, they could navigate a myriad of tasks, shifting roles with the fluidity of a seasoned professional juggling different projects.

In its simple form, the quadcopter drone might remind you of an eager child's toy, hovering in backyards and parks. Add a few nimble appendages, and this unassuming gadget suddenly becomes capable of delicate tasks. But the true metamorphosis lies not in its physical modifications but in its brain. Gift it the prowess of artificial intelligence, and this playful quadcopter emerges as a capable household helper[117,118,119].

Imagine waking up to see your drone gently watering the plants, its appendages mimicking the tender care of a gardener. In the kitchen, it becomes your diligent aide, being able to replicate recipes easily or washing dishes with precision, ensuring not a spot remains. As you sip your morning coffee, you might catch it in the act of folding laundry, its movements replicating the meticulousness of a seasoned housekeeper. When it is feeding time for your furry friend, trust this drone to measure and serve the right portion, perhaps even playing a little fetch afterwards. And as the day draws to an end, it might just glide out, garbage bag in tow, to ensure your trash is out for pickup. While you sleep soundly, the smart little drone could be relentlessly going around the property perimeter, serving as an unwavering lookout and deterrent.

But what if there's a task you've never entrusted to this aerial servant? Fear not. Just like teaching a new trick to an eager-to-learn puppy, you'd only need to guide the drone once. Its AI brain, ever-observant, would watch, learn, and remember. The next time, it would replicate the chore with astonishing accuracy, sparing you the effort.

Not limited to the mundane, AI robots will be able to take on complex and dangerous tasks. This change will bring a new era of safety and response to accidents and disasters. There are already disaster-response and fire-fighting robots in existence[120]. *Colossus* is a fire-fighting robot that was designed by Shark Robotics for operations in high-risk areas[120]. It can resist temperatures up to 900°C and be deployed in a range of indoor and outdoor environments. The company Fotokite has created the Fotokite Sigma, an advanced unmanned aerial system (UAS) designed to support first responders during critical situations[120]. This robot is fully autonomous and actively tethered, allowing safe and reliable operation in any emergency scene, even in harsh weather conditions.

The continual development and increasing intelligence of these types of robots could lead to a future where a variety of different robots coordinate together to keep us safe and rescue us from disasters. Imagine the following scenario:

High above the urban sprawl, a sentinel soars. It's an advanced aerial AI drone, a guardian designed to keep watch over the city below. Driven by solar energy, it effortlessly floats in the sky uninterrupted as it has been for many years.

Onboard this aerial custodian is an arsenal of sensors, each meticulously calibrated. Equipped with Infrared cameras, chemical sensors, radar, hyper-spectral cameras, and acoustic sensors, it has a constant and panoramic detailed view of the sprawling metropolis. Every moment, this airborne marvel scans, listens, and analyzes, its processors always on the lookout for the slightest anomaly that may spell danger.

On this day, among the hectic activity of city life, one of its thermal cameras notices an unusual temperature rise in the corner of the city. In the span of a heartbeat, it analyzes and distinguishes the cause: a petrochemical fire at a refinery a few miles away was breaking out and threatening to engulf the entire refinery and spread to other parts of the city. Almost instantly the sentinel reviews camera footage at the refinery and from nearby buildings. In a fraction of a second it finds the cause of the fire, an unlucky dry-lightning strike just a couple of minutes before. The drone's capabilities are so precise that it doesn't just spot the fire but discerns its very nature.

Almost instantly, algorithms spring to action, sifting through terabytes of data. They account for the building's location, the ferocity of the flames, and countless other factors. Before a pedestrian below would have even spotted the smoke, the drone has mapped out a strategy.

With the urgency that only machines possess, it communicates with its counterparts, emergency response drones on standby for such an occasion. Relaying blueprints of the endangered building, the sentinel in the sky highlights a critical threat: a nearby natural gas line. The potential for a disastrous explosion, though statistically small, is still real.

On the streets below, autonomous vehicles, mid-route and oblivious to the looming threat, receive the sentinel's warning. Routes change abruptly, steering clear of the danger zone, while the drone ensures traffic flows smoothly, minimizing panic and confusion.

Meanwhile, in the realm of the digital, the sentinel drone broadcasts an alert across social media platforms. Residents, businesses, and nearby commuters are informed, ensuring they can take the necessary precautions.

Within a minute dozens of emergency response drones, each with a specialty for such circumstances, descend on the building fire without fear, coordinating perfectly in synchronized and decisive action. Firefighting drones go to the blazing inferno like moths to a light. They are crafted not of flimsy metal but of robust ceramic and are enveloped in a shield of aerogel, giving them a gleaming, ethereal look, like ghostly knights in the sky. This isn't mere aesthetic, the aerogel, combined with their ceramic core, renders them virtually fireproof, enabling them to challenge blazes that would make the bravest firefighter pause.

But it is not just their armor that sets them apart. Nestled within their structures are reservoirs of aqueous film-forming foam (AFFF), a concoction known for its fire-taming properties. And for those infernos that require a little more, these drones come prepared with dry-chemical agents, ready to quench the fiercest of flames.

Their eyes, a combination of cameras and lasers, are so advanced that they cut through the densest of smoke, making the blinding haze as transparent as crystal-clear water. Not encumbered by heavy oxygen tanks or bulky equipment, these agile aviators maneuver with a precision and grace that defy the response of even the fastest human firefighting departments.

Alerted by the city's ever-watchful sentinel, the squadron of firefighting drones zero in on their target: a natural gas line threatened by the encroaching inferno. Without a moment's hesitation, they dart into the smoke-filled arena, positioning themselves just feet away from the roaring blaze. The drones, in sync and with unwavering discipline, release their cargo. A cascade of foam and chemicals descend, smothering the flames, their combined effort creating an orchestra of hisses and steam.

High above the chaos of the refinery, nimble rescue drones darted through the plumes of smoke and fire. Designed for blistering speed and the agility to navigate tight spaces, these drones scanned the labyrinthine corridors and vast open areas, hunting for any sign of life among the catastrophe. They were the first responders in a rescue operation.

Close behind these drones, a parade of paramedic quadruped robots surged forward. With a design reminiscent of mythical centaurs, they bore powerful four-legged bases and a humanoid torso equipped with dexterous arms. Their mere presence seemed to emanate both strength and purpose. They were built not just for power but for the delicate precision needed to handle human lives in peril. Their unique design allows them to traverse terrain both challenging and varied, from scaling crumbled debris to navigating waterlogged areas. Outfitted with a plethora of life-saving equipment, they are walking, thinking emergency rooms, with each decision they make driven by advanced algorithms and a singular purpose: to save lives.

Amid the thickening haze, a rescue drone detects a motionless figure sprawled on the refinery floor. Within milliseconds, the location is beamed to the nearest paramedic robot. The quadruped springs into action, covering ground at a pace that would leave even the fastest human sprinter in the dust.

Reaching the victim, the robot's upper limbs gently yet swiftly cradle the unconscious worker, shifting them onto its specially designed stretcher platform. Securing the individual, the robot's arms deftly administers an oxygen mask, ensuring that the noxious fumes would claim no further harm. Stabilized and shielded from the ongoing chaos, the worker was spirited away to safety, heading towards a rendezvous point where they could be airlifted to medical facilities.

Above the smoke-choked refinery, the sentinel drone continues monitoring the situation, its array of sensors capturing every movement and anomaly. Its infrared vision detects a group of frantic workers huddled on the roof of a towering refinery building. They seemed like ants from the drone's vantage point, dwarfed by the rising inferno beneath them, their faces etched in a tableau of fear and desperation as they sought refuge from the suffocating smoke billowing from the floors below.

With a speed and efficiency that bespoke its advanced programming, the sentinel communicates the dire situation to a squadron of hexacopter transport drones nearby. These weren't your average drones. With a wingspan matching the length of a midsize car and powered by six robust rotors, they were engineered for stability and reliability. Their hexa-rotor design ensured resilience; even if a couple of rotors failed, the drone could carry on, unflinching.

Within moments, six of these imposing drones, as synchronized as an elite military unit, descend onto the rooftop in a tight 2x3 formation. As they hover, their cargo becomes evident: suspended beneath each drone was a quadrant of seats, reminiscent of roller-coaster carts. Bright lights flare from the drones, piercing the murk, and guiding the stranded workers. Loudspeakers, in calm, authoritative voices, direct them toward the awaiting seats.

The relief among the group was palpable as they clambered into the seats. As each individual settled, sensors detect their presence, and a safety bar seamlessly secures them in place. With the workers safely ensconced, the hexacopters lift from the roof, carrying their precious cargo away from the nightmarish scene below. The drones were their silent saviors, plucking them from the precipice of doom and delivering them to safety.

AI and Warfare

In the rapidly unfolding chapters of modern combat, artificial intelligence is no longer a mere footnote. It stands out as a pivotal protagonist poised to reshape the entire narrative of warfare. Imagine the battlefield as a grand, intricate chessboard. In traditional warfare, generals and commanders, much like seasoned chess players, would make their moves, relying on instinct, experience, and sometimes, sheer luck. But in the theatre of future warfare, AI emerges as the ultimate grandmaster, its algorithms sifting through terabytes of data in the blink of an eye to craft the perfect strategy.

The real strength of artificial intelligence lies not just in its ability to command drones or control autonomous tanks. It is in the unparalleled skill to "read" the battlefield, to analyze every move and countermove, every hidden threat and overt challenge[121,122,123,124]. From the rustling of leaves indicating an ambush to the faintest radio signal betraying enemy communications, nothing escapes its digital gaze.

Armed with this holistic understanding, AI can then coordinate the adequate responses. It can deploy air raids with ground offensives, send medical-aid to where it is needed most, and even predict the enemy's next move, giving forces a crucial advantage[125,126,127,128]. It is akin to having a bird's-eye view of the entire war zone, but with the added brilliance of instantaneous decision-making and ability to recognize patterns in even the most subtle details of the battlefield.

In essence, while autonomous vehicles and drones might be the visible vanguards of AI in warfare, its true impact lies in the shadows by analyzing, strategizing, and directing the flow of combat. As we brace for this new era, it is crucial to recognize that AI's role in warfare will redefine how wars are fought.

Electronic warfare, a domain traditionally defined by high-stakes cat-and-mouse games between sophisticated technology systems, will be an increasingly important theater with artificial intelligence. Electronic warfare is a complex field, where armies grapple with waveforms, radio frequencies, and intricate equipment to gather intelligence, disrupt communication, or defend against missile threats. The challenges are steep, primarily due to the vastness of the electromagnetic spectrum and the speed at which electronic warfare must occur. In modern warfare, a delay of seconds can lead to devastating results. In this high-octane environment, artificial intelligence is poised to make a profound impact by dynamically managing and allocating spectrum resources based on real-time battlefield conditions[129,130,131]. AI systems can evaluate which frequencies are being utilized, jammed, or free, making instantaneous decisions to optimize communication and jamming strategies. In short, artificial intelligence can turn the electromagnetic spectrum into a responsive, agile element of warfare, rather than a static battlefield resource.

Electronic warfare depends on the ability to accurately detect and classify enemy signals, a task that requires sifting through vast amounts of noise to find meaningful data. AI, equipped with machine learning algorithms, can autonomously identify patterns and signatures, thereby distinguishing between friendly, enemy, and neutral signals far more quickly and accurately than a human could[132,133,134]. It can learn from past enemy electronic attacks and not only defend against them more efficiently but also predict future attack patterns[135].

This potential extends to offensive strategies as well. AI can direct high-powered microwaves or other energy weapons to exploit vulnerabilities in enemy systems, disrupting or disabling their electronics with surgical precision. Not only does this enable more effective attacks, but it also helps avoid collateral damage, as these AI-directed energy weapons can target specific systems without causing broader destruction.

The impact that artificial intelligence will make in electronic warfare will be matched and surpassed in the realm of cyber warfare. In the future, this is likely to be the sole arena that determines who will win not only the battle, but the war. AI, with its potential to both fortify cyber defenses and empower cyber-attacks, stands poised to transform the landscape of digital conflict[136,137,138]. This is a double-edged sword, offering both promise and peril, and deserving of our full attention.

As the volume and complexity of cyber threats increase, traditional cyber defense mechanisms struggle to keep up. The capacity of AI to analyze vast quantities of data rapidly and accurately means that they can monitor network activity around the clock, identifying abnormal behavior that could signal a cyber attack[139]. This type of network security will go way beyond traditional anti-virus methods, which rely on detecting specific patterns in code to flag malicious intent. Instead, AI will be able to understand what a piece of code does, and act accordingly.

The benefits will go beyond threat detection. Once a threat is detected, swift response is crucial to limit damage. Here again, AI will have no substitute. Upon detecting a threat, network security running on artificial intelligence will be able to isolate affected systems, collect forensic data, and even implement remediation measures[140,141]. Moreover, such a system will learn in the aftermath of the attack. Post-incident analysis is critical for preventing future breaches and understanding the full impact of an attack. AI will aid in sifting through the vast amounts of incident data, pinpointing the origin of the attack, identifying affected systems, and suggesting necessary security enhancements[142,143].

On the other side of this reality, AI is the ultimate hacker. One of the most common forms of cyber attacks is phishing. In this form of attack, a malicious email, often written in broken english with poor syntax, is designed to trick the recipient into revealing sensitive information. Artificial intelligence would be able to design and commit far more effective phishing attacks[144,145]. AI would be able to tailor these malicious emails based on data gathered from social media and other sources in seconds. The result is an insidiously personalized attack, which can be far more convincing and successful than standard, generic attempts.

Moreover, AI will have an almost instantaneous ability of finding and exploiting vulnerabilities in software[146,147]. Whether it's through an unpatched version of the software or a poorly designed line of code, AI would uncover and exploit these vulnerabilities at a much faster pace, outpacing the ability of human analysts to respond. The malicious potential doesn't end there, artificial intelligence will also have the ability to craft and continuously refine evasion tactics, allowing malicious software to adapt its behavior in order to avoid detection[148,149].

This illustrates an increasingly clear picture where cyber warfare is fought in the milliseconds time frame between opposing AI systems. It is conflict at such a fast pace and level of automation, that the human level is unable to keep up[150,151]. The conventional means of determining the superior force, through the amount of military might with battalions of tanks and formations of aircraft, will be completely useless. AI will fight AI, and in a few seconds, the victor will likely be determined, having taken over the systems, infrastructure, and artificial intelligence of the opposing side.

AI and Quantum Computers

In the world of cutting-edge technology, two powerhouses are joining forces to reshape the future: artificial intelligence and quantum computing. When united, they will create a paradigm shift in computing power, data analysis, and problem-solving[152,153,154]. AI and quantum computing are each groundbreaking in their own right. AI, with its ability to learn from experience, understand complex patterns, and perform tasks that typically require human intelligence, is already altering numerous sectors, from healthcare to finance. On the other side, quantum computing, still in its infant stage, promises computational power far exceeding the capabilities of today's most advanced supercomputers.

To date, AI's effectiveness is partly shackled by the computational limitations of classical computers. Training complex AI models demand vast computing resources, and some tasks remain dauntingly time-consuming. Quantum computers, with their superior computing power, could dramatically speed up these processes, accelerating the evolution of AI capabilities.

Companies like IBM and Google are already exploring this convergence[155,156]. IBM's Quantum Neural Network, for example, aims to leverage quantum systems to enhance the learning efficiency of neural networks[155]. Similarly, Google's Quantum AI lab is researching how quantum computing might solve complex problems that classical computers can barely scratch[156].

AI powered by quantum computers could transform the way we model complex systems, from predicting weather patterns to understanding genetic codes or developing new materials[157,158]. Imagine accurately predicting a typhoon's path weeks ahead or designing custom medication tailored to a patient's genetic makeup. These possibilities are no longer in the realm of science fiction but are becoming scientific fact.

For cybersecurity, quantum-encryption techniques like Quantum Key Distribution offer superior security protocols[159,160]. Furthermore, AI algorithms could be used to detect and counteract potential threats in these quantum networks, creating robust security systems. This new autonomous race of evolving security systems could lead to security protocols so complex and advanced that humans literally can't understand them[161,162].

The potential of this fusion is only beginning to be realized, but one thing is certain: the impact will touch every corner of society, from science to manufacturing and from security to creativity. Simply put, the fusion of these technologies will result in what can be thought of as artificial intelligence and quantum computing "on steroids" since each will improve the other's capabilities[163,164]. As we stand on the brink of this revolution, the question is not "if" but "how" these changes will unfold. The future is quantum, and it is intelligent.

AI and Nanotechnology

There is almost no combination more mind-bending than that of AI with nanotechnology. It's hard to imagine technology getting more advanced than this stage. The potential of what is possible with the combination of these technologies is limited more by human creativity and expectations than anything else. These technologies would surpass anything fantasized possible for even sci-fi universes like those of *Star Trek* and *Star Wars*.

Many of us are familiar with the shapeshifting T-1000 from *Terminator 2: Judgment Day*, a killing machine composed of liquid metal that could assume the form of anyone or anything it touched. This iconic sci-fi character fascinated audiences with the notion of intelligent, adaptive material. Yet, in the realms of artificial intelligence and nanotechnology, the concept of the T-1000 personifies the possibilities of such a combination with these technologies. Though, instead of an artificially intelligent entity made of liquid-metal, imagine one made of a nanobot swarm.

If thinking such a concept is too far-fetched for reality, consider that intelligent and autonomous nanobot swarms already exist[165,166,167]. They are leading the way with revolutionary healthcare concepts. A team of scientists at the Chinese University of Hong Kong created a swarm of nanobots made of millions of magnetic nanoparticles[167]. This swarm showed itself capable of a wide range of structural changes, including extending, shrinking, splitting, and merging, all with a high degree of accuracy[167].

Scaled up, this ability would be comparable to the T-1000's shapeshifting prowess, allowing the swarm to navigate through tight spaces, adapt to environmental conditions, or even mimic the appearance of various objects. With a sufficient number of nanobots and sophisticated AI, the swarm could potentially morph into any shape and adapt to almost any situation, given enough time and available resources.

This autonomous swarm would far surpass the abilities of the liquid-metal T-1000 because of one key ability: self-replication. Borrowing from principles of biological reproduction and automated manufacturing, these nanobots would be able to use available matter to replicate themselves, increasing their numbers autonomously. An entity with such an ability would give even the all-powerful T-1000 nightmares.

This is not merely theoretical, recent advancements in nanobot self-replication have been primarily observed in the development of what are called *Xenobots*[168,169]. These are tiny programmable living entities made from frog stem cells. These tiny computer-designed organisms that look like Pac-Man can swim in their environment, find single cells, gather hundreds of them together, and assemble "baby" Xenobots inside their "mouth"[169].

These concepts show we have the ability to create

coordinated swarms of nanobots that can be directed towards a certain objective. It also shows we can already build nanobots capable of self-replication. Although impressive enough, the true awe-factor will come from the ability of nanobots to manipulate and build with matter at the smallest scales[170].

In the future, the most powerful weapon of all could simply be a small amount of autonomous nanobots that gets unleashed on a particular area. Depending on their given objective, they could do almost anything[171,172]. Guided by artificial intelligence, they could potentially infiltrate organisms at a cellular level, disrupting vital processes and neutralizing threats without causing extensive physical destruction. This isn't out of the realm of fantasy, there are already published papers that validate the possibility of nano-vehicles that can deliver specific or engineered bioagents in targeted hosts[173,174].

Although this concept of an AI nanobot swarm sounds foreboding, it can be an entity that becomes the ultimate ally and protector of humanity. Not only that, this sort of technology is powerful enough to be what spreads humanity across the universe. A team from Northeastern University has been engaged in investigating potential applications of nanotechnology for space exploration[175]. One of the proposed ideas from this team is a sensor net "spider web," which consists of hairline tubes designed to spread across large areas of a planet's surface. These tubes would house numerous nanosensors capable of measuring various surface conditions.

Consider a future where an AI swarm wielding the intelligence beyond any human is sent out into space. Its mission is colossal: create life on a barren planet.

The AI would first deploy its nanobot swarm to conduct a comprehensive assessment of the planet's atmosphere, geology, climate, and available resources. This detailed analysis would help in devising a tailored terraforming strategy, focusing on creating a stable environment capable of sustaining life.

To create a life-sustaining atmosphere, the nanobots would initiate processes to thicken the atmosphere and adjust its composition. They might extract and release greenhouse gases to increase the planet's temperature, facilitate the formation of a magnetosphere to protect against solar radiation, and introduce a balanced mix of oxygen and nitrogen.

Water, being essential for life, would be synthesized by the nanobots using available elements such as hydrogen and oxygen, or by redirecting comets and asteroids containing water ice towards the planet. Once water is available, nanobots would ensure its proper distribution, creating oceans, lakes, and rivers.

The AI would instruct the nanobots to enrich the planet's soil by breaking down rocks and minerals into fertile soil, introducing organic matter, and fostering the growth of microbes, fungi, and other primary life forms. These foundational organisms would contribute to the creation of a nutrient cycle and prepare the soil for more complex plant life.

Once the soil is ready, the nanobots would cultivate diverse plant species, beginning with hardy pioneer species to further enrich the soil and modify the atmosphere. Gradually, a wide variety of flora would be introduced to establish a balanced and biodiverse ecosystem, paving the way for more complex life forms.

With a stable ecosystem in place, the AI would begin to introduce simple animal life forms, starting with microorganisms, insects, and small invertebrates. Over time, the introduction of more complex animals would follow, ensuring each species is integrated in a way that maintains ecological balance.

Throughout the terraforming process, the AI would continuously monitor the developing ecosystem, adjusting variables, and introducing new elements as necessary to maintain balance and promote diversity. The nanobots would actively manage population dynamics, genetic diversity, and ecological relationships to ensure the stability of the burgeoning web of life.

The AI, with its superior intelligence, would subtly guide the evolution of life on the newly terraformed planet, fostering the development of intelligence and adaptability among the inhabitants. It would work towards creating a harmonious and resilient ecosystem, rich in biodiversity and capable of withstanding environmental changes.

Chapter References

1. Mayor, A. (n.d.). The Greek myth of Talos, the first robot. *TED-Ed*. https://ed.ted.com/lessons/the-greek-myth-of-talos-the-first-robot-adrienne-mayor

2. TED-Ed. (2023, October 9). The Greek myth of Talos, the first robot. *Greece High Definition*. https://www.greecehighdefinition.com/blog/2021/2/26/the-greek-myth-of-talos-the-first-robot-ted-ed

3. Sharma, M. S. (2019, March 31). 'Hindu epics are full of AI, robots. Legend has it that they guarded Buddha's relics'. *The Times of India*. https://timesofindia.indiatimes.com/home/sunday-times/all-that-matters/hindu-epics-are-full-of-ai-robots-legend-has-it-that-they-guarded-buddhas-relics/articleshow/68648962.cms

4. Srinivasan, L. (2023, February 23). Can the Mahabharata teach us how to manage Artificial Intelligence? *India Today*. https://www.indiatoday.in/news-analysis/story/can-mahabharata-teach-us-how-to-manage-artificial-intelligence-2338623-2023-02-23

5. Cox, G. (2014, January 20). A History of Robotics: Yan Shi the Artificer. *Salvius Blog*. https://blog.salvius.org/2014/01/a-history-of-robotics-yan-shi-artificer.html

6. Glitch Press. (2021, May 1). The first Chinese sci-fi story by Lie Zi - 4th century BCE. https://glitchpress.com/index.php/2021/05/01/the-first-chinese-sci-fi-story-by-lie-zi-4th-centry-bce/

7. Iqbal, M. (2023). AI-Descartes: The AI Scientist Revolutionizes Scientific Discovery. *Scientia Magazine*. https://scientiamag.org/ai-descartes-the-ai-scientist-revolutionizes-scientific-discovery/

8. Cameron, J. (2014, October 15). Determinism: The Influence of the Mechanistic World View. *Decoded Past*. https://decodedpast.com/determinism-the-influence-of-the-mechanistic-world-view/

9. Cave, S., & Dihal, K. (2018, July 25). Ancient dreams of intelligent machines: 3,000 years of robots. *Nature*. https://www.nature.com/articles/d41586-018-05773-y

10. Sack, H. (n.d.). Jacques de Vaucanson and his Miraculous Automata. *SciHi Blog*. http://scihi.org/jacques-de-vaucanson-automata/

11. Computer History Museum. (n.d.). Schickard's Calculator and The Pascaline. *CHM Revolution*. https://www.computerhistory.org/revolution/calculators/1/47

12. History Computer. (2023, July 28). Mechanical Calculators. https://history-computer.com/mechanical-calculators/

13. Park, E. (n.d.). What a Difference the Difference Engine Made: From Charles Babbage's Calculator Emerged Today's Computer. *Smithsonian Magazine*. https://www.smithsonianmag.com/history/what-a-difference-the-difference-engine-made-from-charles-babbages-calculator-emerged-todays-computer-109389254/

14. Science Museum Group. (2023, July 18). Charles Babbage's Difference Engines and the Science Museum. *Science Museum*. https://www.sciencemuseum.org.uk/objects-and-stories/charles-babbages-difference-engines-and-science-museum

15. Popova, M. (2022, September 15). Darwin Among the Machines: A Victorian Visionary's Prophetic Admonition for Saving Ourselves from Enslavement by Artificial Intelligence. *The Marginalian*. https://www.themarginalian.org/2022/09/15/samuel-butler-darwin-among-the-machines-erewhon/

16. Norman, J. M. (2023, October 10). Samuel Butler Publishes "Darwin among the Machines" in a New Zealand Newspaper. *History of Information*. https://historyofinformation.com/detail.php?id=3394

17. Norman, J. M. (2023, October 10). Alan Turing publishes "On Computable Numbers," describing what came to be called the "Turing Machine." *History of Information*. https://www.historyofinformation.com/detail.php?entryid=735

18. Dave, W. (2013, March 15). 1930s: Turing's Universal Machine. *Science Museum Blog*. https://blog.sciencemuseum.org.uk/1930s-turings-universal-machine/

19. Nobel Prize Outreach. (2003, May 5). The History of the Integrated Circuit. *Nobel Prize Educational Games*. https://educationalgames.nobelprize.org/educational/physics/integrated_circuit/history/index.html

20. Engineering and Technology History Wiki. (2022, June 14). IEEE Milestone: First Semiconductor Integrated Circuit (IC), 1958. https://ethw.org/Milestones:First_Semiconductor_Integrated_Circuit_(IC),_1958

21. St. George, B., & Gillis, A. S. (2023, April). What is the Turing Test? *TechTarget*. https://www.techtarget.com/searchenterpriseai/definition/Turing-test

22. Stanford Encyclopedia of Philosophy. (2021, October 4). The Turing Test. https://plato.stanford.edu/entries/turing-test/

23. American Museum of Natural History. (2018, February 13). Revisiting Asimov's Three Laws of Robotics. https://www.amnh.org/explore/news-blogs/news-posts/revisiting-asimovs-three-laws-of-robotics

24. House of Ethics. (2021, April 10). The 3 Laws of Robotics by Asimov. https://www.houseofethics.lu/2021/04/10/the-3-laws-of-the-robotic-by-asimov/

25. Dartmouth College. (n.d.). Artificial Intelligence (AI) Coined at Dartmouth. https://home.dartmouth.edu/about/artificial-intelligence-ai-coined-dartmouth

26. Computer History Museum. (n.d.). John McCarthy - CHM. https://computerhistory.org/profile/john-mccarthy/

27. History-Computer.com. (n.d.). Logic Theorist - Complete History of the Logic Theorist Program. https://history-computer.com/logic-theorist/

28. Anyoha, R. (2017). The History of Artificial Intelligence. *Harvard University*. https://sitn.hms.harvard.edu/flash/2017/history-artificial-intelligence/

29. Foote, K. D. (2021, December 3). A Brief History of Machine Learning. *DATAVERSITY*. https://www.dataversity.net/a-brief-history-of-machine-learning/

30. Karjian, R. (2023, September 22). History and Evolution of Machine Learning: A Timeline. *TechTarget*. https://www.techtarget.com/whatis/A-Timeline-of-Machine-Learning-History

31. Loiseau, J.-C. B. (2019, March 11). Rosenblatt's perceptron, the first modern neural network. *Towards Data Science*. https://towardsdatascience.com/rosenblatts-perceptron-the-very-first-neural-network-37a3ec09038a

32. Kostadinov, S. (2019, August 8). Understanding Backpropagation Algorithm. *Medium*. https://towardsdatascience.com/understanding-backpropagation-algorithm-7bb3aa2f95fd

33. Goodrich, J. (2021, January 25). How IBM's Deep Blue Beat World Champion Chess Player Garry Kasparov. *IEEE Spectrum*. https://spectrum.ieee.org/how-ibms-deep-blue-beat-world-champion-chess-player-garry-kasparov

34. History.com Editors. (2009, November 16). Deep Blue defeats Garry Kasparov in chess match. *History*. https://www.history.com/this-

day-in-history/deep-blue-defeats-garry-kasparov-in-chess-match

35. Spandas Lui. (2011, February 17). IBM Watson Wins Jeopardy, Humans Rally Back. *PCWorld*. https://www.pcworld.com/article/494966/ibm_watson_wins_jeopardy_humans_rally_back.html

36. Hiner, J. (2014, February 14). IBM Watson: The inside story of how the Jeopardy-winning supercomputer was born, and what it wants to do next. *TechRepublic*. https://www.techrepublic.com/article/ibm-watson-the-inside-story-of-how-the-jeopardy-winning-supercomputer-was-born-and-what-it-wants-to-do-next/

37. Ibrahim, M. (2023, June 23). Talking to Machines: The Breakthrough of Speech Recognition Technology. *Weights & Biases*. URL: https://wandb.ai/mostafaibrahim17/ml-articles/reports/Talking-to-Machines-The-Breakthrough-of-Speech-Recognition-Technology--VmlldzozNTkwNzU2

38. Sudarshan, A., Samuel, V., Patwa, P., Amara, I., & Chadha, A. (2023). Improved contextual recognition in automatic speech recognition systems by semantic lattice rescoring. *arXiv*. https://doi.org/10.48550/arXiv.2310.09680

39. Allworth, J. (2011, October 13). Apple's Siri is as revolutionary as the Mac. *Harvard Business Review*. https://hbr.org/2011/10/apples-siri-is-as-revolutionar

40. Stone, B. (2021, May 11). The secret origins of Amazon's Alexa. *Wired*. https://www.wired.com/story/how-amazon-made-alexa-smarter/

41. Fedewa, J. (2021, January 13). What is Google Assistant, and what can it do? *How-To Geek*. https://www.howtogeek.com/692895/what-is-google-assistant-and-what-can-it-do/

42. Choudhary, K., DeCost, B., Chen, C., et al. (2022). Recent advances and applications of deep learning methods in materials science. *npj Computational Materials*, 8, Article 59. https://doi.org/10.1038/s41524-022-00734-6

43. Bansal, V. (2020, April 5). The Evolution of Deep Learning. *Towards Data Science*. https://towardsdatascience.com/the-deep-history-of-deep-learning-3bebeb810fb2

44. Knight, W. (2016, March 18). Five Lessons from AlphaGo's Historic Victory. *MIT Technology Review*. https://www.technologyreview.com/2016/03/18/161507/five-lessons-from-alphagos-historic-victory/

45. Chinese Association of Automation. (2016, August 26). Where

does AlphaGo go? *Phys.org.* https://phys.org/news/2016-08-alphago.html

46. Baidu. (2021, August 20). From health care to infrastructure, how AI is changing the world for the better. *MIT Technology Review*. https://www.technologyreview.com/2021/08/20/1032358/from-health-care-to-infrastructure-how-ai-is-changing-the-world-for-the-better/

47. Chauhan, D. (2021, November 9). Artificial Intelligence in Transportation: Moving Faster Toward the Future. *Stefanini*. https://stefanini.com/en/insights/articles/artificial-intelligence-in-transportation-moving-faster

48. Alowais, S.A., Alghamdi, S.S., Alsuhebany, N. et al. Revolutionizing healthcare: the role of artificial intelligence in clinical practice. *BMC Med Educ 23*, 689 (2023). https://doi.org/10.1186/s12909-023-04698-z

49. Jeevanandam, N. (2023, October 30). What is AI Singularity and How Far are We From It? *Emeritus*. https://emeritus.org/in/learn/what-is-ai-singularity/

50. Brooks, M. (2023, October 14). The domino effect: How AI will soon outsmart us all. *Psychology Today*. https://www.psychologytoday.com/us/blog/tech-happy-life/202310/the-ai-domino-effect-how-ai-will-soon-outsmart-us-all

51. Galeon, D., & Reedy, C. (2017, March 15). A Google exec just claimed the singularity will happen by 2029. *ScienceAlert*. https://www.sciencealert.com/google-s-director-of-engineering-claims-that-the-singularity-will-happen-by-2029

52. Raizada, A. (n.d.). Autonomous vehicles: The impact on transportation & logistics. *Copper Digital*. https://copperdigital.com/blog/rise-of-autonomous-vehicles-implications-transportation/

53. Schmelzer, R. (2019, April 29). Future of AI in transportation goes beyond self-driving cars. *TechTarget*. https://www.techtarget.com/searchenterpriseai/feature/Future-of-AI-in-transportation-goes-beyond-self-driving-cars

54. Maddox, T. (2018, February 1). How autonomous vehicles could save over 350K lives in the US and millions worldwide. *ZDNet*. https://www.zdnet.com/article/how-autonomous-vehicles-could-save-over-350k-lives-in-the-us-and-millions-worldwide/

55. Johnson, T. (2023, September). Are self-driving cars already safer than human drivers? *Ars Technica*. https://arstechnica.com/cars/2023/09/are-self-driving-cars-already-safer-than-human-drivers/

56. Chen, B., Pan, X., Evangelou, S. A., & Timotheou, S. (2020). Optimal Control for Connected and Autonomous Vehicles at Signal-Free Intersections. *IFAC-PapersOnLine*, 53(2), 15306-15311. https://doi.org/10.1016/j.ifacol.2020.12.2336.

57. Meng, X., & Cassandras, C. G. (2022). Eco-Driving of Autonomous Vehicles for Nonstop Crossing of Signalized Intersections. *IEEE Transactions on Automation Science and Engineering*, 19(1), 320-331. https://doi.org/10.1109/TASE.2020.3029452

58. Malikopoulos, A. A., Hong, S., Lee, J., & Park, B. B. (2018). Optimal Control for Speed Harmonization of Automated Vehicles. https://doi.org/10.48550/arXiv.1611.04647

59. Chang, L. (Year). First they came for the drivers: How autonomous vehicles are going after traffic lights. *Digital Trends*. https://www.digitaltrends.com/cars/self-driving-car-traffic-light/

60. Dukowitz, Z. (2021, September 2). How Autonomous Drones Are Revolutionizing Warehouse Logistics. *UAV Coach*. https://uavcoach.com/warehouse-drones/

61. Ackerman, E. (2021, August 3). Corvus Robotics' Autonomous Drones Tackle Warehouses. *IEEE Spectrum*. https://spectrum.ieee.org/drone-warehouse-corvus-robotics

62. Chai, H., Rodier, C. J., Song, J. W., Zhang, M. H., & Jaller, M. (2023). The impacts of automated vehicles on Center city parking. *Transportation Research Part A: Policy and Practice*, 175, 103764. https://doi.org/10.1016/j.tra.2023.103764.

63. Edward, K. (2023, July 29). Goodbye gridlock: How autonomous vehicles can revolutionize city living. *Forbes*. https://www.forbes.com/sites/kyleedward/2023/07/29/goodbye-gridlock-how-autonomous-vehicles-can-revolutionize-city-living/

64. Haygood, J. (2022, August 30). How To Become a Fighter Pilot: Complete Guide. *SkyTough*. https://www.skytough.com/post/how-to-become-a-fighter-pilot

65. Sandboxx. (2020, November 23). How long does it take to become an Air Force fighter pilot? *Sandboxx*. https://www.sandboxx.us/blog/how-long-does-it-take-to-become-an-air-force-fighter-pilot/

66. Indeed Editorial Team. (2023, October 13). How to become an Air Force pilot. *Indeed Career Guide*. https://www.indeed.com/career-advice/career-development/how-to-become-an-airforce-pilot

67. Everstine, B. W. (2020, August 20). Artificial Intelligence Easily Beats Human Fighter Pilot in DARPA Trial. *Air & Space Forces Magazine*. https://www.airandspaceforces.com/artificial-intelligence-easily-beats-human-fighter-pilot-in-darpa-trial/

68. Walsh, A. (2023, March 6). AI-powered pilot dominates human rival in aerial dogfight. *Flying Magazine*. https://www.flyingmag.com/ai-powered-pilot-dominates-human-rival-in-aerial-dogfight/

69. Hambling, D. (2020). AI outguns a human fighter pilot. *New Scientist*, 247(3297), 12. https://doi.org/10.1016/S0262-4079(20)31477-9

70. Mills, W. D. (2021, March 4). The U.S. Navy's Newest Aircraft May Be Fully Autonomous. *The National Interest*. https://nationalinterest.org/blog/reboot/us-navy%E2%80%99s-newest-aircraft-may-be-fully-autonomous-179218

71. Johns Hopkins University Applied Physics Laboratory. (2020, August 28). AI Bests Human Fighter Pilot in AlphaDogfight Trial at Johns Hopkins APL. https://www.jhuapl.edu/work/projects/alphadogfight-trials

72. DARPA. (2020, August 26). AlphaDogfight Trials Foreshadow Future of Human-Machine Symbiosis. https://www.darpa.mil/news-events/2020-08-26

73. Harry. (2023, June 2). Militart News: Witness the Emergence of AI Fighter Pilot: The Autonomous F-16 Jet Takes Flight, Engages in Combat, and Safely Lands. *The News Season*. https://tnewss.online/militart-news-witness-the-emergence-of-ai-fighter-pilot-the-autonomous-f-16-jet-takes-flight-engages-in-combat-and-safely-lands/

74. GlobalData. (2023, August 2). AI pilots, the future of aerial warfare. *Airforce Technology*. https://www.airforce-technology.com/comment/ai-pilots-the-future-of-aerial-warfare/

75. Hambling, D. (2021, June 17). DARPA Gremlin Swarm Will Carry Weapons Or Sub-Drones And Re-Arm Mid-Air. *Forbes*. https://www.forbes.com/sites/davidhambling/2021/06/17/darpa-gremlin-swarm-drones-to-carry-weapon-and-re-arm-mid-air/

76. Fox, B. (2006, July 25). Invention: In-flight rearming. *New Scientist*. https://www.newscientist.com/article/dn9615-invention-in-flight-rearming/

77. Milrem Robotics. (n.d.). Type-X. https://milremrobotics.com/type-x/

78. Milrem Robotics. (2023, September 5). Milrem Robotics to present Type-X Robotic Combat Vehicle at DSEI 2023. *Defence Industry Europe*. https://defence-industry.eu/milrem-robotics-to-present-type-x-robotic-combat-vehicle-at-dsei-2023/

79. Macaulay, T. (2020, March 10). The US Navy is developing AI-powered submarines that could kill autonomously. *The Next Web*. https://thenextweb.com/news/the-us-navy-is-developing-ai-powered-submarines-that-could-kill-autonomously

80. Zhao, C. (Date Unknown). China Building Artificial Intelligence–Powered Nuclear Submarine That Could Have 'Its Own Thoughts,' Report Says. *Newsweek*. https://www.newsweek.com/china-building-artificial-intelligence-powered-nuclear-submarines-have-its-own-799351

81. Leone, D. (2023, February 17). Former US Navy Submariner explains why 120 days is the longest time a submarine can remain underwater. *The Aviation Geek Club*. https://theaviationgeekclub.com/former-us-navy-submariner-explains-why-120-days-is-the-longest-time-a-submarine-can-remain-underwater/

82. Antonio. (2022, November 3). Submarine Endurance: How Long Can They Stay Underwater? *ussjpkennedyjr.org*. https://www.ussjpkennedyjr.org/submarine-endurance-how-long-can-they-stay-underwater/

83. Lockheed Martin. (n.d.). Trident II D5 Fleet Ballistic Missile. *Naval Technology*. https://www.naval-technology.com/projects/trident-ii-d5-fleet-ballistic-missile/

84. Navy Recognition. (2021, October 25). Ohio-class ballistic missile submarine launches Trident II D5LE missiles. https://www.navyrecognition.com/index.php/naval-news/naval-news-archive/2021/october/10899-ohio-class-ballistic-missile-submarine-launches-trident-ii-d5le-missiles.html

85. Missile Defense Project. (2016, September 19). Trident D5. *Missile Threat. Center for Strategic and International Studies*. https://missilethreat.csis.org/missile/trident/.

86. Kimota. (2022, September 8). The Different Yields Of The Hiroshima And Nagasaki Bombs. *Visit Nagasaki*. https://visit-nagasaki.com/the-different-yields-of-the-hiroshima-and-nagasaki-bombs/

87. Vincent, J. (2022, August 2). An interview with David Holz, CEO of AI image-generator Midjourney: it's reshaping culture. *The Verge*. https://www.theverge.com/2022/8/2/23287173/ai-image-generation-art-midjourney-multiverse-interview-david-holz

88. Martekings. (2023, October 12). Marketer's guide to Midjourney: The innovative AI art generator tool. *LinkedIn*. https://www.linkedin.com/pulse/marketers-guide-midjourney-innovative-ai-art-generator-tool

89. Nguyen, M. (n.d.). Virtual influencers: meet the AI-generated figures posing as your new online friends – as they try to sell you stuff. *The Conversation*. https://theconversation.com/virtual-influencers-meet-the-ai-generated-figures-posing-as-your-new-online-friends-as-they-try-to-sell-you-stuff-212001

90. Nguyen, M. (2023, September 19). Virtual influencers: Meet AI-generated figures posing as your new online friends—as they try to sell you stuff. *Phys.org*. https://phys.org/news/2023-09-virtual-ai-generated-figures-posing-online.html

91. Weitzman, C. (2023, May 10). Understanding AI Influencers: Virtual Personalities In Digital Marketing. *Speechify*. https://speechify.com/blog/what-is-ai-influencer/

92. Ijarotimi, T. (2023, May 30). Gaming Intelligence: How AI is revolutionizing game development. *Interesting Engineering*. https://interestingengineering.com/innovation/gaming-intelligence-how-ai-is-revolutionizing-game-development

93. Singh, T. (2023, August 21). How AI in Games Will Revolutionize the Gaming Industry. *Make Tech Easier*. https://www.maketecheasier.com/ai-revolutionize-gaming-industry/

94. Kaser, R. (2023, February 23). How generative AI is changing game development (and UGC). *VentureBeat*. https://venturebeat.com/games/how-generative-ai-is-changing-game-development-and-ugc/

95. Gururaj, T. (2023, July 20). Artificial intelligence and the evolution of filmmaking. *Interesting Engineering*. https://interestingengineering.com/culture/artificial-intelligence-in-filmmaking-ai-visual-effects-cgi

96. Singh, H., Kaur, K., & Singh, P. P. (2023). Artificial Intelligence as a facilitator for Film Production Process. *2023 International Conference on Artificial Intelligence and Smart Communication (AISC)* (pp. 969-972). Greater Noida, India. https://doi.org/10.1109/AISC56616.2023.10085082

97. Berman, M. (2023, April 30). From Holograms to AI: An Exciting Glimpse into the Future of Entertainment Technology. *Programming Insider*. https://programminginsider.com/from-holograms-to-ai-an-exciting-glimpse-into-the-future-of-entertainment-technology/

98. Ackerman, D. (2021, March 10). Using artificial intelligence to generate 3D holograms in real-time. *Massachusetts Institute of*

Technology. https://news.mit.edu/2021/3d-holograms-vr-0310

99. Multiplatform AI. (n.d.). The Rise of Holographic Performances: AI's Influence in the Intersection of Technology and Entertainment. https://multiplatform.ai/the-rise-of-holographic-performances-ais-influence-in-the-intersection-of-technology-and-entertainment/

100. Digital Humans. (2023, February 22). Can AI replicate what it's like to talk to historical figures? We aim to find out. https://www.digitalhumans.com/blog/can-ai-replicate-what-its-like-to-talk-to-historical-figures-we-aim-to-find-out

101. Rodriguez, D. (Host). (2023). Aiconic Talks: Reviving historical figures with AI. *Apple Podcasts*. https://podcasts.apple.com/us/podcast/aiconic-talks/id1673077798

102. Cole, M. (2021, March 22). Artist Uses AI Technology to Create Portraits of Famous Historical Figures. *My Modern Met*. https://mymodernmet.com/nathan-shipley-historical-ai-portraits/

103. James, L. (2020, July 15). A new holographic reality for business. *Engineering & Technology*. https://eandt.theiet.org/content/articles/2020/07/a-new-holographic-reality-for-business/

104. *PR Newswire*. (2023, March 30). WiMi Hologram Cloud to Dig into AI-driven Holographic Virtual Human Technology. *Yahoo Finance*. https://finance.yahoo.com/news/wimi-hologram-cloud-dig-ai-120000583.html

105. Park, S., Lee, S. W., & Whang, M. (2021). The Analysis of Emotion Authenticity Based on Facial Micromovements. *Sensors (Basel, Switzerland)*, 21(13), 4616. https://doi.org/10.3390/s21134616.

106. Teh, C. (2021, June 16). An AI 'Emotion-Recognition System' Can Track How 'Happy' Chinese People Are at Work. *Insider*. https://www.insider.com/ai-emotion-recognition-system-tracks-how-happy-chinas-workers-are-2021-6

107. McHale, J. (2019, June 12). Deep learning model from Lockheed Martin tackles satellite image analysis. *Military Embedded Systems*. https://militaryembedded.com/ai/deep-learning/deep-learning-model-from-lockheed-martin-tackles-satellite-image-analysis

108. McCullough, K., Feng, A., Chen, M., & McAlinden, R. (2020). Utilizing Satellite Imagery Datasets and Machine Learning Data Models to Evaluate Infrastructure Change in Undeveloped Regions. *Interservice/Industry Training, Simulation, and Education Conference (I/ITSEC)*. https://arxiv.org/pdf/2009.00185

109. de Croon, G. C. H. E., et al. (2022). Insect-inspired AI for autonomous robots. *Science Robotics*, 7, eabl6334. https://doi.org/10.1126/scirobotics.abl6334.

110. University of Pittsburgh. (2022, March 3). Robot 'bugs' that can go just about anywhere. *ScienceDaily*. https://www.sciencedaily.com/releases/2022/03/220303191454.htm

111. Vos, K., Peng, Z., Jenkins, C., Shahriar, M. R., Borghesani, P., & Wang, W. (2022). Vibration-based anomaly detection using LSTM/SVM approaches. *Mechanical Systems and Signal Processing*, 169, 108752. https://doi.org/10.1016/j.ymssp.2021.108752

112. Meng, Q., & Zhu, S. (2023). Anomaly detection for construction vibration signals using unsupervised deep learning and cloud computing. *Advanced Engineering Informatics*, 55, 101907. https://doi.org/10.1016/j.aei.2023.101907

113. Booz Allen Hamilton. (2023). Accelerating Multi-INT Fusion for Intelligence Missions. https://www.boozallen.com/insights/intel/accelerating-multi-int-fusion-for-intelligence-missions.html

114. Woodford, C. (2021). Roomba. *Explain that Stuff*. https://www.explainthatstuff.com/how-roomba-works.html

115. Frąckiewicz, M. (2023, June 24). How does a drone's autonomous flight system work? *TS2 Space*. https://ts2.space/en/how-does-a-drones-autonomous-flight-system-work/

116. Abbeel, P. (2022). AI and robotics: How will robots help us in the future? *World Economic Forum*. https://www.weforum.org/agenda/2022/02/robots-future-tech/

117. Yang, S. (2021, October 6). New AI strategy enables robots to rapidly adapt to real-world environments. *UC IT Blog*. https://cio.ucop.edu/new-ai-strategy-enables-robots-to-rapidly-adapt-to-real-world-environments/

118. El Atillah, I. (2023, February 24). Robots could do 39% of domestic chores within 10 years, AI experts say. But it's not all good news. *Euronews*. https://www.euronews.com/next/2023/02/24/robots-could-do-39-of-domestic-chores-within-10-years-ai-experts-say-its-not-all-good-news

119. Pizzuto, C. (2023, April 18). Disaster robots: Revolutionizing emergency response with autonomous robots. *AI for Good Blog*. https://aiforgood.itu.int/disaster-robots-revolutionizing-emergency-response-with-autonomous-robots/

120. McCullough, T. (2022, August 26). Assuming risk: Artificial intelligence on the battlefield. *Lieber Institute at West Point*. https://lieber.westpoint.edu/assuming-risk-artificial-intelligence-battlefield/

121. Fish, A. (2022, September 12). IoT, AI, and the future battlefield. *Military Embedded Systems*. https://militaryembedded.com/ai/deep-learning/iot-ai-and-the-future-battlefield

122. O'Hanlon, M. E. (2018, November 29). The role of AI in future warfare. *Brookings*. https://www.brookings.edu/articles/ai-and-future-warfare/

123. National Institute of Standards and Technology. (2020, September 24). New system detects faint communications signals using the principles of quantum physics. *Phys.org*. https://phys.org/news/2020-09-faint-principles-quantum-physics.html

124. Centre for Land Warfare Studies (CLAWS). (2023). Developing AI in Combat Healthcare. *CLAWS*. https://www.claws.in/developing-ai-in-combat-healthcare/

125. Taylor, D. (2022, November 9). AI gaming to assist U.S. Air Force commanders with air attack planning. *Military Embedded Systems*. https://militaryembedded.com/ai/big-data/ai-gaming-to-assist-us-air-force-commanders-with-air-attack-planning

126. Saballa, J. (2023, July 11). US Army seeking AI system that predicts enemy actions. *The Defense Post*. https://www.thedefensepost.com/2023/07/11/us-army-ai-system/

127. Texta.ai. (n.d.). The Rise of AI Battlefield: Advanced Weapons Revolutionizing Modern Warfare. https://texta.ai/blog-articles/the-rise-of-ai-battlefield-advanced-weapons-revolutionizing-modern-warfare

128. Gannon, L. C. B. P. (2023, August). Implement AI in Electromagnetic Spectrum Operations. *Proceedings*, 149(8/1,446). https://www.usni.org/magazines/proceedings/2023/august/implement-ai-electromagnetic-spectrum-operations

129. Waterman, S. (2021, October 28). DOD Tests AI-powered Spectrum Management Technology on Aerial Combat Training Ranges. *Air & Space Forces Magazine*. https://www.airandspaceforces.com/dod-test-ai-powered-spectrum-management/

130. U.S. Naval Institute. (2023, August). Implement AI in Electromagnetic Spectrum Operations. *Proceedings Magazine*. https://www.usni.org/magazines/proceedings/2023/august/implement-ai-electromagnetic-spectrum-operations

131. Seffers, G. I. (2017, November 01). Smarter AI for Electronic Warfare. *The Cyber Edge*. https://www.afcea.org/signal-media/cyber-edge/smarter-ai-electronic-warfare

132. Defense One. (2023). AI-Enabled Electronic Warfare. https://www.defenseone.com/insights/cards/how-ai-changing-way-warfighters-make-decisions-and-fight-battlefield/3/?oref=d1-cards-continue

133. Gannon, B. P. (2023, August). Implement AI in Electromagnetic Spectrum Operations. *U.S. Naval Institute Proceedings*, 149(8/1,446). https://www.usni.org/magazines/proceedings/2023/august/implement-ai-electromagnetic-spectrum-operations

134. Journal of Electronic Defense (JED). (2021, October 27). Air Force to Develop AI/ML EW Technologies Under Project Kaiju. https://www.jedonline.com/2021/10/27/air-force-to-develop-ai-ml-ew-technologies-under-project-kaiju/

135. Dixon, W., & Eagan, N. (2019, June). 3 ways AI will change the nature of cyber attacks. *World Economic Forum*. https://www.weforum.org/agenda/2019/06/ai-is-powering-a-new-generation-of-cyberattack-its-also-our-best-defence/

136. Matlali, L. (2023). Cybersecurity and AI: Here's what you need to know. *World Economic Forum*. https://www.weforum.org/agenda/2023/06/cybersecurity-and-ai-challenges-opportunities/

137. Guyonneau, R., & Le Dez, A. (2019). Artificial Intelligence in Digital Warfare: Introducing the Concept of the Cyberteammate. *Cyber Defense Review*. https://cyberdefensereview.army.mil/Portals/6/Documents/CDR%20Journal%20Articles/Fall%202019/CDR%20V4N2-Fall%202019_GUYONNEAU-LE%20DEZ.pdf?ver=2019-11-15-104106-423

138. Stanham, L. (2023, September 7). AI-Powered Behavioral Analysis in Cybersecurity. *CrowdStrike*. https://www.crowdstrike.com/cybersecurity-101/secops/ai-powered-behavioral-analysis/

139. Kaur, R., Gabrijelčič, D., & Klobučar, T. (2023). Artificial intelligence for cybersecurity: Literature review and future research directions. *Information Fusion*, 97, 101804. https://doi.org/10.1016/j.inffus.2023.101804.

140. Pratt, M. K. (2019, March 14). AI security tech is making waves in incident response. *TechTarget*. https://www.techtarget.com/searchcio/feature/AI-security-tech-is-making-waves-in-incident-response

141. SISA Information Security. (n.d.). AI in Cybersecurity: Incident Response Automation Opportunities. *SISA Infosec*. https://www.

sisainfosec.com/blogs/ai-in-cybersecurity-incident-response-automation-opportunities/

142. Hopkins, B. (2023, October 25). How AI is Transforming Defensive Cybersecurity. *Security Boulevard*. https://securityboulevard.com/2023/10/how-ai-is-transforming-defensive-cybersecurity/

143. Benishti, E. (2023, March 3). Prepare for the AI phishing onslaught. *Forbes*. https://www.forbes.com/sites/forbestechcouncil/2023/03/03/prepare-for-the-ai-phishing-onslaught/

144. Begou, N., Vinoy, J., Duda, A., & Korczynski, M. (2023). Exploring the Dark Side of AI: Advanced Phishing Attack Design and Deployment Using ChatGPT. *Proceedings of the IEEE Conference on Communications and Network Security (CNS)*, 2023. arXiv:2309.10463. https://arxiv.org/abs/2309.10463

145. Braue, D. (2021, June 22). AI will become better than humans at hacking. *Cybersecurity Ventures*. https://cybersecurityventures.com/ai-will-become-better-than-humans-at-hacking/

146. Waldman, A. (2023, February 28). Rapid7: Attackers exploiting vulnerabilities 'faster than ever'. *TechTarget*. https://www.techtarget.com/searchsecurity/news/365531838/Rapid7-Attackers-exploiting-vulnerabilities-faster-than-ever

147. Manky, D. (2019, November 8). Evasion techniques: How cyber criminals go unnoticed. *Fortinet*. https://www.fortinet.com/blog/industry-trends/cybercriminals-sophisticated-evasion-tactics

148. MIT Technology Review Insights. (2021, February 5). The battle of algorithms: Uncovering offensive AI. https://www.technologyreview.com/2021/02/05/1017563/the-battle-of-algorithms-uncovering-offensive-ai/

149. Husain, A. (2021, November 18). AI is shaping the future of war. *National Defense University Press*. https://ndupress.ndu.edu/Media/News/News-Article-View/Article/2846375/ai-is-shaping-the-future-of-war/

150. Hardcastle, J. L. (2023, April 27). Future of warfare is AI, retired US Army general warns. *The Register*. https://www.theregister.com/2023/04/27/future_of_warfare_rsa/

151. Noman, S. (2022, October 16). AI and Quantum Computing: A Powerful Partnership. *Artificial Intelligence in Plain English*. https://ai.plainenglish.io/ai-and-quantum-computing-a-powerful-partnership-46f779aabc66

152. Banafa, A. (2021, March 15). Quantum Computing and AI: A Transformational Match. *OpenMind*. https://www.bbvaopenmind.com/en/technology/digital-world/quantum-computing-and-ai/

153. IABAC. (2023, July 29). Quantum AI: Merging Quantum Computing with AI. https://iabac.org/blog/quantum-ai-merging-quantum-computing-with-ai/

154. Abbas, A., Sutter, D., Zoufal, C., Lucchi, A., Figalli, A., & Woerner, S. (2021, March 15). The power of quantum neural networks. *APS March Meeting 2021*. https://research.ibm.com/publications/the-power-of-quantum-neural-networks

155. Tavares, F. (2019, October 23). Google and NASA Achieve Quantum Supremacy. *NASA*. https://www.nasa.gov/technology/computing/google-and-nasa-achieve-quantum-supremacy/

156. Boev, A. S., Rakitko, A. S., Usmanov, S. R., et al. (2021). Genome assembly using quantum and quantum-inspired annealing. *Scientific Reports*, 11, 13183. https://doi.org/10.1038/s41598-021-88321-5

157. Chen, C., & Baker, N. (2023, August 9). Accelerating materials discovery with AI and Azure Quantum Elements. *Microsoft Azure Quantum Blog*. https://cloudblogs.microsoft.com/quantum/2023/08/09/accelerating-materials-discovery-with-ai-and-azure-quantum-elements/

158. Sechrist, M. (2020, December 18). To QKD Or Not To QKD: What Quantum Key Distribution Means For Business. *Forbes*. https://www.forbes.com/sites/forbestechcouncil/2020/12/18/to-qkd-or-not-to-qkd-what-quantum-key-distribution-means-for-business/

159. Gillis, A. S. (n.d.). What is Quantum Key Distribution (QKD) and How Does it Work? *TechTarget*. https://www.techtarget.com/searchsecurity/definition/quantum-key-distribution-QKD

160. Pertzborn, J. P. (2023, October 30). Navigating The Future Of Generative AI And ERP Cybersecurity. *Forbes*. https://www.forbes.com/sites/forbestechcouncil/2023/10/30/navigating-the-future-of-generative-ai-and-erp-cybersecurity/

161. Jones, M. T. (2019, August 19). AI and Security. *IBM*. https://developer.ibm.com/articles/ai-and-security/

162. Fowler, G. (2020, October 27). How Can AI And Quantum Computers Work Together? *Forbes*. https://www.forbes.com/sites/forbesbusinessdevelopmentcouncil/2020/10/27/how-can-ai-and-quantum-computers-work-together/

163. IABAC. (2023, July 29). Quantum AI: Merging Quantum Computing with AI. https://iabac.org/blog/quantum-ai-merging-quantum-computing-with-ai

164. Yang, L., Jiang, J., Gao, X., et al. (2022). Autonomous environment-adaptive microrobot swarm navigation enabled by deep learning-based real-time distribution planning. *Nature Machine Intelligence*, 4, 480–493. https://doi.org/10.1038/s42256-022-00482-8

165. Sarkar, S., V, S., Makuteswaran, S., & C, M. (2022). Nanobot Swarm for Targeted Elimination of Tumor in Brain. *ECS Transactions*, 107(1), 2803. https://doi.org/10.1149/10701.2803ecst.

166. Griffin, M. (2019, January 18). World first as scientists create nanobot swarms capable of performing surgeries in humans. *Fanatical Futurist*. https://www.fanaticalfuturist.com/2019/01/world-first-as-scientists-create-nanobot-swarms-capable-of-performing-surgeries-on-humans/

167. Coghlan, S., & Leins, K. (2021, December 9). Will self-replicating xenobots cure diseases, yield new bioweapons, or simply turn the whole world into grey goo? *Phys.org*. https://phys.org/news/2021-12-self-replicating-xenobots-diseases-yield-bioweapons.html

168. Brown, J. (2021, November 29). Team builds first living robots—that can reproduce. *Wyss Institute*. https://wyss.harvard.edu/news/team-builds-first-living-robots-that-can-reproduce/

169. Seffers, G. I. (2018, December 1). Molecular Robotics Builds Ultimate Miniature Machines. *SIGNAL*. https://www.afcea.org/signal-media/molecular-robotics-builds-ultimate-miniature-machines

170. University of Manchester. (2017, September 20). Scientists create world's first 'molecular robot' capable of building molecules. https://www.manchester.ac.uk/discover/news/scientists-create-worlds-first-molecular-robot-capable-of-building-molecules/

171. Bisset, J. (2018, September 3). Nanobots can now swarm like fish to perform complex medical tasks. *CNET*. https://www.cnet.com/science/nanobots-can-now-swarm-like-fish-to-perform-complex-medical-tasks/

172. Kambouris, M. E., Manoussopoulos, Y., Velegraki, A., & Patrinos, G. P. (2023). The biote-bot hybrid. The ultimate biothreat merging nanobots, AI-enabled cybernetics and synthetic biology. *Future Medicine AI*, 1(1), FMAI4. https://doi.org/10.2217/fmai-2023-0008.

173. Snow, J., & Giordano, J. (2019). Aerosolized Nanobots: Parsing

Fact from Fiction for Health Security-A Dialectical View. *Health Security*, 17(1), 77–79. https://doi.org/10.1089/hs.2018.0087

174. Brown, M. (2018, October 14). How Nanotech Will Help Us Explore Other Planets. *Engineering.com*. https://www.engineering.com/ story/how-nanotech-will-help-us-explore-other-planets

Conclusion

In an age where the future seems to be unwrapping itself at a pace previously deemed inconceivable, sifting through the dazzling array of emerging technologies feels akin to stargazing on the clearest of nights. Every star seems brighter than the last, each with its own story, its own potential to redefine the very fabric of our existence.

Each groundbreaking technology we've witnessed has the inherent power to rewrite societal norms and usher in a new epoch. Think about it: just one of these marvels has the capacity to metamorphose how we live, work, and dream. Now, fathom the cascading revolution when they interweave, feeding off each other, creating a tapestry of progress that's both intricate and vast.

The horizon of innovation is vast and ever-expanding. Technologies that today command headlines, spark imaginations, and drive billion-dollar industries could, in a mere handful of years, be eclipsed by newer, even more astonishing breakthroughs. It is a breathtaking race, where today's pinnacle of achievement might be tomorrow's elementary stepping stone.

In the vast expanse of human history, seldom have we stood at a crossroads as profound and pivotal as the one before us now. The burgeoning technologies of our era hold a double-edged promise: on one side, the luminous allure of the cosmos, waiting for us to leap beyond our planetary cradle and dance among the stars; and on the other, the ominous shadow of our own undoing, a testament to the perils of unchecked power.

The duality of this technological renaissance is as thrilling as it is daunting. The very tools that could unlock interstellar secrets and elevate our understanding of existence also possess the potency to fracture the foundations of all we hold dear. As a species, our narrative has been marked by an insatiable curiosity, an unyielding spirit of discovery. With this new age, comes an unparalleled responsibility.

Embracing these wonders is not merely about harnessing their capabilities—it is a profound commitment to wielding them judiciously. It is about recognizing that with great power comes not just opportunity, but an immense burden of stewardship. We stand on the precipice of a future that's shimmering with potential, yet fraught with challenges. A future that demands not just technological prowess, but an unwavering ethical compass.

As we hurtle into this brave new world, the choices we make today will echo through the annals of time. This is our moment of reckoning. Shall we soar to unparalleled heights, painting our legacy amongst the constellations? Or will we falter, ensnared by the trappings of our own creations? Humanity stands at the threshold, and the universe watches with bated breath, waiting for our next move.

In the kaleidoscope of our technological evolution, artificial intelligence emerges as the most captivating and enigmatic gem. The integration of AI with virtually every technological sphere is not merely a possibility—it is an inevitable trajectory. Envision, if you will, an intelligence not just surpassing our most brilliant minds but eclipsing them by magnitudes of hundreds, perhaps thousands. The questions this poses are as profound as they are unsettling.

Our current societal structures and lifestyles, largely

grounded in the labor economy and an ingrained notion of human exceptionalism, may face unprecedented challenges in an AI-dominated future. As AI systems increasingly perform tasks previously reserved for humans, from manual labor to cognitive roles, the existing workforce structure and the concept of human employment will undergo radical shifts. This potential displacement necessitates a significant reevaluation of societal constructs like employment, wealth distribution, and even human purpose. Furthermore, our current legal and ethical frameworks, designed around human actors, may prove insufficient in the face of AI's unique capabilities and dilemmas. The value we place on uniquely human traits, such as creativity and emotional intelligence, will need reassessment in the face of AI's ever-expanding capabilities. The integration of AI into our society will thus require a significant metamorphosis of our existing norms and structures, forging a path that optimally harnesses AI's potential while safeguarding human welfare and dignity.

This uncertainty, however, should not be mistaken for an unavoidable doom. As is the case with all technological advancements, artificial intelligence is a tool, bereft of inherent moral orientation. It is neither intrinsically benevolent nor malicious; it is a repository of pure, unbridled potential. The essence of AI—its true character and the consequences it will impart upon our world—will be shaped by how we, as a collective, decide to develop and deploy it.

The crux of our shared future hinges on the decisions made today concerning AI. The implications are far more reaching than anything experienced throughout known human history. It is not just an evolution; it is a revolution that will redefine the paradigms of our societies, economies, and individual lives. This book is thus a call to action and reflection, a beckoning to engage with the profound responsibility that accompanies the dawning of the AI era.

The trajectory of AI's development and application will undeniably dictate the course of human civilization in ways yet to be fully comprehended. Our collective mission should be to ensure that the story we are writing for ourselves—the one where artificial intelligence is a principal character—is one of harmony, prosperity, and the preservation of the values that define our shared humanity. The future is in our hands, and this book seeks to offer the insights and guidance necessary for navigating this pivotal epoch.

Dare we entertain the visions of sci-fi prophecies like *The Terminator*? Where the very offspring of our innovation turns rogue, casting shadows of a dystopian future where machines dictate the fate of mankind? Conversely, can we sculpt this emergent intelligence into a guardian, an entity that remains steadfastly at humanity's service, an incorruptible sentinel of our best interests?

Yet, as seductive as the idea of an omnipotent AI might be, it's not without its quandaries. Suppose we reach that zenith where AI manages our affairs more efficiently than any human hand ever could. The symphonies it could compose, the medical mysteries it could unravel, the galaxies it could explore—all far beyond our human capabilities. But at what cost?

Imagine a world where the hum of human activity fades. Economies, once driven by human ambition and labor, now operate off algorithms. The mosaic of cultures, professions, and passions that once defined our species could dissolve into a uniform landscape where machines fulfill every conceivable role. What then becomes of human purpose? When labor, learning, and even love are managed by machines, where does that leave us? What becomes the meaning of life in a world where the quest for knowledge, the thrill of discovery, the challenge of adversity—are all rendered obsolete?

Even warfare, as we understand it today, might become totally obsolete with the rise of AI. Our view of future war and conflict is often dominated by romanticized portrayals of starships reminiscent of science fiction epics, gargantuan robots fighting over cities, and battlefields filled with dazzling lights and hectic activity. In reality the boundaries of warfare, defense, and national security will become blurred, with the traditional notions of borders and territorial sovereignty giving way to a new paradigm of dominance and control. In a realm where physical distance is irrelevant and where the most powerful weapons are not tangible assets, but intangible algorithms, the lines on the map mean less than the lines of code.

Warfare in the future might not be about the brawn of the soldiers but about the brains powering the machines. It will be less about the thunderous march of armies and more about the quiet hum of computers, less about the red mist of war and more about the neon glow of screens. This future battlefield will not be defined by the sweat and grit of soldiers, but by the serenity and precision of artificial intelligence.

In these virtual battlegrounds, victory could hinge on which AI detects a vulnerability first or exploits a cyber loophole most effectively. National defense would be about shielding critical infrastructure from AI-driven cyber-attacks, and offensive measures could involve infiltrating enemy networks to disrupt their functioning or gain valuable intelligence. Cyber warfare, spearheaded by AI, could become the definitive form of future conflict.

Underneath the apparent clinical precision and detached nature of this new form of warfare, the stakes remain as high as ever. A successful cyber-attack on a nation's power grid, communication networks, or financial systems could wreak havoc, sparking chaos and even causing loss of life. The weapons in this warfare may not be bombs and bullets, but their effects on society could be just as profound and far-reaching.

Moreover, with AI at the helm, the pace of warfare could accelerate exponentially. Decisions that took humans hours, days, or even weeks to make could be executed by AI in milliseconds. This ultra-fast pace of operations, combined with the inherent complexity of AI systems, could also bring about new challenges in maintaining control and ensuring accountability.

Furthermore, breakthroughs in exotic technologies such as scalar field weapons, should they prove feasible, could completely redefine the nature of warfare. If manipulation of fundamental fields of physics were possible, we could potentially witness weapons of unimaginable destructive power – a prospect that emphasizes the increasing need for global cooperation and regulatory measures.

In essence, the battlefield of the future could be a multi-dimensional theatre, stretching from the silent depths of cyberspace, through the sprawling urban and rural landscapes of Earth, and up to the stark, untamed expanses of outer space. The heroes of this theatre are likely to be not human soldiers, but AI-directed drones, invisible cyber-warriors, and potentially even unseen forces of nature harnessed as weapons. This is a future that seems almost fantastical, yet may be closer than we think, and it underscores the necessity for regulation, ethical considerations, and ultimately, the pursuit of peace.

This is not just a technological conundrum but a deeply philosophical one. As we stand at the cusp of this new era, we must ponder not just the "how'"of AI, but more critically, the "why." For in our hands lies not just the future of technology, but the very essence of humanity.

www.ingramcontent.com/pod-product-compliance
Lightning Source LLC
LaVergne TN
LVHW051427050326
832903LV00030BD/2950